POE'S MAJOR CRISIS

POE'S MAJOR CRISIS

His Libel Suit and New York's Literary World

Sidney P. Moss

Duke University Press

Durham, N. C. 1970

L.C.C. card no. 74–100089
I.S.B.N. 0–8223–0217–9

PRINTED IN THE UNITED STATES OF
AMERICA BY THE SEEMAN PRINTERY

For Abraham Golinkin

. . . let this be my Kaddish

PREFACE

In this book I present documents concerning Poe that have been declared "unlocated" or "inaccessible," or whose existence others have not suspected or that they did not trouble to track down. These documents, together with those that others have uncovered, enable us to see the jigsaw puzzle of Poe's libel suit with its pieces in place for the first time.

The lawsuit, given its causes and consequences, constituted Poe's major crisis, whether of a biographical or literary nature, and deserves study in its own right. But it is also a dramatic device for reporting in depth Poe's last years. Moreover, the case serves as a stereoscopic viewer for seeing New York's literary world in three-dimensional perspective, and this book is, therefore, as much concerned with literary history and journalism as with biography, for Poe has to be projected against his background if he is to be understood. What especially drew me to the documentary method I adopted is that it gives the reader an acute sense of reality, a sense of being on the scene, something that a secondhand account fails to accomplish.

There are many obligations a researcher contracts in the course of his investigations, not the least of which are to the scholars who preceded him, and my Bibliography records my more palpable debts. There are other obligations I am pleased to acknowledge here, since Poe materials are scattered in libraries throughout the United States. A major one is to the people who manage the National Union Catalog and who publish its lists, the *Union List of Newspapers* and the *Union List of Serials*. My other major obligations are to the Library of Congress, the New York Public Library, the New York Historical Society, the Boston Public Library, the American Antiquarian Society, and the University of Virginia Library. The staffs of these libraries, as well as those of other libraries, who have proved cooperative and generous of their time are too many to thank here by name, but I have, I trust, thanked each of them individually.

There are special favors, however, that I have received from certain people and organizations that, with special pleasure, I record here:

Professor Frank Adams who, however offhandedly, suggested the project.

Professor Alan M. Cohn, Head of the Humanities Library at Southern Illinois University, who again proved one of the most able research librarians in the country.

Professors Eugene E. Bridwell, Jr., Kathleen D. Eads, and Hensley C. Woodbridge, also of Southern Illinois University Library, who helped me in many valuable ways.

Mr. Nathan Behrin, a court reporter of the New York Supreme Court for almost fifty years and until recently Historian of the National Shorthand Reporters' Association, who with his special experience was able to clarify for me many of the legal questions concerning the libel suit.

Mr. Terence S. Martin and *Mr. James W. Mock*, graduate students in English at Southern Illinois University, who helped me to check the accuracy of the transcription of the documents.

Mrs. Carol Lawson for collaborating with me in translating E.-D. Forgues's article on Poe.

The American Philosophical Society for a summer grant in 1966 to enable me to study the Duyckinck Manuscript Collection in the New York Public Library.

The Department of English, the College of Liberal Arts and Sciences, and the Graduate School of Southern Illinois University for the support they have given me in this and other projects.

I am also obliged to the editors of *The American Book Collector*, the *Poe Newsletter*, and *Papers on Language and Literature* for permission to use some of the information that I first published in their journals. I am obliged, too, to the University of South Carolina Press for permission to reprint a Simms letter that appears in *The Letters of William Gilmore Simms*, Volume 2, collected and edited by Mary C. Simms Oliphant, Alfred Taylor Odell, and T. C. Duncan Eaves, copyright 1953 by the University of South Carolina Press.

CONTENTS

During the Lawsuit

After the Lawsuit

INTRODUCTION

The concatenation of events that thoroughly discredited Poe with his audience and that accounts for his being hooted and almost literally starved out of the literary profession was that which led to and followed his libel suit against the owners of the New York *Mirror*. Poe seemed headed for ruin in any case. He had damaged himself badly by his Boston Lyceum "hoax"; by what, given the conventions of the time, was considered his extraordinarily poor taste in quarreling publicly with a lady, Miss Cornelia Walter, editress of the Boston *Transcript*; by his wrangle with Longfellow and his circle, the "Five of Clubs"; by his continual slanging match with Lewis Gaylord Clark, editor of the *Knickerbocker* magazine, and with members of the New York literary clique; by his abusive criticism of the Transcendentalists as well as the Boston coterie of the *North American Review*; and by the scandal arising from his involvement with Frances Osgood and Elizabeth Ellet.[1] But the events leading to and following his lawsuit proved the ordeal that finally ended his brilliant, if erratic and notorious, career and that shortened his life.

One wonders what Poe would have done differently if he had had the chance to relive his career. Given his character and sense of independence, he would, no doubt, have persisted in refusing to join the New York literary establishment, much as an alliance with that group would have ensured him material success and have added to his contemporary reputation as a poet and writer of fiction. Surely, however, knowing their disastrous consequences, he would have chosen to avoid certain actions or at least have modified them considerably. Given a second chance, he would not have accepted the invitation to speak at the Boston Lyceum. He would not, I also believe, have befriended the flirtatious Mrs. Osgood and would unquestionably have avoided the malicious Mrs. Ellet. Above all, he would not have written those lampoons that appeared in "The Literati of New York City," especially the one of Thomas Dunn English which led to his libel suit, an action that, in turn, all but ended his career.

1. For a detailed discussion of these events, see Moss, *Poe's Literary Battles*. Full citations of this and other works pertinent to the libel suit appear in the Bibliography.

But second chances are given to no one, and the literary historian, while he may deplore them, can only reconstruct the circumstances and reenact the choices that led in this instance to a most unfortunate outcome for Poe, his enemies, and the literary world in general.

Since the causes and consequences of his libel suit constitute the major crisis in Poe's literary career, I have considered it important to collect the pertinent documents and present them here, wherever reasonable, in the order in which the events they disclose occurred. I was tempted for a time to preface these documents with an introduction that would put them all in focus and that would make the general assessment due them. Notwithstanding that I accomplished this task,[2] I have decided not to use that kind of introduction here on the grounds that it would deprive the reader of a measure of suspense as the documents and the events they disclose unfold before him, and would infringe upon his privilege of forming his own judgment. I have then, apart from the headnotes, which are designed to put each document in context and to explain whatever in the document requires explanation, allowed the record to speak for itself, a record that reveals the literary world in which Poe worked and the choices he made, and that shows as nothing else can how Poe was cannibalized by the enemies he helped to create.

One cautionary note needs to be added before we turn to the record itself. The image of Poe reflected in these documents should not be taken as the image of Poe that appears throughout his entire career. Such simplification would not be true of Wordsworth, Carlyle, or Whitman, and it is not true of Poe either. Though cruel and untrustworthy at times, Poe as a critic was principled at heart, as I have tried to show elsewhere, so much so that, without flagrant exaggeration, one could make a case for his being a martyr to the cause of the literary profession in America. And whatever reservations one may have about the man as a man, poet, critic, and writer of fiction—and I have my share of them—one must concede what is of ultimate importance, that Poe ranged himself on the side of the artist; that he urged support of worthy authors; that he called for a respectable criticism; that he exhorted publishers to exercise standards other than commercial ones; and that he struggled to provide an audience for deserving books. Though, despite his fifteen-year struggle made at great personal cost, he lost that battle, the loss was finally ours, for we

2. Moss, "Poe, Hiram Fuller and the Duyckinck Circle."

can see the shambles of that defeat everywhere about us, in literary cliquism and log-rolling, in literary commercialism, in irresponsible criticism, and, worst of all, in an audience whose taste has been all but irredeemably corrupted.

These documents then, which are at once concerned with literary history, with American journalism of the 1840s, and with biography, reflect only one image of Poe and that far from his best. As literary history, this study revives the personalities that figured so largely in the period and that made their impact upon Poe's life and career. As a study in journalism, it exposes the coteries that were formed haphazardly to defend or attack a man, and the defamatory techniques that editors so easily employed, devices to which Poe often lent himself by his weaknesses of character. As biography, it shows the kind of hack work, such as "The Literati of New York City," that Poe cranked out to earn a livelihood, as well as the notoriety he courted and the persecution he had to cope with in consequence, if he was to survive in the journalistic and literary world that could not pay him enough for his poems and fiction.

In the words of a contemporary who was an authority in the matter, "Poe was sensitive to opinion. He sought, . . . as I often witnessed, with an intense eagerness the smallest paragraph in a newspaper touching himself or his writings."[3] The paragraphs that Poe might not have found for himself, others probably found for him, for New York's editorial and publishing world, concentrated within eight short square blocks around City Hall, was then as provincial as a small town today. No doubt Poe did not see every document presented here, but there is little doubt that he saw many of them.

3. From a diary entry made on 1 November 1875 by Evert A. Duyckinck. The diary is in the Duyckinck Manuscript Collection in the New York Public Library.

TOWARD THE LAWSUIT

1. May 1846: "The Literary Snob": Two Versions
Lewis Gaylord Clark and Cornelia Wells Walter

[When the Broadway Journal, *heavily in debt and invested with Poe's entire capital, became defunct, Poe's only means of support was his pen. He contrived, therefore, to bring off a journalistic sensation that would make him the author to publish. In a series of sketches he would distinguish between the popular opinion of contemporary New York authors and the opinion expressed about them in private literary society, for, as he said, "the very editors who hesitate at saying in print an ill word of an author personally known, are usually the most frank in speaking about him privately. In literary society, they seem bent upon avenging the wrongs self-inflicted upon their own consciences. Here, accordingly, the quack is treated as he deserves . . . by way of striking a balance" ("Author's Introduction" to "The Literati of New York City").*

To create this sensation, Poe had to exploit private gossip among the literati, something he was in an ideal position to do. For in 1845 the fantastic success of "The Raven," the publication of two of his books, and the undoubted fact that he looked the poet, which the lady, if not the gentleman, writers found irresistible, became his entrée into the fashionable literary salons of New York. There the Raven held forth, spellbinding the ladies, charming them with his attentions, and listening to their views—as well as those of their guests—concerning their fellow authors and editors. That Poe was a leading critic and could and did say flattering things about them in print only enhanced his attractiveness as a literary lion.

But invitations to the salons ceased abruptly when in 1846 he published—or, more accurately, threatened to publish—what had been intended as privileged communications. His threatened betrayal, for he attributed the gossip he purveyed to no one in particular, made him seem a cad and a hack, and cost him his entrée into literary society. Now he became, in turn, the subject of spiteful gossip and outright abuse. Lewis Gaylord Clark, as editor of the popular Knickerbocker *magazine and self-*

appointed custodian of New York literary reputations, greeted the first installment of "The Literati of New York City" by calling its author a "literary snob" (in nineteenth-century parlance, a low-class person vulgarly struggling for position and éclat) "to-day in the gutter, to-morrow in some milliner's magazine" (Godey's Lady's Book in which "The Literati" was appearing) ". . . who seems to invite the 'Punchy' writers among us to take up their pens and impale him for public amusement." (Clark's article appears below.)

Poe, obviously, succeeded all too well in creating the journalistic sensation he wanted. He could hardly have failed in the endeavor. As James Russell Lowell doggerelled in A Fable for Critics (a work that owed as much to Poe as Poe owed to The Dunciad): "So the excellent Public is hereby assured that the sale of my book is already secured. For there is not a poet throughout the whole land but will purchase a copy or two out of hand, in the fond expectation of being amused in it, by seeing his betters cut up and abused in it." The irony is that the very success of "The Literati" cost Poe his livelihood as well as a great many of his friends, so that by winter, as we shall see, he became the object of public charity. For the thirty-eight authors and editors he noticed, not to mention their colleagues and friends or the purveyors of gossip whose confidence he had threatened to violate, were frequently more outraged than pleased at his sketches, and they pilloried him from all sides.

Now a pariah, Poe, just about the time "The Literati" first appeared, gave up his house at 85 Amity Street (now 85 West Third Street) and moved to Fordham, a village about thirteen miles out of the city, where he passed the three remaining years of his life in order, as Sarah Helen Whitman put it, to recover "that peace which had been so fatally perilled by the irritations and anxieties of his New York life."

Poe, no doubt, would have agreed that he had practiced a dubious morality in betraying, or threatening to betray, the confidences of his friends for "The Literati"; but he would also have argued that his object, for all the impurity of his motives and the "occasional words of personality" (part of his subtitle to "The Literati") that adulterated his purpose, was indubitably moral—the purification of American criticism.

Clark had a number of reasons for writing the article below besides the ones mentioned. Not only had Poe lampooned Charles F. Briggs (known to readers of the Knickerbocker as Harry Franco) in his first installment of "The Literati," but he was preparing to treat Clark himself, *a literary enemy of long standing, in like fashion. Informed by Godey that he had been "booked" for the series (Document 5), Clark decided to beat Poe to the punch, especially as the series, widely known because of Godey's "advertisements and placards," threatened to be widely read.*

Not to be outdone, Miss Walter, editress of the Boston Transcript, *who had been attacking Poe with fair regularity since October 1845 for his performance at the Boston Lyceum and his subsequent quarrel with her, decided to copy Clark's attack. The two articles, printed side by side, appear below. Clark's statement was made in the well-known "Editor's Table" of the* Knickerbocker *in May 1846; Miss Walter's version of Clark's statement was made in the Boston* Daily Evening Transcript *on 5 May 1846. "Mrs. Louisa Godey" is, of course, a slur upon Louis Godey, the owner of* Godey's Lady's Book. *The papers in* Punch *on "The Snobs of England" were written by Thackeray, although they appeared anonymously.]*

Clark in the Knickerbocker	*Miss Walter in the* Transcript
	THE LITERARY SNOB. The Knickerbocker occasionally serves up in its "editor's table" rare bits of opinion which well answer the purpose of palpable *hits* for individuals. The last number, alluding to a series of
PUNCH is giving a series of papers on 'The Snobs of England,' and if we had a PUNCH in this country, the example would be immediately imitated, as a matter of course, because we imitate every thing English but the inimitable, and PUNCH is unhappily of this class of subjects. The 'snobs' however are not among American impossibilities, and we are in daily expectation of seeing some periodical come out with an article on SNOBS, by way of novelty. There is a wandering specimen of 'The Literary Snob' continually ob-	papers given in *Punch* upon the "Snobs of England," remarks that "if we had a Punch in this country, the example would be immediately imitated. The 'Snobs' are by no means among American impossibilities. Indeed, there is a wandering specimen of 'The Literary Snob'

truding himself upon public notice; to-day in the gutter, to-morrow in some milliner's magazine; but in all places, and at all times, magnificently snobbish and dirty, who seems to invite the 'Punchy' writers among us to take up their pens and impale him for public amusement. Mrs. Louisa Godey has lately taken this snob into her service in a neighboring city, where he is doing his best to prove his title to the distinction of being one of the lowest of his class at present infesting the literary world. The 'Evening Gazette and Times' speaks of our literary 'snob' as one 'whose *idiosyncracies* have attracted some attention and compassion of late;' and adds: 'We have heard that he is at present in a state of health which renders him not completely *accountable* for all his peculiarities!' We do not think that the 'ungentlemanly and unpardonable personalities of this writer,' of which our contemporary complains, are worthy of notice, simply because they are so notoriously false that they destroy themselves. The sketch for example of Mr. Briggs, ('Harry Franco,') in the paper alluded to, is *ludicrously* untrue, in almost every particular. Who that knows 'Harry Franco,' (whose prose style Washington Irving pronounced 'the freshest, most natural and graphic he had met with,') would

continually obtruding himself upon public notice; today in the gutter, tomorrow in some milliner's magazine; but in all places, and at all times, magnificently snobbish and dirty, who seems to invite the 'Punchy' writers among us to take up their pens and impale him for public amusement. Mrs Louisa Godey has lately taken this snob into her service in a neighboring city, where he is doing his best to prove his title to the distinction of being one of the lowest of his class at present infesting the literary world. The Evening Gazette speaks of him as one 'whose *idiosyncracies* have attracted some attention and compassion of late because he is at present in a state of health which renders him not completely *accountable* for all his peculiarities!' " The same individual is famous for indulging in gross falsehoods, and these have recognize his *physical* man from our 'snob's' description? But after all, why should one speak of all this? Poh! POE! Leave the 'idiosyncratic' man 'alone in his glory.' become so common with him that wherever seen in print they are ever met by the reader, with the simple exclamation Poh! POE!

---

2. *21 April 1846: "New Publications"*
William G. King

[*As he made clear, Lewis Gaylord Clark was not the first to mock the initial installment of "The Literati" and denigrate its author. That distinction probably belongs to King, the editor of the New York* Gazette *and* Times, *from whose notice of Godey's Lady's Book Clark quoted, using his "typographical tricks," as Evert Duyckinck called them, to emphasize certain suggestive words.*

The Gazette *and* Times *was able to say that Poe was "at present in a state of health which renders him not completely accountable for all his peculiarities" because Poe had recently adopted an extreme "solution" to escape the persecution of Mrs. Elizabeth Ellet. He explained that he had maligned the lady in a seizure of insanity (see headnote to Document 89).*

Ernest Helfenstein, William Cranston, and William Simmons, mentioned in the article below, were dilettantes whose reputations are extinct. Mrs. Caroline Kirkland is best known for her narratives of pioneer life. In 1845 her Western Clearings *appeared with Poe's* Tales *and* The Raven and Other Poems *in Duyckinck's* Library of American Books. *Mrs. Sarah Josepha Hale was widely known as the literary editor of* Godey's Lady's Book. *Timothy Shay Arthur was the editor of* Arthur's Ladies' Magazine, *which merged with* Godey's *in May 1846, as the* Gazette *and* Times *noted, the fateful month that saw the first installment of "The Literati" sketches. Arthur's many temperance tales were forerunners of his* Ten Nights in a Bar-Room, *a book whose popularity was first exceeded by* Uncle Tom's Cabin.]

NEW PUBLICATIONS. GODEY'S LADY'S BOOK, which has contracted a matrimonial alliance with ARTHUR'S MAGAZINE, has the month of May for its Honey moon, which it spends in the company of Ernest Helfenstein, William Cranston, Mrs. Kirkland, Mrs. Hale, Mr. Simmons, T. S. Arthur and others. We are sorry to see admitted in such company, such a piece of gratuitous and unpardonable impertinence as the paper on "The Literati of New York City." We hoped and believed till now that the ungentlemanly and unpardonable personalities, and intrusion into the private matters of living men, which appear at the close of each of these sketches was confined to the columns of the vilest and most unprincipled presses in this country and England, and are heartily sorry to be undeceived.

The unfortunate writer of this paper, a gentleman whose idiosincracies [sic] have attracted some attention and compassion of late, is, we regret to hear, at present in a state of health which renders him not completely accountable for all his peculiarities. The Editor should, we think, have considered this.

---

3. 20 April 1846: Godey's Lady's Book for May
Hiram Fuller

[When the first installment of "The Literati" appeared, Fuller, as editor of the New York Evening Mirror, applauded what he recognized would be a journalistic hit. Apart from his reservations, he observed that Poe "always writes with spirit and a commendable degree of independence," and in encouraging him he predicted there would be "great sport. . . ."

His notice, appearing prior to Lewis Clark's, Miss Walter's, and William King's, was unique for its essential cordiality. But that cordiality proved to be ephemeral, for Fuller by degrees became Poe's deadliest enemy.

For identification of the figures mentioned by Fuller, see "The Literati." For more information about Fuller, see headnotes to Documents 9 and 61.

GODEY's LADY's BOOK having swallowed Arthur's Magazine, presents in the May number unusual attractions. The leading article, and the one calculated to make the most noise, is from the pen of Edgar A. Poe on the 'Literati of New York.' The following gentlemen are the subjects of dissection number one: George Bush, George H. Colton, N. P. Willis, William M. Gillespie, Charles F. Briggs, William Kirkland and Doctor John W. Francis. The juxtaposition of names in this list is quite amusing. But as personalities are always popular, we think this kind of gossip will prove a happy hit for the publisher—though the friends of the gentlemen discussed would have been puzzled to recognize the portraits had the names been omitted. Dr. Francis and Mr. Kirkland are the only characters that are not caricatured. One is grossly abused and another as grossly flattered, while some are but superficially touched. Mr. Poe makes sad mistakes in his attempts at minute description of personal appearance, height, figure, age, foreheads, noses, &c. But he always writes with spirit, and a commendable degree of independence, and we hope that next month, he will dish us up a lady or two, just by way of adding a plum to his pudding. He now assumes to be master of the literary ring, so let him trot out the whole menagerie and show up the lions and kangaroos, parrots, cockatoos and all. As the Spirit of the Times would say, there is great sport in prospect. Poets, look to your laurels!

---

4. 29 April 1846: "The Knickerbocker for May"
Hiram Fuller

[*Unlike Miss Walter (Document 1), Fuller was laconic concerning Lewis Clark's statement about Poe when he alluded to it in the* Evening Mirror. *"The way old 'Knick' touches up Poe is a 'caution'" was all he wrote.*

To bear out the prediction he had earlier made, that Poe's "Literati" series would "prove a happy hit," Fuller noted the extraordinary fact that Louis Godey, the publisher of Godey's Lady's Book, *was "compelled . . . to print a second edition."*

Fuller erred in writing "April number"; it should be "May number," since the "Literati" series commenced with that number.]

THE KNICKERBOCKER FOR MAY is already on our table. It is particularly rich. The way old 'Knick' touches up Poe is 'a caution.' By the way, we notice that the article on the 'New York Literati' in the April number of Godey's Lady's Book has compelled the publisher to print a second edition. There is nothing in this country that sells so well as literary scandal.

Any man who will go into it with a 'perfect looseness' may make his fortune.

---

5. *8 May 1846: A Card: "Edgar A. Poe and the New York Writers—Lewis Gaylord Clark"*
   Louis A. Godey

[*Besides the fact that he and his magazine had been slurred by Clark in the* Knickerbocker, Godey *was incensed at Clark's treatment of Poe. He therefore decided to expose Clark's motives in writing "The Literary Snob." Since the June number of* Godey's *would not appear for another two weeks* (Godey's *was regularly in the hands of New York booksellers by the twentieth of the month), he paid to have a Card placed in the* Evening Mirror *soon after the* Knickerbocker *appeared.*

In retrospect, it is surprising that Hiram Fuller, editor of the Mirror, *accepted Godey's Card, since he was to prove Poe's most militant enemy.*]

EDGAR A. POE AND THE NEW YORK WRITERS—LEWIS GAYLORD CLARK.— When during a recent visit to New York, the subscriber informed Mr. Lewis Gaylord Clark that Mr. Poe had him 'booked' in his 'Opinions of the New York Literati,' he supposed that he was giving Mr. Lewis Gaylord Clark a very agreeable piece of information; as it must have been quite apparent to the gentleman himself, that his natural position was not among the literati, but *sub-literati* of New York; and he ought to have been greatly surprised and gratified to find himself placed in such agreeable company. But it seems that, on the contrary, the information that Mr. Lewis Gaylord Clark received has put him in a perfect agony of terror. His desperation is laughably exhibited in the insane attack he has made on Mr. Poe, in the Knickerbocker for May, where Mr. Poe is represented as imbecile from physical infirmity, and at the same time is threatened with impalement. It would undoubtedly afford the public much amusement to witness an attempt on the part of Mr. Lewis Gaylord Clark to impale Edgar A. Poe; and if Mr. Lewis Gaylord Clark will exhibit his talents at invective in this way, and prove that his article is written without assistance, it shall incontinently be inserted in the subscriber's Magazine, without note or comment.

Mr. Lewis Gaylord Clark says, 'We do not think that the ungentle-manly and unpardonable personalities of this writer are worthy of notice, simply because they are so notoriously false that they destroy themselves.' Some people make blunders because their education has been neglected; but it takes a born blockhead to make such a blunder as this. It is simply saying, 'Mr. Poe's are unworthy of notice and destroy themselves; there-fore we now make them the subject of special notice, and are doing our utmost to destroy him, even descending to the heartless and cruel insinu-ation, that illness has weakened the powers of his mind.' Such an argu-ment is the very essence of absurdity.

The subscriber has been repeatedly advised to discontinue the publi-cation of 'Mr. Poe's articles on the New York Literati.' It will be readily perceived, however, that such a course on his part would be as indelicate and unjust towards Mr. Poe, as it would be ungrateful towards the pub-lic, who have expressed distinct and decisive approbation of the articles in that unmistakeable way which a publisher is always happy to recog-nize.   L. A. GODY [sic],
                                    Proprietor of the Lady's Book.

---

6. 20 May 1846: "The Authors and Mr. Poe"
Louis A. Godey

[Before "The Literati" papers were printed, the prediction was that they would "raise some commotion in the literary emporium," to quote Godey's Lady's Book of May 1846. As early as 7 March 1846 the Daily Tribune reported the statement of a "New-York correspondent of a Washington paper" as follows: He "says that Mr. Poe is engaged on a work which will embrace his opinions of the various New-York literati, and thinks that it will create a sensation, and that the uproar which attended Pope's Dun-ciad was nothing to the stormy confusion of the literary elements which will war and rage 'with red lightning winged,' when the book (?) makes its appearance."

Now, despite the success of the series and the strong statement he had made on May 8 (preceding document), Godey was prompted to print a disclaimer when the second installment of "The Literati" appeared ("We . . . do but publish Mr. Poe's opinions, not our own"). He would, in fact, *make a more forceful disclaimer in his September number: "We hear of some complaints having been made by those writers who have already been noticed by Mr. Poe. Some of the ladies have suggested that the publisher has something to do with them. This we positively deny, and we as positively assert, that they are published as written by Mr. Poe, without any alteration or suggestion from us."*

The phenomenon of the May edition of Godey's *being "exhausted before the first of May" is attested by William H. Graham, a New York bookseller, who ran the following advertisement in the* Daily Tribune *of April 25: "EDGAR A. POE and the New-York Literati.—The great excitement caused by publication of No. 1 of the above remarkable papers, exhausted our supply of the May no. of Godey's Lady's Book. We have this morning received a few more, and will be in the constant receipt of them until the extraordinary demand is fully supplied.*

"The June No. will contain several more notices, and they will be continued monthly."

Godey's Lady's Book *was regularly in the hands of New York booksellers on the twentieth of the month; hence the above date that is attributed to the June number.*]

THE AUTHORS AND MR. POE.—We have received several letters from New York, anonymous and from personal friends, requesting us to be careful what we allow Mr. Poe to say of the New York authors, many of whom are our personal friends. We reply to one and all that we have nothing to do but publish Mr. Poe's opinions, *not our own.* Whether we agree with Mr. Poe or not is another matter. We are not to be intimidated by a threat of the loss of friends, or turned from our purpose by honeyed words. Our course is onward. The May edition was exhausted before the first of May, and we have had orders for hundreds from Boston and New York, which we could not supply. The first number of the series (with autographs) is republished in this number, which also contains No. 2. The usual quantity of reading matter is given in addition to the notices.

Many attempts have been made and are making by various persons to forestall public opinion. We have the name of one person. Others are busy with reports of Mr. Poe's illness. Mr. Poe has been ill, but we have letters from him of very recent dates, also a new batch of the *Literati,* which show anything but feebleness either of body or mind. Almost every paper that we exchange with has praised our new enterprise—the Union [of *Godey's Lady's Book* and *Arthur's Ladies' Magazine*]—and spoken in high terms of No. 1 of Mr. Poe's opinions.

---

7. 22 May 1846: "The Hornet's Nest Disturbed"
Hiram Fuller, Joseph C. Neal, and "Mustard Mace"

[*"Mustard Mace" wrote the skeltonic verse below which, introduced by Neal, was first published in the Philadelphia* Saturday Gazette, *and then, with Fuller's introduction, was reprinted in the* Evening Mirror *of May 22.*

The statement that Poe was "not, just now, / Where you may cow / The slaves who bow," was true enough, however wretched the lines; and the prediction that "A storm may brew / That harm may do / Yourself unto," proved sound, though Poe, however smitten, never sued "for quarter. . . ."]

THE HORNET'S NEST DISTURBED.—The following clever thing we clip from Neal's Saturday Gazette:

Poetical Warrings.—We cannot say from whom the subjoined emanates; but as literary warfare is 'a deed in fashion,' we give it for the sake of keeping up a healthy excitement among those who wield the pen and ride deadly passages, quill in rest. It is certainly a remarkable specimen of ingenious construction, while it talks to Mr. Poe with considerable seriousness on the subject of the sharp criticism in which that gentleman is prone to indulge—caustic all round:

Dictator Poe,
Of Scribblers' Row!
(I name you so
Because you show
You're fain to crow
O'er every foe
Who will not go
Your feet below.)
Beware lest you
A storm may brew
That harm may do

Yourself unto,
And you may rue,
And learn to sue
For quarter to[o].
The folks you smite
With rare delight,
May find your might
Of brain is slight,
And in a fight
Show spite for spite,
And trip you quite.

A pretty plight!
'Twould serve you right,
You waspish wight!

Pray let me hint
To you, in print,
You're not among
A slavish throng,
Where every tongue,
Or old or young,
Wags somehow wrong.
You're not, just now,
Where you may cow
The slaves who bow
With blenched brow.

What have you wrought
In things of thought
To give you claim
To extra fame?
You've growled and fought,
Much further—aught?

Think you Lenore
Has merits more
Than was before
Found in the store
Of po'sy lore?
Think you, you stand
At the right hand
Of all the band
Of masters grand,
In po'sy land?
Your Raven's fine
In many a line;
Yet I opine
The various Nine
Have wreaths to twine
For brows that shine
More bright than thine.

Go, take your place,
With modest grace,
Among your race.

Yours,   MUSTARD MACE.

---

8. 26 May 1846: "Mr Poe and the New York Literati"
Hiram Fuller

*[When the first installment of "The Literati" appeared, Fuller reviewed
it rather cordially (Document 3). Later, on May 16 in his Weekly Mirror,
he even reprinted passages from the essays dealing with William Kirkland
and Dr. John W. Francis, commenting, "They are very just." This tribute
is explained by the fact that Kirkland was Fuller's close friend and Dr.
Francis was everyone's, because, as Poe accurately remarked, the latter's
bonhomie was irresistible. When Kirkland died some months later, Fuller
wrote in the Evening Mirror (26 October 1846) that a "daily intercourse"
with the man—Kirkland had been a regular contributor to the Mirror
during the last two years of his life—"has impressed us with the profound-*

est convictions of his worth, and with such reverence for his many virtues as we have but rarely experienced towards our fellow men."

But when the second installment of "The Literati" appeared, Fuller did a complete turnabout and joined Lewis Clark, Miss Walter, and William King in condemning the sketches. He had announced his intention to do so in the Evening Mirror *of May 20.* "GODEY'S LADY'S BOOK FOR JUNE," *he wrote, "is on our table. As we purpose giving in a day or two a thorough review of 'Poe's Literati,' which is continued in the present number, with a reprint of his former article, we shall not notice it particularly to-day. The writer of course would not object to the same treatment which he so liberally deals to others." Now Fuller reviewed the two installments, fully determined to discredit them and their author. In the process he maligned Louis Godey for continuing to publish "The Literati" and expressed his resentment of Nathaniel P. Willis, under whose auspices and those of George Pope Morris he had served as part-owner and junior editor of the* Mirror *before buying them out.*

This article also appeared in the Weekly Mirror *on May 30.*]

MR POE AND THE NEW YORK LITERATI.—By force of advertisements and placards, Mr. Godey succeeded a month ago in apprising that portion of the public—a rather small one, by the by—who take an interest in literary matters, that Mr. Poe was coming down, upon the New York literati, in a series of papers in a Philadelphia magazine, with the force of a 'thousand of brick' and two or three thousand trip hammers, which would infallibly grind them—the literati of New York—into dust and powder, and create a sensation in the world, which it would be impossible to allay, by any possible amount of extra editions of the Lady's Book. Those who knew Mr. Poe only smiled at such an announcement, and those who knew Mr. Godey, if there be any such in New York, put as much faith in the advertisement as they do in the announcement on the cover of his Lady's Book, that it is the best magazine in the world, and that it has the greatest number of subscribers. Mr. Poe's articles were to have still greater currency given them by uniting the Lady's Book with Arthur's Magazine, and publishing them with the latest Paris fashions, Americanized and expressed from Paris. A still greater impetus was to be given to Mr. Poe's opinions; they were even to be accompanied with autographs of the New York Literati. It is said that all Division street was put in an uproar by this tremendous announcement, and two milliner's apprentices never slept a wink one whole night, for thinking about it. Some of the students in Dr. Anthon's grammar school made a pilgrimage to Bloomingdale to gaze upon the asylum where Mr. Poe was reported to be confined, in consequence of his immense mental efforts having turned his brain; and a certain great writer on small subjects, in Ann street, had serious thoughts of calling him the American Tasso; as to the New York literati, they all sat in their garrets shaking in their shoes, with their wives and children clinging to their knees, in fear. In short there was an earthquake among the literati and milliners. Mr. Godey was in Philadelphia all the while, as calm as a demon, smoking his cigar and writing advertisements of 2d Editions, and Mr. Poe was almost anywhere and in any situation which the mind could conceive.

At last the 'honest opinions' of Mr. Poe, and the Americanized fashions expressed from Paris, appeared together, and Mr. Godey himself says they are creating a great sensation throughout the country,—which we believe: But the sensation, so far as we have had an opportunity of observing, has been one of disgust. We never before saw so much froth on so small a quantity of small beer. Mr. Godey, in a card published in the Mirror, a few day's since, said that he had been advised to publish no more of Mr. Poe's opinions, and we are surprised that he, Mr. Godey, did not take the advice; because we are sure that none but a very sincere friend could have advised him to do so very sensible a thing. His enemies, if he have any, and we do not see how so amiable a gentleman can have any, would have advised him to act directly contrary. It was a capital thought in Mr. Poe to call his opinions of the New York literati *honest*, to distinguish them from his other judgments, and because nobody but himself would ever be likely to apply such an epithet to them. People were looking for a furious unbottling of carboy's of vitriol, torrents of aqua fortis, and demi-john's of prussic acid. But instead of these biting, withering and scorching elements, what was our astonishment to find only a few slender streams of sugar house molasses and Godfrey's cordial, trickling through the soft pages of Mr. Godey's Lady's Book. We were as much disappointed as though we had mixed a salad with *eau sucre*, instead of white vinegar. We had heard that Mr. Poe wrote with an antique stylus dipped in gall and mustard, and we find him using a crow quill and ink, 'warranted free from corrosive qualities.' Mr. Poe said a true thing of himself, in the preface to his opinions, in these words:

'We place on paper, without hesitation, a tissue of flatteries, to which in society we could not give utterance, for our lives, without either blushing or laughing outright.'*

In the two numbers already published of Mr. Poe's 'honest opinions,' there are notices of fourteen gentlemen and one lady; of the fifteen persons, not more than half were ever heard of before as literati. The sketches are extremely slight, and of not the least consequence to anybody; three or four of them had already appeared in the Democratic Review, where they died a natural death. The opinion on Mr. Willis, who has no particular claim that we know of to be considered one of the literati of New York city, is the only one which makes any show of ability of analysis, or of knowledge. Of its fairness, the following extract will attest:

'His success (for in point of fame, if of nothing else, he has certainly been successful) is to be attributed, one-third to his mental ability, and two-thirds to his physical temperament—the latter goading him into the accomplishment of what the former merely gave him the means of accomplishing.'

'Mr. Willis speaks French with some fluency, and Italian not quite so well,' says Mr. Poe, with a grand *comme il faut* air, as though he could speak French and Italian himself, which everybody knows he cannot do. But Mr. Poe thinks that Mr. Willis showed the greatest degree of ability, and gave the best evidence of possessing genius, by publishing a string of affidavits and certificates from my Lord knows who, in London, and the proprietors of certain tailors shops and boarding-houses in New York, in favor of his moral character, which had been attacked by the Courier & Enquirer. Well, if such 'management' as this be an evidence of genius, we know many a genius acting in the capacity of scullion, who always carry with them a certificate of character wherever they go. But Mr. Poe has a variety of ways of testing genius. He thinks the author of Tecumseh [George H. Colton] a genius, because he succeeded in obtaining 2500 subscribers for his Magazine [the *American Review*] in the first year of its establishment. One of his opinions is of a pot companion [William M. Gillespie?], contained in half a dozen lines, whose name appears for the

* Fuller, of course, is quoting out of context here for the sake of "exposing" Poe. In the "Author's Introduction" to "The Literati," Poe charged that two kinds of opinion exist in regard to contemporary authors—one popular and clique-manufactured; the other, private and honest. In respect to manufactured reputations, he maintained that editors—the "we" of this passage—were guilty of publishing a "tissue of flatteries. . . ."

first and probably for the last time, associated with the literati. Another is of somebody who, Mr. Poe says, never wrote three consecutive lines of grammatical English in his life [Charles F. Briggs, known as Harry Franco]. If this be true, his name has no right to be placed in a catalogue of the New York literati, nor of any other literati; but true or false, the opinion furnishes a key to Mr. Poe's 'honesty,' and affords sufficient evidence that he can be guilty of the meanness of making attacks on individuals to gratify personal malice, as some of his 'tissues of flatteries' prove that he can be a toady when he has any thing to gain.

As to the independence for which we have heard Mr. Poe commended, we certainly have never seen so small an amount of that commodity in a literary review as is contained in his 'honest opinions.' There is but one mark of it in the whole series of his 'literati,' and that is so purely personal as to appear the very reverse. His patronising notices of Dr. Bush, Mr. Verplanck, and Dr. Anthon, are really the most laughable things in their way that we ever saw in print. He is about as capable of measuring either of these gentlemen as the frog in the fable of showing the dimensions of an ox. If he didn't burst in the attempt, we came near doing so when looking at him.

We hope that Mr. Poe gets well paid for his 'honest opinions,' for we are sure that a man must be sadly in want of money who resorts to such methods of raising it, and we hope also that they may be the means of giving increased circulation to Mr. Godey's book, for the same reason. Mr. Poe is the last man in the country who should undertake the task of writing 'honest opinions' of the literati. His infirmities of mind and body, his petty jealousies, his necessities even, which allow him neither time nor serenity for such work, his limited information on local subjects, his unfortunate habits, his quarrels and jealousies, all unfit him for the performance of such a duty, as the specimens already published abundantly prove. The folly and nonsense of Mr. Poe's attempt are sufficiently apparent, but to any one who has read the sketches by Hazlitt of some of his contemporaries, they must appear monstrous. It is a matter of no consequence what the 'literati' themselves think of their delineator, no man is a proper judge of his own picture, but to gain the admiration or respect of the world, some degree of integrity, benevolence and power of characterization must be evinced. And these are just the qualities in which Mr. Poe's opinions are lamentably deficient. We have no thought of reviewing Mr. Poe's opinions, or we could enumerate numerous misstatements which are altogether inexcusable in such sketches. Opinions, whether they are called honest by their author or not, are always received under protest. We do not adopt another man's opinion as an article of faith; but there should be no guesses at facts, which, to be of any value, must be truths.

Although we have laughed at Mr. Godey's expressed—Americanized—Paris fashions, we have no wish to underrate his Lady's Book, nor to dispute his announcement that it is "decidedly the most valuable monthly magazine now published," for we know but little about it.

To conclude, after the fashion of our Thersitical Magazinist, Mr. Poe is about 39. He may be more or less. If neither more nor less, we should say he was decidedly 39. But of this we are not certain. In height he is about 5 feet 1 or two inches, perhaps 2 inches and a half. His face is pale and rather thin; eyes gray, watery, and always dull; nose rather prominent, pointed and sharp; nostrils wide; hair thin and cropped short; mouth not very well chiselled, nor very sweet; his tongue shows itself unpleasantly when he speaks earnestly, and seems too large for his mouth; teeth indifferent; forehead rather broad, and in the region of ideality decidedly large, but low, and in that part where phrenology places conscientiousness and the group of moral sentiments it is quite flat; chin narrow and pointed, which gives his head, upon the whole, a balloonish appearance, which may account for his supposed light-headedness; he generally carries his head upright like a fugleman on drill, but sometimes it droops considerably. His address is gentlemanly and agreeable at first, but it soon wears off and leaves a different impression after becoming acquainted with him; his walk is quick and jerking, sometimes waving, describing that peculiar figure in geometry denominated by Euclid, we think, but it may be Professor Farrar of Cambridge, Virginia fence. In dress he affects the tailor at times, and at times the cobbler, being in fact excessively nice or excessively something else. His hands are singularly small, resembling birds claws; his person slender; weight about 110 or 115 pounds, perhaps the latter; his study has not many of the Magliabechian characteristics, the shelves being filled mainly with ladies magazines; he is supposed to be a contributor to the Knickerbocker, but of this nothing certain is known; he is the author of Politian, a drama, to which Professor Longfellow is largely indebted, it is said by Mr Poe, for many of his ideas. Mr. Poe goes much into society, but what society we cannot positively say; he formerly lived at West Point; his present place of residence is unknown. He is married.

---

9. *15 and 30 June 1846: Poe's Letter to Joseph M. Field and Field's Article on Poe*

[*Poe felt that Fuller's description of him as a cretin was damaging, so he wrote to Field, the editor of the* Saint Louis Daily Reveille, *pleading that he "say a few words in condemnation" of the attack and "do away with the false impression of my personal appearance" that Fuller may have created. He also requested Field to enlist in his behalf the New Orleans* Daily Picayune, *the most famous newspaper in the South, and that he make laudatory comments on his work, for which he provided Field with copy.*

Poe seems to have gone far afield to get help, but he knew that the New York papers, including the Mirror, *"exchanged" with the* Reveille *and* Picayune, *and might reprint their articles, as they sometimes did. "Exchanging" before the era of wire services was common practice. Fuller, for example, said that he printed an extra two thousand copies a week of both* Mirrors *at a cost of $1,300 a year for purposes of exchange, and complained that some editors "refuse to* exchange papers *unless the difference in the subscription price be paid in advance." Despite the fact that the* Reveille *and* Picayune *cooperated with Poe, no New York paper republished their articles on him. Poe was reduced to sending clippings of the* Reveille *article to Louis Godey, who did not reprint it, and to Thomas Chivers.*

Little is known about Poe's relation to Field. From this one extant letter Poe wrote to Field, we know only that they met ("You have seen me and can describe me as I am"); that Poe knew about Field's connection with the Picayune—*he had been its European correspondent in 1840; and that they had exchanged journals. Field mentioned or quoted from the* Broadway Journal *on occasion, and Poe remarked in his letter, "I have frequently seen in 'The Reveillé' notices of myself. . . ." These notices appeared on 24 September, 10 and 29 October, 9 November, and 4 December 1845, as well as on 12 April 1846.*

Poe's remarks about Fuller's "swindling transactions" in Providence and cowardly behavior as a husband must remain in doubt, though in an article published subsequently (Document 24), Poe wrote: "Mr. Fuller is a pitiful man. Much is he to be pitied for his . . . Providential escapes— for the unwavering conjugal chivalry which, in a public theatre—but I pause. Not even in taking vengeance on a Fuller can I stoop to become a Fuller myself." All that I have been able to uncover is that Fuller had been the principal of Green Street Seminary in Providence, where he had as his assistant the gifted Margaret Fuller, no kin of his; that he afterward became a bookseller in Providence for several years before he moved to New York in 1843, where he joined the staff of the Mirror; *and that in October 1844 he improved his social and financial position by marrying Emilie Louise, daughter of John F. Delaplaine, an affluent New Yorker. But Poe's statement that Nathaniel Willis and George Pope Morris had to abandon the* Mirror *because they found Fuller disreputable seems untrue. As Fuller was only a junior editor and part-owner of the* Mirror, *they could have bought him out. (For more information on this matter, see headnote to Document 61.)*

Poe resorted to ruse in his letter. He did not explain to Field that Miss Barrett's remarks were made to him in a private letter. Instead, he changed her use of the second person to the third to give the impression that her remarks were taken from an essay-review. Of less significance but equally self-revealing is the fact that Poe was thirty-seven when he wrote this letter, not thirty-three as he alleges in his footnote.

That Poe had to seek editorial assistance in St. Louis is indicative of his loss of reputation in New York.

Poe's letter appears in Ostrom, II, 318–20.]

Poe's Letter to Field	*Field's Statement in the* Reveille
(Confidential) New-York : June 15. 46. Dear Field, I have frequently seen in "The Reveillé" notices of myself, evincing a kindly feeling on your part which, believe me, I reciprocate in the most cordial manner. This conviction of your friendship induces me now to beg a favor of you. I en-	EDGAR A. POE.—Certainly one of the most original geniuses of the country is Edgar A. Poe, and the only fault we have to find with him is, that he is wasting his time at present in giving his *"honest* opinions" touching his contemporaries —the maddest *kind* of honesty, in our opinion. Poe's papers upon the "New York Literati," published in

close an article from "The New-York Mirror" of May 26 th. headed "Mr Poe and the N.Y. Literati". The attack is editorial & the editor is Hiram Fuller. He was a schoolmaster, about 3 years ago, in Providence, and was forced to leave that city on account of several swindling transactions in which he was found out. As soon as Willis & Morris discovered the facts, they abandoned "The Mirror", preferring to leave it in his hands rather than keep up so disreputable a connexion. This Fuller ran off with the daughter of a respectable gentleman in this city & was married. The father met the couple in the Park theatre (the Park, I think) and was so carried away by indignation at the disgrace inflicted upon his family by the marriage, that he actually struck Mrs Fuller repeated blows in the face with his clenched fist—the husband looking calmly on, and not even attempting to interfere. I pledge you the honor of a gentleman that I have not exaggerated these facts in the slightest degree. They are here notorious.

All that I venture to ask of you in the case of this attack, however, is to say a few words in condemnation of it, and to do away with the false impression of my personal appearance* it *may* convey, in those parts

* I am 33 years of age—height 5 ft. 8. [Poe's note. Poe, of course, was 37 years old at this time.]

Godey's Magazine, have stirred up, as might have been expected, any amount of ill temper. The *Evening Mirror* takes the lead in the attack upon the author, who is very sick, by-the-bye, and unable to make battle, as is his wont. The Mirror, among other things, seeks to make Poe ridiculous by a false description of his personal appearance. We won't stand this. Instead of being "five foot one," &c, the poet is a figure to compare with any in manliness, while his features are not only intellectual, but handsome. As to his mental "presentment," the British journals are admitting his merits in the most unequivocal manner.

of the country where I am not individually known. You have seen me and can describe me as I am. Will you do me this act of justice, and influence one or two of your editorial friends to do the same? *I know you will.*

I think the "N. O. Picayune", which has always been friendly to me, will act in concert with you.

There is, also, an incidental service of great importance, just now, which you have it in your power to render me. That is, to put the following, editorially, in your paper:

A long and highly laudatory review of his Tales, written by *Martin Farquhar Tupper*, author of "Proverbial Philosophy", "The Crock of Gold" etc., appeared in a late number of "The London Literary Gazette". "The Athenaeum", "The British Critic["], "The Spectator", "The Popular Record"[,] "Churton's Literary Register", and various other journals, scientific as well as literary, have united in approbation of Tales & Poems. "The Raven" is copied in full in the "British Critic" and "The Athenaeum". "The Times" —the matter of fact *"Times!"*—copies the "Valdemar Case". The world's greatest poetess, *Elizabeth Barrett Barrett*, says of Mr Poe:—"This *vivid* writing!—this power *which is felt*! 'The Raven' has produced a *sensation*—a 'fit horror'—here in England. Some of my friends are

A long and highly laudatory review of his "Tales," written by *Martin Farquhar Tupper*, author of "Proverbial Philosophy," "The Crock of Gold," &c., appeared in a late number of "The London Literary Gazette." "The Athenaeum," "The British Critic," "The Spectator," "The Popular Record," "Churton's Literary Register," and various other journals, scientific as well as literary, have united in approbation of "Tales and Poems." "The Raven" is copied, in full, in the "British Critic" and "The Athenaeum." "The Times" —the matter of fact *Times!*—copies the "Valdemar Case." The world's greatest poetess, *Elizabeth Barrett*, says of Mr. Poe: "This *vivid* writing!—this power *which is felt*! 'The Raven' has produced a *sensation*— a 'fit horror'—here in England. *All are*

[23]

taken by the fear of it and some by the music—but all are taken. I hear of persons absolutely *haunted* by the 'Nevermore', and one acquaintance of mine who has the misfortune of possessing a 'bust of Pallas' never can bear to look at it in the twilight. Our great poet, Mr Browning, the author of 'Paracelsus', 'The Pomegranates' etc. is enthusiastic in his admiration of the rhythm."

After all this, Mr Poe may possibly make up his mind to endure the disapprobation of the editor of the *Mirror*.

Miss Barrett continues:—"Then there is a tale of his which I do not find in this volume, but which is going the rounds of the newspapers, about Mesmerism (The Valdemar case) throwing us all into 'most admired disorder', or dreadful doubts as to 'whether it can be true'. The *certain* thing in the tale in question is the *power* of the writer and the faculty he has of making horrible improbabilities seem near & familiar."

If you can oblige me in this case, you may depend on my most earnest reciprocation when where & how you please.

Cordially yours

Edgar A Poe.

P.S. Please *cut out* anything you may say and en[close i]t to me in a letter. A newspaper wil[l] not be [li]kely to reach me.

[24]

taken. I hear of persons absolutely *haunted* by the 'Nevermore,' and one acquaintance of mine, who has the misfortune of possessing a 'bust of Pallas,' never can bear to look at it in the twilight. Our great poet, Mr. Browning, the author of 'Paracelsus,' 'The Pomegranates,' &c, is enthusiastic in his admiration of the rhythm."

After all this, Mr. Poe may possibly make up his mind to endure the disapprobation of the editor of the *Mirror*.

Miss Barrett continues: "Then there is a tale of his which I do not find in this volume, but which is going the rounds of the newspapers about Mesmerism, ('The Valdemar Case,') throwing us all into 'most admired disorder,' or dreadful doubts as to whether it can be true. The *certain* thing in the tale in question is the *power* of the writer, and the faculty he has of making horrible improbabilities seem near and familiar."

We heartily wish Mr. Poe a speedy restoration to health and "honestly" regarding his literary combats as only tending to harass and weaken energies which were given for nobler struggles, we exclaim with the dramatist:

—— *"Honesty?*

'Tis a ragged virtue; prithee, no more of it."

I have been very seriously ill for some months* and, being thus utterly unable to defend myself, must rely upon the chivalry of my friends. Fuller knows of my illness & depends upon it for his security. I have never said a word about the vagabond in my life. Some person, I presume, has hired him to abuse me.

*—am now scarcely able to write even this letter—

---

10. *April 1846: Letter to Poe*
   Elizabeth Barrett Barrett

[*The curious reader will want to read the letter below, if only to see what use Poe made of Miss Barrett in his letter to Field. For Poe was less than candid with Field in respect to the poetess. He had dedicated* The Raven and Other Poems *to her ("To the noblest of her sex, . . . to Miss Elizabeth Barrett Barrett, of England, I dedicate this volume, with the most enthusiastic admiration and with the most sincere esteem"), though apparently she had received only the combined* Tales and Poems *that Wiley and Putnam had issued as a single volume, inscribed in Poe's handwriting, "To Miss Elizabeth Barrett Barrett, With the Respects of Edgar A. Poe." In gratitude she had written him the letter below, from which Poe quoted liberally, changing her use of the second person to the third to give the impression that her letter was an essay-review. Apart from this deception and the fact that he italicized certain phrases and omitted others, his quotations from her letter are substantially correct.*

The source of this letter is Harrison, XVII, 229–30.]

5 Wimpole St., April, 1846.

Dear Sir,—Receiving a book from you seems to authorize or at least encourage me to try to express what I have felt long before—my sense of the high honor you have done me in [illegible] your country and of mine, of the dedication of your poems. It is too great a distinction, conferred by a hand of too liberal generosity. I wish for my own sake I were worthy of it. But I may endeavour, by future work, to justify a little what I cannot deserve anywise, now. For it, meanwhile, I may be grateful—because gratitude is the virtue of the humblest.

After which imperfect acknowledgment of my personal obligation may I thank you as another reader would thank you for this vivid writing, this power which is felt! Your "Raven" has produced a sensation, a "fit horror," here in England. Some of my friends are taken by the fear of it and some by the music. I hear of persons haunted by the "Nevermore," and one acquaintance of mine who has the misfortune of possessing a "bust of Pallas" never can bear to look at it in the twilight. I think you will like to be told our great poet, Mr. Browning, the author of "Paracelsus," and the "Bells and Pomegranates," was struck much by the rhythm of that poem.

Then there is a tale of yours ("The Case of M. Valdemar") which I do not find in this volume, but which is going the round of the newspapers, about mesmerism, throwing us all into "most admired disorder," and dreadful doubts as to whether "it can be true," as the children say of ghost stories. The certain thing in the tale in question is the power of the writer, and the faculty he has of making horrible improbabilities seem near and familiar.

And now will you permit me, dear Mr. Poe, as one who though a stranger is grateful to you, and has the right of esteeming you though unseen by your eyes—will you permit me to remain

Very truly yours always,

Elizabeth Barrett Barrett

---

11. *20 June 1846: "Thomas Dunn English"*

Edgar A. Poe

[*The third installment of "The Literati" contained Poe's outrageously playful sketch of English, the antic spirit of which English himself had encouraged in Poe. Companions in the Philadelphia days, they had become companions again in New York when Poe, conducting his "Little Longfellow War" in the* Broadway Journal, *found an ally in English's* Aristidean, *a monthly magazine that began and ended its career in 1845.*

All the articles in English's journal were anonymous and, except for internal evidence, there was no way for the contemporary reader to identify an article until the Index appeared in the last number providing the titles and initials of contributors. If there was doubt as to the initials TDE or EAP, English's card of gratitude listing his "collaborators" dispelled it.

There was a great deal of editorial hanky-panky between Poe and English, both of whom liked to gibbet dunces. Both the Broadway Journal, once Poe owned it, and the Aristidean listed 304 Broadway as the address of their respective editorial offices. At this address English kept what he called chambers, and his friend, Thomas H. Lane, who had a financial hand in both magazines, had a room adjoining his. The Aristidean listed "Lane & Co." as the proprietor, and Lane purchased a half-interest in the Broadway Journal just before its demise. (Poe's valedictory told subscribers that "Mr. Thomas H. Lane is authorized to collect all money due to the Journal.") Whatever other role Lane played—perhaps that of an appreciative audience—one can at least imagine Poe and English in the apartment at their writing desks, hilariously spurring each other to greater and greater excesses as they collaborated in lampooning one dunce or another. The devastating ten-page review of "Henry B. Hirst's Poems," a poet they used to pal with in Philadelphia, is a prime example of their being carried away by near-manic humor. (The article, though initialed TDE in the Index to the Aristidean, is entirely in Poe's style, which suggests at least that Poe wrote the final version.) Similarly, the articles on "Longfellow's Poems" and "Poe's Tales," the first initialed EAP, the other for obvious reasons initialed TDE, go to fantastic lengths to prove Poe infinitely superior to Longfellow. The article on Longfellow stated—and one can hear the wild laughter in the background: ". . . We were not a little surprised to hear Mr. Poe . . . claim for the Professor a pre-eminence over all poets of this country. . . . We will make an even wager . . . that the rash opinion would not be given again."

In addition to this kind of hanky-panky, Poe and English in the Broadway Journal, whether individually or collaboratively, lauded certain articles in the Aristidean or the magazine as a whole. On 4 October 1845, for example, one of them wrote: "There is a scorching review of Hirst's Poems—a good thing for everybody but Mr. Hirst;—this is a very laughable article."

Alliance between the two men came to an abrupt end in 1846 when Poe appeared at English's apartment begging for a pistol to defend him-

self against Colonel William Lummis, whose sister, Mrs. Elizabeth Ellet,
he had outraged by saying in the presence of witnesses that she had
written compromising letters to him (see headnote to Document 89). En-
glish refused Poe the pistol, urging him instead to retract his unfounded
charges if he wished to save his skin. Affronted by the insult that he was
a rank liar, Poe had a fist fight with English, a fight that both men con-
tinued, at Poe's instigation, in the journalistic arena.

English not only encouraged Poe in the craft of ridicule, but he be-
came in turn the object of his ridicule. Moreover, when he charged that
Poe had taken money from him under false pretenses (the loan of thirty
dollars to help buy the Broadway Journal, *for which sum he was alleged-*
ly promised an interest in the magazine), Poe was able to retort that En-
glish had not fully reimbursed him for his contributions to the Aristidean,
in particular for his article on American poetry.

This sketch of English was published in the July number of Godey's
Lady's Book *which appeared on June 20.*]

THOMAS DUNN ENGLISH

I have seen one or two brief poems of considerable merit with the
signature of *Thomas Dunn English* appended. For example—
"AZTHENE.
"A sound melodious shook the breeze
    When thy beloved name was heard:
    Such was the music in the word
    Its dainty rhythm the pulses stirred.
But passed forever joys like these.
    There is no joy, no light, no day;
    But black despair and night alway,
        And thickening gloom:
And this, Azthene, is my doom.

"Was it for this, for weary years,
    I strove among the sons of men,
    And by the magic of my pen—
    Just sorcery—walked the lion's den
Of slander void of tears and fears—
And all for thee? For thee!—alas,

As is the image on a glass
So baseless seems,
Azthene, all my earthly dreams."

I must confess, however, that I do not appreciate the "dainty rhythm" of such a word as "Azthene," and, perhaps, there is a little taint of egotism in the passage about "the magic" of Mr. English's pen. Let us be charitable, however, and set all this down under the head of "pure imagination" or invention—one of the first of poetical requisites. The *inexcusable* sin of Mr. E. is imitation—if this be not too mild a term. Barry Cornwall and others of the *bizarre* school are his especial favorites. He has taken, too, most unwarrantable liberties, in the way of downright plagiarism, from a Philadelphian poet whose high merits have not been properly appreciated—*Mr. Henry B. Hirst.*

I place Mr. English, however, on my list of New York *literati*, not on account of his poetry, (which I presume he is not weak enough to estimate very highly,) but on the score of his having edited for several months, "with the aid of numerous collaborators," a monthly magazine called "The Aristidean." This work, although professedly a "monthly," was issued at irregular intervals, and was unfortunate, I fear, in not attaining at any period a very extensive circulation.

I learn that Mr. E. is not without talent; but the fate of "The Aristidean" should indicate to him the necessity of applying himself to study. No spectacle can be more pitiable than that of a man without the commonest school education busying himself in attempts to instruct mankind on topics of polite literature. The absurdity in such cases does not lie merely in the ignorance displayed by the would-be instructor, but in the transparency of the shifts by which he endeavours to keep this ignorance concealed. The editor of "The Aristidean," for example, was not laughed at so much on account of writing "lay" for "lie," etc. etc., and coupling nouns in the plural with verbs in the singular—as where he writes above,

"—— so baseless *seems*,
Azthene, all my earthly *dreams*—"

he was not, I say, laughed at *so much* for his excusable deficiencies in English grammar (although an editor should certainly be able to write *his own name*) as that, in the hope of disguising such deficiency, he was perpetually lamenting the "typographical blunders" that "in the most unaccountable manner *would* creep into his work.["] Nobody was so stupid as to suppose for a moment that there existed in New York a single proof-reader—or even a single printer's devil—who would have permitted *such* errors to escape. By the excuses offered, therefore, the errors were only the more obviously nailed to the counter as Mr. English's own.

I make these remarks in no spirit of unkindness. Mr. E. is yet young—certainly not more than thirty-five—and might, with his talents, readily improve himself at points where he is most defective. No one of any generosity would think the worse of him for getting private instruction.

I do not personally know Mr. English. He is, I believe, from Phila-delphia, where he was formerly a doctor of medicine, and subsequently took up the profession of law; more latterly he joined the Tyler party and devoted his attention to politics. About his personal appearance there is nothing very observable. I cannot say whether he is married or not.

---

12. *"Thomas Dunn Brown" (the Revised Version of "Thomas Dunn English")*
Edgar A. Poe

[*On 15 December 1846 Poe wrote that the "unexpected circulation" of "The Literati" "suggested to me that I might make a hit and some profit, as well as proper fame, by extending the plan into that of a book on American Letters generally, and keeping the publication in my own hands. I am now at this—body & soul" (Document 58). The projected book, though it had many provisional titles, was to be called* Literary America: Some Honest Opinions about Our Aut[h]orial Merits and Demerits with Occasional Words of Personality. *The three extant chapters on Richard Adams Locke, Christopher Pearse Cranch, and Thomas Dunn English— now called Thomas Dunn Brown, a nickname with which he was tagged in Philadelphia and to which English perversely referred in* The John-Donkey *he co-edited in 1848 ("Punch is certainly 'Dunn brown' by . . . this modern speaking Ass")—explain why Poe never finished the book. Mere elaborations of their originals, they do not go beyond the "critical gossip" which Poe recognized as the chief fault of "The Literati."*

Upon Poe's death in 1849, Rufus Wilmot Griswold, though an enemy of Poe, acted as Poe's literary executor. The third of his four-volume edi-tion of the dead man's works was The Literati *(1850). Whether he wanted to smear Poe's memory by republishing the New York sketches, as seems* evident by his "Memoir of the Author" that introduces the volume, or whether he felt the sketches would make the edition more salable, he substituted without explanation the essay "Thomas Dunn Brown" for the original "Thomas Dunn English." Since the two essays are often confused with each other (see, for instance, Hervey Allen, Israfel, page 549, and Frances Winwar, The Haunted Palace, page 298), it is reprinted here.]

THOMAS DUNN BROWN.

I HAVE seen one or two scraps of verse with this gentleman's *nom de plume** appended, which had considerable merit. For example:

> A sound melodious shook the breeze
>> When thy beloved name was heard:
>> Such was the music in the word
>> Its dainty rhythm the pulses stirred [.]
> But passed forever joys like these.
>> There is no joy, no light, no day;
>> But black despair and night *al-way*
>>> And thickening gloom:
> And this, Azthene, is my doom.
>
> Was it for this, for weary years,
>> I strove among the sons of men,
>> And by *the magic of my pen—*
> Just sorcery—walked the lion's den
> Of slander void of tears and fears—
>> And all for thee? For thee!—alas,
>> As is the image on a glass
>>> So baseless *seems,*
> Azthene, all my early [*sic*] *dreams.*

I must confess, however, that I do not appreciate the "dainty rhythm" of such a word as "Azthene," and, perhaps, there is some taint of egotism in the passage about "the magic" of Mr. Brown's pen. Let us be charitable, however, and set all this down under the head of the pure imagination or invention—the first of poetical requisites. The *inexcusable* sin of Mr. Brown is imitation—if this be not too mild a term. When Barry Cornwall, for example, sings about a "dainty rhythm," Mr. Brown forthwith, in B flat, hoots about it too. He has taken, however, his most unwarrant-

* Thomas Dunn English [Poe's note].

able liberties in the way of plagiarism, with Mr. Henry B. Hirst, of Phila-delphia—a poet whose merits have not yet been properly estimated.

I place Mr. Brown, to be sure, on my list of literary people not on account of his poetry, (which I presume he himself is not weak enough to estimate very highly,) but on the score of his having edited, for several months, "with the aid of numerous collaborators," a magazine called "The Aristidean." This work, although professedly a "monthly," was issued at irregular intervals, and was unfortunate, I fear, in not attaining at any period more than about fifty subscribers.

Mr. Brown has at least that amount of talent which would enable him to succeed in his father's profession—that of a ferryman on the Schuyl-kill—but the fate of "The Aristidean" should indicate to him that, to pros-per in any higher walk of life, he must apply himself to study. No spec-tacle can be more ludicrous than that of a man without the commonest school education, busying himself in attempts to instruct mankind on topics of polite literature. The absurdity, in such cases, does not lie merely in the ignorance displayed by the would-be instructor, but in the trans-parency of the shifts by which he endeavors to keep this ignorance con-cealed. The "editor of the Aristidean," for example, was not the public laughing-stock throughout the five months of his magazine's existence, so much on account of writing "lay" for "lie," "went" for "gone," "set" for "sit," etc. etc., or for coupling nouns in the plural with verbs in the singular—as when he writes, above,

—— so baseless *seems*,
Azthene, all my earthly *dreams*—

he was not, I say, laughed at *so much* on account of his excusable de-ficiencies in English grammar (although an editor should undoubtedly be able to write *his own name*) as on account of the pertinacity with which he exposed his weakness, in lamenting the "typographical blun-ders" which so unluckily *would* creep into his work. He should have re-flected that there is not in all America a proof-reader so blind as to permit *such* errors to escape him. The rhyme, for instance, in the matter of the "dreams" that "seems," would have distinctly shown even the most un-educated printers' devil that he, the devil, had no right to meddle with so obviously an *intentional* peculiarity.

Were I writing merely for American readers, I should not, of course, have introduced Mr. Brown's name in this book. With us, *grotesqueries* such as "The Aristidean" and its editor, are not altogether unparalleled, and are sufficiently well understood—but my purpose is to convey to foreigners some idea of a condition of literary affairs among us, which otherwise they might find it difficult to comprehend or to conceive. That Mr. Brown's blunders are really such as I have described them—that I have not distorted their character or exaggerated their grossness in any respect—that there existed in New York, for some months, as conductor of a magazine that called itself *the organ of the Tyler party*, and was even mentioned, at times, by respectable papers, a man who obviously *never went to school*, and was so profoundly ignorant as not to know that he could not spell—are serious and positive facts—uncolored in the slightest degree—demonstrable, in a word, upon the spot, by reference to almost any editorial sentence upon any page of the magazine in question. But a single instance will suffice:—Mr. Hirst, in one of his poems, has the lines,

> Oh Odin! 'twas pleasure—'twas passion to see
> Her serfs sweep like wolves on a lambkin like me.

At page 200 of "The Aristidean" for September, 1845, Mr. Brown, commenting on the English of the passage, says:—"This lambkin might have used better language than '*like me*'—unless he intended it for a specimen of choice Choctaw, when it may, for all we know to the contrary, pass muster." It is needless, I presume, to proceed farther in a search for the most direct proof possible or conceivable, of the ignorance of Mr. Brown—who, in similar cases, invariably writes—"like I."

In an editorial announcement on page 242 of the same "number," he says:—"This and the three succeeding *numbers brings* the work up to January and with the two *numbers* previously published *makes* up a volume or half year of *numbers*." But enough of his absurdity:—Mr. Brown had, for the motto on his magazine cover, the words of Richelieu,

> ——— Men call me cruel;
> I am not:—I am *just*.

Here the two monosyllables "an ass" should have been appended. They were no doubt omitted through "one of those d——d typographical blunders" which, through life, have been at once the bane and the antidote of Mr. Brown.

I make these remarks in no spirit of unkindness. Mr. B. is yet young—certainly not more than thirty-eight or nine—and might readily improve himself at points where he is most defective. No one of any generosity would think the worse of him for getting private instruction.

I do not personally know him. About his appearance there is nothing very remarkable—except that he exists in a perpetual state of vacillation between mustachio and goatee. In character, a *windbeutel*.

---

13. 23 *June 1846: "A Card: Mr. English's Reply to Mr. Poe" (with an Introduction by Hiram Fuller)*
Thomas Dunn English

[Unlike the other literati featured in Poe's sketches—Lewis Gaylord Clark was to prove an exception—English did not vent his anger in private. Roused by Poe's tone of contempt and his charges of plagiarism and ignorance, not to mention Poe's mocking disclaimer that he made "these remarks in no spirit of unkindness," English sent his reply to all the New York papers, if we can believe Hiram Fuller, but only the Morning Telegraph and Evening Mirror published it—on June 23. (Fuller also printed the reply in the Weekly Mirror on June 27.) Poe could not help hearing that the Telegraph had published English's reply. The Daily Tribune, for instance, carried this statement on 24 July 1846: "We understand that Mr. Poe has commenced a libel-suit against the proprietor of the Evening Mirror for republishing the Card of Mr. English from the Telegraph." But Poe chose to ignore that fact, for there is nothing in the record to suggest that he settled with the publisher of the Telegraph out of court.

English's so-called card was not a card at all, for English had not paid for its insertion; nor was it, like Godey's legitimate card (Document 5), buried among the advertisements. Rather, it was featured on the "news and gossip" page and prefaced by Fuller himself.

In his reply English made two actionable statements. The first was that Poe had obtained money from him under false pretenses, a matter of an alleged loan of thirty dollars to help Poe buy the Broadway Journal from John Bisco, the publisher, and that allegedly was to have given English an interest in the magazine. The second libel was that Poe had committed forgery. In his deposition (Document 76) English explained that Poe's victim was his uncle, though Poe, of course, had none. The other charges English made were execrable perhaps but not libelous. He

charged Poe with irresponsible conduct in respect to New York Univer-
sity and with discreditable behavior at the Boston Lyceum; of having
slandered an "esteemed authoress, of the South," Mrs. Elizabeth Ellet,
who, Poe had alleged, had written compromising letters to him; and he
concluded by returning Poe's charges of plagiarism and ignorance, to
which he added another, that Poe was "thoroughly unprincipled, base
and depraved. . . ."]

THE WAR OF THE LITERATI.—We publish the following terrific rejoinder of one of Mr. Poe's abused *literati*, with a twinge of pity for the object
of its severity. But as Mr. Godey, 'for a consideration,' lends the use of
his battery for an attack on the one side, it is but fair that we allow our
friends an opportunity to exercise a little 'self-defence' on the other.

[A CARD]
MR. ENGLISH'S REPLY TO MR. POE.

As I have not, of late, replied to attacks made upon me through the
public press, I can easily afford to make an exception, and still keep my
rule a general one. A Mr. Edgar A. Poe has been engaged for some time
past in giving to the public, through the medium of the *Lady's Book*,
sketches of what he facetiously calls the 'literati of New York city.' These
he names by way of distinction, I presume, from his ordinary writings,
'*honest* opinions.' He honors me by including me in the very numerous
and remarkably august body he affects to describe. Others have con-
verted the paper on which his sketches are printed to its legitimate use—
like to like—but as he seems to covet a notice from me, he shall be
gratified.

Mr. Poe states in his article, 'I do not personally know Mr. English.'
That he does not know me is not a matter of wonder. The severe treatment he received at my hands for brutal and dastardly conduct, rendered
it necessary for him, if possible, to forget my existence. Unfortunately, I
know him; and by the blessing of God, and the assistance of a grey-goose
quill, my design is to make the public know him also.

I know Mr. Poe by a succession of his acts—one of which is rather costly. I hold Mr. Poe's acknowledgement for a sum of money which he obtained of me under false pretences. As I stand in need of it at this time,
I am content he should forget to know me, provided he acquits himself
of the money he owes me. I ask no interest, in lieu of which I am willing
to credit him with the sound cuffing I gave him when I last saw him.

Another act of his gave me some knowledge of him. A merchant of this city had accused him of committing forgery. He consulted me on the mode of punishing his accuser, and as he was afraid to challenge him to the field, or chastise him personally, I suggested a legal prosecution as his sole remedy. At his request, I obtained a counsellor who was willing, as a compliment to me, to conduct his suit without the customary retaining fee. But, though so eager at first to commence proceedings, he dropped the matter altogether, when the time came for him to act—thus virtually admitting the truth of the charge.

Some time before this, if I mistake not, Mr. Poe accepted an invitation to deliver a poem before a society of the New York University. About a week before the time when this poem was to be pronounced, he called on me, appearing to be much troubled—said he could not write the poem, and begged me to help him out with some idea of the course to pursue. I suggested that he had better write a note to the society, and frankly state his inability to compose a poem on a stated subject. He did not do this, but—as he always does when troubled—drank until intoxicated; and remained in a state of intoxication during the week. When the night of exhibition came, it was gravely announced that Mr. Poe could not deliver his poem, on account of severe indisposition!

His next affair of a similar kind, was still more discreditable. Unmindful of his former act, he accepted an invitation to deliver a poem before a Boston institution—the Lyceum, I think. When I remonstrated with him on undertaking a task he could not perform, he alleged that he was in want of the money they would pay him, and would contrive to 'cook up something.' Want of ability prevented him from performing his intention, and he insulted his audience, and rendered himself a laughing-stock, by reciting a mass of ridiculous stuff, written by some one, and printed under his name when he was about 18 years of age. It had a peculiar effect on his audience, who dispersed under its infliction; and when he was rebuked for his fraud, he asserted that he had intended a hoax. Whether he did or not is little matter, when we reflect that he took the money offered for his performance—thus committing an act unworthy of a gentleman, though in strict keeping with Mr. Poe's previous acts.

But a series of events occurred in January last, which, while they led to my complete knowledge of Mr. Poe, has excited his wrath against me, and provoked the exhibition of impotent malice now under my notice.

Mr. Poe having been guilty of some most ungentlemanly conduct, while in a state of intoxication, I was obliged to treat him with discourtesy. Some time after this, he came to my chambers, in my absence, in search of me. He found there, a nephew of one of our ex-presidents. To that gentleman he stated, that he desired to see me in order to apologise to me for his conduct. I entered shortly after, when he tendered me an apology and his hand. The former I accepted, the latter I refused. He told me that he came to beg my pardon, because he wished me to do him a favor. Amused at this novel reason for an apology, I replied that I would do the favor, with pleasure, if possible, but not on the score of friendship. He said that though his friendship was of little service his enmity might be dangerous. To this I rejoined that I shunned his friendship and despised his enmity. He beseeched a private conversation, so abjectly, that, finally, moved by his humble entreaty, I accorded it. Then he told me that he had villified a certain well known and esteemed authoress, of the South, then on a visit to New York; that he had accused her of having written letters to him which compromised her reputation; and that her brother (her husband being absent) had threatened his life unless he produced the letters he named. He begged me for God's sake to stand his friend, as he expected to be challenged. I refused, because I was not willing to mix myself in his affairs, and because having once before done so, I had found him at the critical moment, to be an abject poltroon. These reasons I told him. He then begged the loan of a pistol to defend himself against attack. This request I refused, saying that his surest defence was a retraction of unfounded charges. He, at last, grew exasperated, and using offensive language, was expelled from the room. In a day or so, afterwards, being confined to his bed from the effect of fright and the blows he had received from me, he sent a letter to the brother of the lady he had so vilely slandered, denying all recollection of having made any charges of the kind alleged, and stating that, if he had made them, he was laboring under a fit of insanity to which he was periodically subject. The physician who bore it said that Mr. Poe was then suffering under great fear, and the consequences might be serious to the mind of his patient, if the injured party did not declare himself satisfied.—The letter being a full retraction of the falsehood, he, to whom it was addressed, stopped further proceedings, and the next day Mr. Poe hastily fled from town.

I can, if necessary, give some facts connected with the last mentioned circumstances, which show Mr Poe's conduct in a still baser view. And I can detail the history of my assailant's deeds in Philadelphia and New York. I have not room here, but, if Mr. Poe desires it, he can be accommodated at any future time.

I am not alone in my knowledge of Mr. Poe. The kennels of Philadelphia streets, from which I once kindly raised him, have frequently had the pleasure of his acquaintance; the 'Tombs,' of New York, has probably a dim remembrance of his person; and if certain very eminent and able authors and publishers, in this city, do not know him as I do, I am much mistaken—and so are they.

His review of my style and manner is only amusing when contrasted with his former laudation, almost to sycophancy, of my works. Whether he lied then or now, is a matter of little moment. His lamentation over my lack of common English education is heart-rending to hear. I will acknowledge my deficiencies with pleasure. It is a great pity he is not equally candid. He professes to know every language and to be a proficient in every art and science under the sun—when, except that half Choctaw, half-Winebago he habitually uses, and the art and science of 'Jeremy-Diddling,' he is ignorant of all. If he really understands the English language, the sooner he translates his notices of the New York literati, into it, the better for his readers.

Mr. Poe has announced his determination to hunt me down. I am very much obliged to him, and really wish he would hurry to begin. That he has a fifty fish-woman-power of Billingsgate, I admit; and that he has issued his bull, from his garret of a Vatican, up some six pair of stairs, excommunicating me from the church literary, is evident. But he overrates his own powers. He really does not possess one tithe of that greatness which he seems to regard as an uncomfortable burthen. He mistakes coarse abuse for polished invective, and vulgar insinuation for sly satire. He is not alone thoroughly unprincipled, base and depraved, but silly, vain and ignorant—not alone an assassin in morals, but a quack in literature. His frequent quotations from languages of which he is entirely ignorant, and his consequent blunders expose him to ridicule; while his cool plagiarisms from known or forgotten writers, excite the public amazement. He is a complete evidence of his own assertion, that 'no spectacle can be more pitiable than that of a man without the commonest school education, busying himself in attempts to instruct mankind on topics of polite literature.' If he deserves credit for any thing, it is for his frankness in acknowledging a fact, which his writings so triumphantly demonstrate.

THOMAS DUNN ENGLISH

---

14. 24 June 1846: "Quarrel among the Literati"
Morning News

[*The earliest published reaction to English's "Card" was recorded in the* Morning News, *which, according to Fuller, was "issued from the Mirror building" (*Evening Mirror, 1 May 1846*).*]

QUARREL AMONG THE LITERATI.—Edgar A. Poe attacked Thomas Dunn English most ridiculously in a late number of Godey's Lady's Book, and Mr. English, in the papers of yesterday, replied in a most caustic and fearful article. When Mr. Poe attacked English he took hold of the wrong man.

---

15. 25 June 1846: "Quarrels among the Literati"
Public Ledger

[*Another reaction to English's "Reply to Mr. Poe" was registered in the* Philadelphia *Public Ledger. The article was noncommittal on the whole, though the columnist observed that English "carves up" Poe "in the most caustic manner imaginable."*
"To catch a tartar" is to attack someone more powerful than oneself and thereby to get more than one bargained for. The "Resaca de la Palma affair" is an allusion to the battle fought there by General Mariano Arista and General Zachary Taylor in the previous month, on May 8 and 9. Because of the retreat of the Mexican forces at Resaca (Resaca de Guerrero), General Arista was replaced by General Pedro Ampudia.]

QUARRELS AMONG THE LITERATI.—The New York Literati are by the ears again, and are saying all sorts of complimentary things of each other in the tartest possible manner. Mr. Edgar A. Poe, poet and critic, well known in this city, recently attacked Thomas Dunn English, formerly of

Philadelphia, in a late number of Godey's Lady's Book. But Mr. Poe evidently waked up the wrong passenger and caught a tartar, for Mr. English is out in a terrific rejoinder upon Mr. Poe, and carves him in the most caustic manner imaginable. This is the first brush between the literary combatants, and if English's assault does not prove a Resaca de la Palma affair to Mr. Poe, he will muster his intellectual forces, and give his adversary another battle.

---

16. *26 June 1846: To the Editor of the* Mirror
"Justitia"

[*From a subscriber in Troy came a letter responding to the publication of English's "Card," which Fuller printed in the* Evening Mirror *without comment. "Justitia" is, of course, Latin for "justice."*]

Troy, June 24th, 1846

DEAR SIR.—In inserting Mr. English's card relative to Edgar A. Poe, you "have done the State some service." Mr. Poe may consider his "position defined." I think no one can deny that Mr. Thomas Dunn English has left Mr. Poe *done brown.*

Yours truly,
Justitia.

---

17. *27 June 1846: "Literary Quarrel"*
John S. Du Solle

[*Du Solle, editor of the Philadelphia* Spirit of the Times, *also recorded his reaction to English's "Reply to Mr. Poe" in his newspaper.*

Judging from the reports, English had a reputation for pugnacity. The Morning News *said that Poe had taken hold of the wrong man. The* Public Ledger *likewise said that Poe had "caught a tartar." And now Du Solle, who had known the man when he lived in Philadelphia, said that English was "back upon the literary meat-axe," an allusion to English's treatment of Henry A. Wise (see headnote to Document 20).*]

LITERARY QUARREL.—Mr. Poe, in an article in the July number of the Lady's Book, made an ungenerous attack upon Thomas Dunn English, and among other things asserted that he did not know Mr. E. The latter is back upon the literary meat-axe in a style which shows pretty conclusively that he knows Mr. Poe very well.

---

18. 27 June 1846: "Literary Squabble"
George Pope Morris

[*Another reaction to English's "Reply to Mr. Poe" came from Morris, who was asked by correspondents of his* National Press *to reprint English's article. He refused on the grounds that it was "one of the most savage and bitter things we ever read. . . ."*

Morris's reply was not altogether unpredictable. His notices of Poe had been favorable when he and Hiram Fuller edited the Evening Mirror *upon the departure of Nathaniel Willis for Europe in October 1845. On October 13, for instance, he announced Poe's scheduled appearance before the Boston Lyceum, though he never afterward alluded to Poe's controversial performance there or to its scandalous aftermath except once, and that on the whole approvingly. "The Broadway Journal of to-day," he wrote on November 22, "contains a long tale by the editor, a long attack by the editor, and a long defense of the editor—each excellent of its kind." (The "long attack" was Poe's assault upon the Boston newspaper editors who were then harrying him for his alleged hoax at the Boston Lyceum; the "long defense" was William Gilmore Simms's article on Poe reprinted from the Charleston* Southern Patriot *of 10 November 1845.) Morris's review of* The Raven *volume on November 21 was almost ecstatic, yet he said he was doing but "bare justice to the author." And on November 18 he reprinted Poe's preface to* The Raven *volume under the title "Sentiments of a True Poet" and commented: "We like the spirit that dictated it."*

*The notices of his associate, marked by an asterisk to denote "the contributions of Mr. Fuller the junior editor of the paper" (*Evening Mirror, *October 31), were not nearly so cordial in respect to Poe. He said Poe's tales belong "to that somewhat peculiar style of writing, which . . . we will risk a pun—and name the new school of Poe-lite literature" (October*

18), and he quarreled with a writer in Godey's Lady's Book *who declared Poe to be "one of the most accomplished authors in America" and ranked in England "among the classic writers of the mother tongue" (November 27).*

For reasons that are not clear, Morris and Willis sold their interest in the Evening Mirror *and* Weekly Mirror *in January 1846 to Fuller and his brother-in-law, Augustus W. Clason, Jr. Morris did not remain idle, however; he founded the* National Press: A Journal for Home, *and Willis, upon his return to New York in March 1846 again became Morris's partner, at which time the weekly changed its name to the* Home Journal.]

LITERARY SQUABBLE.—The reply of Mr. English to Mr. Poe is one of the most savage and bitter things we ever read—so much so that we are obliged to decline the requests of several correspondents to publish it in these columns. We condemn all literary squabbles—they are in very bad taste; but when attacks are made, rejoinders will follow.

---

19. *24 July 1846: Letter to Evert A. Duyckinck*
Rufus W. Griswold

[Griswold commented on English's "Card" in the course of a brief letter to Duyckinck, a comment all the more telling for coming from Poe's self-acknowledged enemy, though allowance should be made for the fact that Griswold knew that Poe was Duyckinck's friend.

The Simms works Griswold alludes to are The Wigwam and the Cabin *and* Views and Reviews in American Literature, History and Fiction. *They were not published in the* Library of Choice Reading, *which was devoted to works by foreign authors, but in the* Library of American Books, *both of which series were conducted by Duyckinck as editor for the New York publishers, Wiley and Putnam. Harnden and Company, like Gay and Company, was a private express firm that shipped mail and packages at cheaper rates than the government post office.*

This letter is in the Duyckinck Collection of the New York Public Library.]

Dear Sir

If your leisure will permit you to write a review of Mr Simms's works, based on the late publications by him in The Library of Choice Reading, I will have it inserted in Graham's Magazine. I am sure the task would be an agreeable one to you, and its fulfilment would be pleasing to Mr Simms as well as to me.

I asked Mr [illegible] to endeavor to purchase for me a copy of the Paris edition of Irving, and in case of inability to do so, to beg the use of yours, a few days, upon its return by Mr Poe. It could be sent me by Harnden, and by the same means returned safely. Speaking of Poe reminds me of the brutal article in the Mirror, which it is impossible on any grounds whatever to justify in the slightest degree.

I, who have as much cause as any man to quarrel with Poe, would sooner have cut off my hand than used it to write such an ungentlemanly Card, though every word were true. But my indignation of this treatment even of an enemy exceeds my power of expression.

I am yours ever very truly
Rufus W. Griswold

E. A. Duyckinck, Esq.
New York

---

20. 27 June 1846: Letter to Henry B. Hirst
Edgar A. Poe

[Whatever the reactions to English's "Card," Poe seemed undisturbed by them. Instead, he proceeded to write a counterreply for which he began collecting information. The first person he apparently approached for this purpose was Hirst, a Philadelphia poet who had been a bon camarade of Poe and English. Hirst had been of service to him before: he had written the biographical sketch of Poe that appeared in the Philadelphia Saturday Museum on 4 March 1843.

Poe felt that Hirst would prove cooperative, for in his sketch of English he had written: English "has taken . . . most unwarrantable liberties, in the way of downright plagiarism, from a Philadelphia poet whose high merits have not been properly appreciated—Mr. Henry B.

Hirst." *Poe conveniently forgot his collaboration with English in the dev-astating article on Hirst published in the* Aristidean *(see headnote to Document 11). English would not forget, however; he would frequently deride Hirst in the* John-Donkey *by calling him Miss Henriette B. Hirst, as in this example: "Miss Henriette has been shining, like a defunct mack-erel" (22 April 1848).*

The Honorable Sandy Harris whom Poe mentions seems to be Ira Harris, who became a Supreme Court justice in 1848. John S. Du Solle was the editor of the Philadelphia Spirit of the Times, *who had already indicated that he was less than sympathetic to Poe (Document 17). Henry A. Wise, a congressman, had acted as one of President Tyler's closest ad-visers. Tyler had appointed Wise to be minister to France, but the ap-pointment was rejected by the Senate. English's "attack on H. A. Wise" which Poe requests from Hirst was published in the* Public Ledger *on 14 November 1842. English was provoked by Wise because under the name of "Hawkeye," Wise had criticized the factionalism of the Philadelphia Democrats, in which activity English and his father were involved. En-glish's response to Wise's article was much like his response to Poe's sketch of himself. He called Wise a "sneaking coward," a "covert assassin," "an anonymous libeller," and a man "whose name is a stench in the nos-trils of the great American people." (See Gravely, pages 147–9, for the full article.)*

Hirst's letter, assuming that he replied, is not extant, nor does the evidence indicate that Poe waited for Hirst's information since Poe's letter to Hirst and his "Reply to Mr. English and Others" (Document 24) are both dated June 27.

The letter below appears in Ostrom, II 321–2.]

New : York—June 27. 46.

My Dear Hirst,

I presume you have seen what I said about you in "The New-York Literati" and an attack made on me by English, in consequence. *Vive la Bagatelle!*

I write now, to ask you if you can oblige me by a fair account of your duel with English. I would take it as a great favor, also, if you would get from Sandy Harris a statement of the fracas with *him*. See Du Solle, also, if you can & ask him if he is willing to give me, for publication, an account of his kicking E. out of his office.

I gave E. a flogging which he will remember to the day of his death—

and, luckily, in the presence of witnesses. He thinks to avenge himself by lies—but I shall be a match for him by means of simple truth.

Is it possible to procure me a copy of E's attack on H.A. Wise?

Truly yours,
Poe

---

21. 29 June 1846: Letter to Evert A. Duyckinck
Edgar A. Poe

[*Once he had prepared his "Reply to Mr. English and Others," Poe wanted a friend's reaction to it. He therefore sent the article to Duyckinck with a covering letter, a portion of which is printed below. Still hesitating to appear downtown, he continued to use Mrs. C.—Maria Clemm—as his courier.*

Little in this letter requires explanation. Louis Godey was, of course, the owner of Gody's Lady's Book *in which "The Literati" was still appearing. Cornelius Mathews was Duyckinck's closest friend. Harnden was a private express company.*

What Duyckinck may have written in answer to this letter is unknown, nor has my study of the Duyckinck Manuscript Collection unearthed anything, though Duyckinck sometimes kept fair copies of his letters. One item of interest appears as an undated entry in his Notebooks. Poe's "Sketches of the New York Literati," Duyckinck remarked, consist of "1/3 acute sense, 1/3 wanton ingenuity, 1/3 sheer rigmarole." Another undated item lists Poe as second only to Hawthorne under the rubric "American Tale Writers."

This letter appears in Ostrom, II, 323.]

Monday 29.

My Dear Mr Duyckinck,

I am about to send the "Reply to English" (accompanying this note) to Mr Godey—but feel anxious that some friend should read it before it goes. Will you be kind enough to look it over & show it to Mathews? Mrs C. will then take it to Har[n]den. The *particulars* of the reply I would not wish mentioned to *any* one—of course you see the necessity of this. . . .

---

22. 26 June 1846: Godey's Lady's Book for July
Hiram Fuller

[*Vexed with Godey for continuing to publish the "Literati" sketches, Fuller in the* Evening Mirror *found fault with almost everything in his magazine. The exception he made was the "very clever essay from William Kirkland," a close friend of his (see headnote to Document 8).*

According to Godey, the advice he received to discontinue the "Literati" sketches was far from friendly, notwithstanding Fuller's suggestion. "We are not," Godey wrote in the May number of his magazine, "to be intimidated by a threat of the loss of friends, or turned from our purpose by honeyed words" or by the many attempts that "have been made and are making by various persons to forestall public opinion."

John Waters, mentioned by Fuller, was the pen name of Henry Cary. Poe had discussed him in a "Marginalia" piece printed in the April number of the Democratic Review. *While the "Literati" article on Cary derives largely from the "Marginalia" piece, the "Marginalia" piece is much more indulgent, for Poe turned the "Literati" article into an attack on Charles F. Briggs, who had flattered Cary.*

Poe's statement that John Waters did not write the song ("Give Me the Old") attributed to him by Griswold in Poets and Poetry of America *is correct, despite Fuller's labeling Poe's "honest opinion" an "impudent falsehood." Griswold in the eighth edition of his anthology, which appeared in 1847, conceded as much in a footnote to the poem: "In earlier editions, the above poem has been attributed to* HENRY CAREY *[sic], the elegant essayist, whose writings are published under the signature of 'John Waters;' but I learn that he is not the author of it" (page 528).*

As for James Aldrich's "A Death-Bed," Poe had demonstrated on various occasions that it derived from Thomas Hood's "The Death-Bed." In "the compass of eight short lines," he showed, there were "ten or twelve peculiar identities of thought and identities of expression" between the two poems.

Fuller is correct in suggesting that Poe, never having seen Henry Cary, was reduced to saying there is "nothing remarkable" about his person. In a letter dated 30 January 1846 Poe had asked a correspondent, presumed to be Evert Duyckinck, for "a few memoranda" respecting Cary's "personal appearance, age, residence, etc."

[46]

*For articles which, to use Fuller's words, "contrast very amusingly"
with this one, see Documents 52 and 57.*

The notice below also appeared in the Weekly Mirror *on July 4.*]

GODEY'S LADY'S BOOK. JULY.—This Philadelphia Magazine was promptly issued on the 20th June, with a dreadful caricature of the fashions for
ladies' dresses, which the editor calls 'Paris Fashions Americanised;' a
term equally insulting to France and America. If Mr. Walsh don't take
the matter up, we trust Mons. Michelet will. Mr. Godey is clearly indict-
able for slander. There are, besides the fashion plate, a leaf of tissue
paper containing some patterns for chemisettes and night-gowns, and
two engravings, very poor indeed, even for a Philadelphia Magazine.
Among the literary contents is a very clever essay from William Kirkland,
on the character and opinions of the late Rev. Sydney Smith. The essay
is well written, and seems to be quite out of place in Mr. Godey's Lady's
Book. . . .

Mr. Godey continues the publication of the insane riff-raff, which Mr.
Poe calls his 'honest opinions' of the New York Literati, in spite of the
friendly advice which he says has been given him to discontinue them.

Mr. Poe gives an opinion of John Waters, which contrasts very amusingly with an opinion expressed in the April number of the Democratic
Review, and re-asserts the impudent falsehood that John Waters did not
write the song quoted by Mr. Griswold, as a specimen of his poetic
talents, in the 'Poets.' He also re-asserts for the twentieth or thirtieth
time, that Mr. Aldrich plagiarised from Hood in his little poem entitled
'A Death Bed,' and amusingly says of this gentleman and Mr. Cary, that
there is 'nothing remarkable' about their persons. The truth is, Mr. Poe
knows no more about them than of the man in the moon.

---

23. 10 July 1846: Untitled Article in the Evening Mirror
   Hiram Fuller

[*An unidentified Philadelphia newspaper ironically observed that the
"Mirror has published one number without once referring to Poe's . . .
'New York Literati,' " a notice to which Fuller responded.*

References to Poe and "The Literati" appeared more frequently in the

Mirror *than is apparent here, for I have recorded only the more cogent ones. For instance, on 1 June 1846 Fuller, reflecting on "the belligerent state of things," wrote: "Look . . . at the literary world! . . . See the most 'trenchant' critic of the age! the Longinus of Lilliput! 'taking off' his unhappy compeers and exhibiting them in a peep show. . . . The unhappy 'literati of New York' are being exhibited in portraiture by an artiste belonging to the same school as Dick Tinto, who could 'take your portrait in five minutes, sir—even if I see you passing in a mail coach—but it won't be like you.'" Or, again, on 1 July 1846 he praised Lewis Clark for making "up a very readable monthly, considering that he is not one of the 'New York* Literati.'" Elsewhere, in the same number, he said that Mrs. Mary Gove, who was scheduled to give a lecture, was "one of Mr. Poe's New York* Literati. . . ." Similarly, on 15 August 1846, in suggesting that an article be done on New York publishers, Fuller remarked that the names of some of them are familiar in places "where it is possible that some of the great names enumerated by Mr. Poe in his 'literati of New York city,' have not been heard."*

Harry Franco, mentioned in the article below, was the pen name of Charles F. Briggs, who had not yet become a member of the Mirror *staff (see headnote to Document 89).]*

"The New York Mirror has published one number without once referring to Poe's Notices of the New York Literati. Who is it about this establishment winces so dreadfully? Can it be Mr. Harry Franco Briggs?"

We found this odd paragraph in one of the small Philadelphia dailies, and are quite at a loss to surmise its meaning. We have probably taken more notice of Poe's articles in Godey's Magazine than any other paper in this city, and have done what we could to help them into circulation. We have not only announced them on the first day of their publication, but good naturedly copied the reply of Mr. English to Mr. Poe, from the Morning Telegraph. It is true that we have copied but one or two of Mr. Poe's notices, but they were the only ones we have seen which contained truth enough to render them fit for our columns. We are not aware of harboring any body about our establishment who would be likely to "wince" at anything which can emanate from Mr. Poe, who was once employed upon our paper, and of course is well known to us. We know exactly what degree of importance to attach to his statements of facts, and his estimates of the merits of his friends or enemies. The gentleman whose name is unwarrantably used by our Philadelphia contemporary is not, nor ever was, attached to our establishment. If he "winces dreadfully" at Mr. Poe's articles, he is more susceptible than we had supposed him to be.

---

24. 10 July 1846: "Mr. Poe's Reply to Mr. English and Others"
Edgar A. Poe

[*Poe felt he had two major advantages over English at this point in the controversy. The first was superior polemical power. As he later told Godey, "I have never written an article upon which I more confidently depend for literary reputation than that Reply" (Document 32). The second was command of a much larger audience than English could muster. He assumed, of course, that Godey, who was still running "The Literati" sketches, would publish his reply. Exactly what the circulation of both the* Evening Mirror *and* Weekly Mirror *was cannot be determined, but it was significantly less than the "one hundred thousand readers" that* Godey's Lady's Book *claimed in its February 1847 number.*

Poe erred in both expectations. His reply only detracted from his reputation and Godey, fearful of consequences, sent the article to the Philadelphia Spirit of the Times *(then called the* Times*), a newspaper with little circulation, paying ten dollars to have it printed and charging Poe with the cost. With these delays Poe's reply, though dated June 27, made a belated appearance on July 10.*

In the article Poe ignored English's charges in regard to New York University and the Boston Lyceum and was evasive about Mrs. Ellet. He preferred to concentrate instead upon the two libelous accusations, that of having committed forgery and of having taken money from English under false pretenses, accusations that, he said, were "criminal, and with the aid of 'The Mirror' I can have them investigated before a criminal tribunal." Poe knew he had never given English an "acknowledgment for a sum of money," as English had charged, and he could defy him "to produce such acknowledgement." He knew too that if English could somehow establish his indebtedness to him, for English apparently did give John Bisco, the publisher of the Broadway Journal, *thirty dollars on Poe's account, he could demonstrate that "Mr. English is indebted to me*

*in what (to me) is a considerable sum," the amount he would have re-
ceived had English paid him for his article on American poetry published
in* The Aristidean. *(Poe's contributions to English's magazine are discussed in the headnote to Document 11.)]*

[COMMUNICATED.]
MR. POE'S REPLY TO MR. ENGLISH
AND OTHERS.

NEW YORK, June 27.

To the Public.—A long and serious illness of such character as to render quiet and perfect seclusion in the country of vital importance, has
hitherto prevented me from seeing an article headed "The War of the
Literati," signed "Thomas Dunn English," and published in "The New
York Mirror" of June 23d. This article I might, and should indeed, *never*
have seen but for the kindness of Mr. Godey, editor of "The Lady's Book,"
who enclosed it to me with a suggestion that certain portions of it might
be thought on my part to demand a reply.

I had some difficulty in comprehending what *that was*, said or written
by Mr. English, that could be deemed answerable by any human being;
but I had not taken into consideration that I had been, for many months,
absent and dangerously ill—that I had no longer a journal in which to defend myself—that these facts were well known to Mr. English—that he is
a blackguard of the lowest order—that it would be silly truism, if not
unpardonable flattery, to term him either a coward or a liar—and, lastly,
that the magnitude of a slander is usually in the direct ratio of the little-
ness of the slanderer, but, above all things, of the impunity with which
he fancies it may be uttered.

Of the series of papers which have called down upon me, while supposed defenceless, the animadversions of the pensive [Hiram] Fuller, the
cultivated [Lewis Gaylord] Clark, the "indignant [Charles F.] Briggs,"
and the animalcula with moustaches for antenna that is in the
capital habit of signing itself in full, "Thomas Dunn English"—of this
series of papers all have been long since written, and *three* have been
already given to the public. The circulation of the Magazine in which
they appear cannot be much less than 50,000; and, admitting but 4 readers to each copy (while 6 would more nearly approach the truth) I may
congratulate myself on such an audience as has not often been known in
any similar case—a monthly audience of *at least* 200,000, from among

the most refined and intellectual classes of American society. Of course, it will be difficult on the part of "The Mirror" (I am not sure whether 500 or 600 be the precise number of copies it *now* circulates)—difficult, I say, to convince the 200,000 ladies and gentlemen in question that, individually and collectively, they are block-heads—that they do not rightly comprehend the unpretending words which I have addressed to them in this series—and that, as for myself, I have no other design in the world than misrepresentation, scurrility, and the indulgence of personal spleen. What has been printed is before my readers; what I have written besides, is in the hands of Mr. Godey, and shall remain unaltered. The word "Personality," used in the heading of the series, has of course led astray the quartette of dunderheads who have talked and scribbled themselves into convulsions about this matter—but no one else, I presume, has distorted the legitimate meaning of my expression into that of private *scandal* or personal *offence*. In sketching individuals, every candid reader will admit that, while my general aim has been accuracy, I have yielded to delicacy even a little too much of verisimilitude. Indeed, on this score should I not have credit for running my pen through certain sentences referring, for example, to the brandy-nose of Mr. Briggs (since Mr. Briggs is only one third described when this nose is omitted) and to the family resemblance between the whole visage of Mr. English and that of the best-looking but most unprincipled of Mr. Barnum's baboons?

It will not be supposed, from anything here said, that I myself attach any importance to this series of papers. The public, however, is the best judge of its own taste; and that the spasms of one or two enemies have given the articles a notoriety far surpassing their merit or my expectation—is, possibly, no fault of mine. In a preface their very narrow scope is defined. They are loosely and inconsiderately written—aiming at nothing beyond the gossip of criticism—unless, indeed, at the relief of those "*necessities*" which I have never blushed to admit and which the editor of "The Mirror"—the quondam associate of gentlemen—has, in the same manner, never blushed publicly to insult and to record.

But let me return to Mr. English's attack—and, in so returning, let me not permit any profundity of disgust to induce, even for an instant, a violation of the dignity of truth. What is *not false*, amid the scurrility of this man's statements, it is not in my nature to brand as false, although oozing from the filthy lips of which a lie is the only natural language. The errors and frailties which I deplore, it cannot at least be asserted that I have been the coward to deny. Never, even, have I made attempt at *extenuating* a weakness which is (or, by the blessing of God, *was*) a calamity, although those who did not know me intimately had little reason to regard it otherwise than as a crime. For, indeed, had my pride, or that of my family permitted, there was much—very much—there was everything—to be offered in extenuation. Perhaps, even, there was an epoch at which it might not have been wrong in me to hint—what by the testimony of Dr. Francis and other medical men I might have demonstrated, had the public, indeed, cared for the demonstration—that the irregularities so profoundly lamented were the *effect* of a terrible evil rather than its cause.—And now let me thank God that in redemption from the physical ill I have forever got rid of the moral.

It is not, then, my purpose to deny any part of the conversation represented to have been held *privately* between this person and myself. I scorn the denial of *any* portion of it, because *every* portion of it *may* be true, by a very desperate possibility, although uttered by an English. I pretend to no remembrance of anything which occurred—with the exception of having wearied and degraded myself, to little purpose, in bestowing upon Mr. E. the "fisticuffing" of which he speaks, and of being dragged from his prostrate and rascally carcase by Professor Thomas Wyatt, who, perhaps with good reason, had his fears for the vagabond's life. The *details* of the "conversation," as asserted, I shall not busy myself in attempting to understand. The "celebrated authoress" is a mystery. With the exception, perhaps, of Mrs. Stephens, Mrs. Welby, and Miss Gould—three ladies whose acquaintance I yet hope to have the honor of making—there is *no* celebrated authoress in America with whom I am not on terms of perfect amity at least, if not of cordial and personal friendship. That I "offered" Mr. English "my hand" is by no means impossible. I have been too often and too justly blamed by those who have a right to impose bounds upon my intimacies, for the weakness of "offering my hand," without thought of consequence, to any one whom I see *very* generally reviled, hated, and despised.

Through this mad quixotism arose my first acquaintance with Mr. English, who introduced himself to me in Philadelphia—where, for one or two years, I remained under the impression that his real name was Thomas *Done Brown*.

I shall not think it necessary to maintain that I am *no* "coward." On a point such as this a man should speak only through the acts, moral and physical, of his whole private life and his whole public career. But it is a matter of common observation that your *real* coward never fails to make it a primary point to accuse all his enemies of cowardice. A poltroon charges his foe, by instinct, with precisely that vice or meanness which the pricking of his (the poltroon's) conscience, assures him would furnish the most stable and therefore the most terrible ground of accusation against himself. The Mexicans, for example, seldom call their antagonists anything *but* cowards. It is the "stop thief!" principle, exactly,—and a very admirable principle it is.

Now, the origin of the nick-name, "Thomas *Done Brown*," is, in Philadelphia, quite as thoroughly understood as Mr. English could desire. With even the inconceivable amount of brass in his possession, I doubt if he *could* in that city, pronounce aloud that simple word, "coward," if his most saintly soul depended upon the issue.

> Some have been beaten till they know
> What wood a cudgel's of, by the blow—
> Some kicked until they could tell whether
> A shoe were Spanish or neat's leather.

These lines in "Hudibras" have reference to the case of Mr. English. His primary thrashing, of any note, was bestowed upon him, I believe, by Mr. John S. DuSolle, the editor of "The Spirit of the Times," who could not very well get over acting with this indecorum on account of Mr. E's amiable weakness—a propensity for violating the privacy of a publisher's MSS. I have not heard that there was any resentment on the part of Mr. English. It is said, on the contrary, that he shed abundant tears, and took the whole thing, in its proper light—as a sort of favor. His second chastisement I cannot call to mind in all its particulars. His third I was reduced to giving him myself, for indecorous conduct at my house. His fourth, fifth, sixth, seventh, eighth, ninth, and tenth, followed in so confused a manner and in so rapid a succession, that I have been unable to keep an account of them; they have always affected me as a difficult problem in mathematics. His eleventh was tendered him by the Hon. Sandy Harris, who (also for an insult to ladies at a private house) gave him such a glimpse of a Bowie knife as saved the trouble of a kick—having even more vigorous power of propulsion. For his twelfth lesson, in this course, I have always heard him express his gratitude to Mr. Henry B. Hirst. Mr. English *could* not help stealing Mr. Hirst's poetry. For this reason Mr. Hirst (who gets out of temper for trifles) threw, first, a pack of cards in

Mr. English's face; then knocked that poet down; then pummeled him for not more than twenty minutes; (in Mr. E's case it cannot be *well* done under twenty-five, on account of callosity—the result of too frequent friction on the parts pummeled); then picked him up, set him down, and wrote him a challenge, to come off on the following morning. Of course, this challenge Mr. English *accepted*;—the fact is he *accepts* everything, from a kick to a piece of gingerbread—the smallest favors thankfully received. At the hour appointed Mr. Hirst was on the ground. In regard to Mr. English's whereabouts on the occasion I never could put my hand upon a record that was at all precise. It must be said, however, in his defence, that there is not a better shot in all America than Mr. Hirst. With a pistol, at fifty yards, I once saw him hit a *chicken* in full flight. Mr. English *may* have witnessed this identical exploit—if so, as a "bird of a feather" he was excusable in staying at home. My own opinion, nevertheless, is, that he would have been at the rendezvous without fail, if his breakfast could have been got ready for him in time.

I do not think that Mr. English was ever afterwards flogged, or even challenged, in Philadelphia—but I cannot hope that he would ever "take me by the hand" again, were I to omit mention of that last and most important *escapade* which induced him at length to desert, in disgust, the city of his immense forefathers.

There are, no doubt, one or two persons who have heard of one Henry A. Wise. At all events *Mr. English* had heard of him, and he resolved that nobody else should *ever* hear of him—this Mr. Wise—or even *think* of him, again. That Mr. Wise had never heard of Mr. English (probably on account of his being always called Mr. Brown) was no concern of Mr. English's. He wrote an "article"—I *saw* it. He put "the magic of his name" —his three names—at the bottom of it. He printed it. He handed it for inspection to all the inhabitants of Philadelphia. He then buttoned up his coat—took under the tails of it seven revolvers—and dispatched the article, duly addressed, with his compliments, to "the Hon. Henry A. Wise," who then resided at the house of the President.

Now, I never could understand precisely how or why it was that the Hon. Henry A. Wise did not repair forthwith from Washington to Philadelphia, with a company of the U. S. Artillery—the loan of which his interest could have obtained of Mr. Tyler—why he did not come, I say, to Philadelphia, engage Mr. English, take him captive, cut off his goatee, put him on a high stool, and insist upon his reading (upside down) the whole of that "Sonnet to Azthene" in which the poet sings about his "dreams" that "seems" and other English peculiarities. The punishment would have been scarcely more than adequate to the offence. The Philippic written by Mr. E. was, in fact, *very* severe. It called Mr. Wise "a poltroon"—an "ass," if I remember—and "a dirty despicable vagabond"—of that I feel particularly sure. There occurs then, of course, a question in metaphysics—"*why* did not the Hon. Henry A. Wise repair to Philadelphia and take Mr. Thomas Dunn Brown by the nose?["] Perhaps the legislator had a horror of moustaches. But then neither did he write. Not even *one word did he say*—absolutely *not one—nothing!* Mr. Brown's distress was, not altogether that he could not get himself kicked, but that he could not get any kind of a reason for the omission of the kicking.

This affair is to be classed among the "Historical Doubts"—among the insoluble problems of History. However—Mr. Wise felt himself everlastingly ruined, and soon after, as Minister to France, went, a broken-hearted man, into exile.

Mr. Brown abandoned the city of his birth. He has never been the same person since—that is to say he has been a person beside himself. He finds it impossible to recover from a chronic attack of astonishment. When he dies, the coroner's verdict will be "*Taken* by Surprise." This matter will account for Mr. English's inveterate habit of rolling up the whites of his eyes.

About the one or two other *unimportant* points in this gentleman's attack upon myself, there is, I believe, very little to be said. He asserts that I have complimented his literary performances. The sin of having, at one time, attempted to patronize him, is, I fear, justly to be laid to my charge;—but his goatee was so continual a source of admiration to me that I found it impossible ever to write a serious line in his behalf. And then the Imp of Mischief whispered in my ear, telling me how great a charity it would be to the public if I would only put the pen into Mr. English's own hand, and permit him to kill himself off by self-praise. I listened to this whisper—and the public should have seen the zeal with which the poet labored in the good cause. If in this public's estimation Mr. English did not become at once Phoebus Apollo, at least it was no fault of Mr. English's. I solemnly say that in no paper of mine did there ever appear one word about this gentleman—unless of the broadest and most unmistakeable irony—that was not printed from the MS. of the gentleman himself. The last number of "The Broadway Journal" (the work having been turned over by me to another publisher) was edited by Mr. English. The editorial portion was wholly his, and was one interminable Pæan of his own praises. The truth of all this—if any one is weak enough to care a penny about *who* praises or who damns Mr. English—will no doubt be corroborated by Mr. Jennings, the printer.

I am charged, too, unspecifically, with being a plagiarist on a very extensive scale. He who accuses another of what all the world knows to be *especially* false, is merely rendering the accused a service by calling attention to the *converse* of the fact, and should never be helped out of his ridiculous position by any denial on the part of his enemy. We want a Magazine paper on "The Philosophy of Billingsgate." But I am really ashamed of indulging even in a sneer at this poor miserable fool, on any mere topic of literature alone.

He says, too, that I "seem determined to hunt him down." He said the *very same thing* to Mr. Wise, who had not the most remote conception that any such individual had ever been born of woman. "Hunt him down!" Is it possible that I shall ever forget the paroxysm of laughter which the phrase occasioned me when I first saw it in Mr. English's MS? "Hunt him down!" What idea *can* the man attach to the term "*down?*" Does he really conceive that there exists a deeper depth of either moral or physical degradation than that of the hog-puddles in which he has wallowed from his infancy? "Hunt him down!" By Heaven! I should, in the first place, be under the stern necessity of hunting him *up*—up from among the dock-loafers and wharf-rats, his cronies. Besides, "hunt" is not precisely the word. "Catch" would do better. We say "hunting a buffalo"—"hunting a lion," and, in a dearth of words, we might even go so far as to say "hunting a pig"—but we say "catching a frog"—"catching a weasel"—"catching an English"—and "catching a flea."

As a matter of course I should have been satisfied to follow the good example of Mr. Wise, when insulted by Mr. English, (if this indeed be the person's name) had there been nothing more serious in the blatherskite's attack than the particulars to which I have hitherto alluded. The two passages which follow, however, are to be found in the article referred to:

"I hold Mr. Poe's acknowledgments for a sum of money which he obtained from me under false pretences."

And again:

"A merchant of this city had accused him of committing forgery, and as he was afraid to challenge him to the field, or chastise him personally, I suggested a legal prosecution as his sole remedy. At his request I obtained a counsellor who was willing, as a compliment to me, to conduct his suit without the customary retaining fee. But, though so eager at first to commence proceedings, he dropped the matter altogether when the time came for him to act—thus virtually admitting the truth of the charge."

It will be admitted by the most patient that these accusations are of such character as to justify me in rebutting them in the most public manner possible, even when they are found to be urged by a Thomas Dunn English. The charges are criminal, and with the aid of "The Mirror" I can have them investigated before a criminal tribunal. In the meantime I must not lie under these imputations a moment longer than necessary. To the first charge I reply, then, simply that Mr. English is indebted *to me* in what (to me) is a considerable sum—that I owe him nothing—that in the assertion that he holds my acknowledgment for a sum of money under *any* pretence obtained, he lies—and that I defy him to produce such acknowledgment.

In regard to the second charge I must necessarily be a little more explicit. "The merchant of New York" alluded to, is a gentleman of high respectability—Mr. *Edward I.* [*sic*] *Thomas*, of Broad Street. I have now the honor of his acquaintance, but some time previous to this acquaintance, he had remarked to a common friend that he had heard whispered against me an accusation of forgery. The friend, as in duty bound, reported this matter to me. I called at once on Mr. Thomas, who gave me no very thorough explanation, but promised to make inquiry, and confer with me hereafter. Not hearing from him in what I thought due time, however, I sent him (unfortunately by Mr. English, who was always in my office for the purpose of doing himself honor in running my errands) a note, of which the following is a copy:

OFFICE OF THE BROADWAY JOURNAL, ETC.
EDWARD J. THOMAS, Esq.

Sir:—As I have not had the pleasure of hearing from you since our interview at your office, may I ask of you to state to me distinctly, whether I am to consider the charge of *forgery* urged by you against myself, in the presence of a common friend, as originating with yourself or Mr. [Park] Benjamin?

Your ob. serv't.,

(Signed) EDGAR A. POE.

The reply brought me was verbal and somewhat vague. As usual, my messenger had played the bully, and, as *very* usual, had been treated with contempt. The idea of *challenging* a man for a charge of *forgery* could only have entered the head of an owl or an English:—of course I had no resource but in a suit, which one of Mr. E's friends offered to conduct for me. I left town to procure evidence, and on my return found at my house a letter from Mr. Thomas. It ran thus:

NEW YORK. July 5, 1845.

E.A. POE, Esq., New York,

Dear Sir:—I had hoped ere this to have seen you, but as you have not called, and as I may soon be out of the city, I desire to say to you that, after repeated effort, I saw the person on Friday evening last, from whom the report originated to which you referred in your call at my office. [The contemptuous silence in respect to the communication sent *through Mr. E.* will be observed.] He denies it *in toto*—says he does *not know it* and never said so—and it undoubtedly arose from the misunderstanding of some word used. It gives me pleasure thus to trace it, and still more to find it destitute of foundation in truth, as I thought would be the case. I have told Mr. Benjamin the result of my inquiries, and shall do so to —— [the lady referred to as the common friend]* by a very early opportunity—the only two persons who know anything of the matter, as far as I know.

I am, Sir, very truly your friend and obed't. st.

(Signed) EDWARD J. THOMAS.

Now, as this note was most satisfactory and most kind—as I neither wished nor could have accepted Mr. Thomas' money—as the motives which had actuated him did not seem to me malevolent—as I had heard him spoken of in the most flattering manner by one whom, above all others, I most profoundly respect and esteem—it does really appear to me hard to comprehend how even so malignant a villain as this English could have wished me to proceed with the suit.

In the presence of witnesses I handed him the letter, and, without

---

* The bracketed statements are Poe's interpolations.

meaning anything in especial, requested his opinion. In lieu of it he gave me his advice:—*it was that I should deny having received such a letter and urge the prosecution to extremity*. I promptly ordered him to quit the house. In his capacity of hound, he obeyed.

These are the facts which, in a court of justice, I propose to demonstrate—and, having demonstrated them, shall I not have a right to demand of a generous public that it brand with eternal infamy that wretch, who, with a full knowledge of my exculpation from so heinous a charge, has not been ashamed to take advantage of my supposed inability to defend myself, for the purpose of stigmatising me as a felon!

And of the gentleman who (also with a thorough knowledge of the facts, as I can and will show) prostituted his filthy sheet to the circulation of this calumny—of *him* what is it necessary to say? At present—nothing. He heads Mr. English's article with a profession of *pity* for myself. Ah yes, indeed! Mr. Fuller *is* a *pitiful* man. Much is he to be pitied for his countenance (that of a fat sheep in a reverie)—for his *Providential* escapes—for the unwavering conjugal chivalry which, in a public theatre ——but I pause. Not even in taking vengeance on a Fuller can I stoop to become a Fuller myself.

The fact is, it is difficult to be angry with this man. Let his self-complacency be observed! How absolute an unconsciousness of that proverbial mental imbecility which serves to keep all the little world in which he moves, in one sempiternal sneer or giggle!

Mr. Fuller has fine eyes—but he should put them to use. He should turn them inwardly.—He should contemplate in solemn meditation, that vast arena within his sinciput which it has pleased Heaven to fill with hasty pudding by way of brains. He needs, indeed *self*-study, *self*-examination—and for this end, he will not think of me officious if I recommend to his perusal Heinsius' admirable treatise *"On the Ass."*

EDGAR A. POE.

---

25. *11 July 1846:* *"Quarrel among the Literati"*
Morning News

[*The first published reaction to Poe's "Reply to Mr. English and Others," expressed by the New York* Morning News *in somewhat garbled form, was far from favorable.*]

QUARREL AMONG THE LITERATI.—Poe has at last replied to the card of Mr. English, and it is a most terrific, absolutely bitterness and satire unadulterated [*sic*]. Poe states that he will prosecute the *Mirror* for publishing the card of Mr. E. This is rather small business for a man who has reviled nearly every literary man of eminence in the United States.

---

26. *12(?) July 1846: "Mr. Poe and Mr. English" and "The Literary War"* Joseph C. Neal

[*Responding to the requests of "some of Mr. Poe's friends" in Philadelphia, Neal, the editor of the Philadelphia* Saturday Gazette, *reprinted Poe's "Reply to Mr. English and Others" in full, though he thought the affair "in bad taste." The article occupied so much space that, as Neal said on another page, news of the "literary war" had crowded out news of the Mexican War, which had officially begun on 13 May 1846.*

Only Neal's remarks on Poe's reply are reprinted here, not the reply itself, which Neal reproduced faithfully and which appears as Document 24.

I have been unable to date the two documents below except by conjecture, for I cannot locate a copy of the Saturday Gazette *containing these items and have had to rely upon John Ingram's clippings from the Gazette (in the Alderman Library of the University of Virginia), which he mistakenly dated 27 June 1846. June 27 was the date of composition Poe assigned to the article; the article itself appeared in the* Spirit of the Times *on July 10.*]

MR. POE AND MR. ENGLISH.—We publish on our first page to day, by particular request of some of Mr. Poe's friends in this city, a reply from that gentleman to Mr. English's letter in the New York Mirror. With the merits of this quarrel we have nothing to do, and we may add that we consider the whole affair one of very little importance to the public. Mr. E.'s letter was very severe upon the private character of Mr. Poe, and the latter retaliates in the same spirit. All this is, to our notion, in bad taste, yet we cannot well refuse the assailed an opportunity to exculpate himself.

As the war has actually commenced we suppose it will be prosecuted

[60]

to the (literary) death, both the combatants having entered into it with a zeal and spirit that, with Fa[h]renheit ranging at 90 and upwards, will not be apt to cool off without the application of some tempering process. Whether much or any thing is to be gained by either of the gentlemen in this controversy it is useless to speculate. Their friends will probably watch the progress of affairs with some interest, and the public, if it reads them, will enjoy a laugh for which they must jointly pay unless the victorious party—as is proposed in our war with Mexico—makes the vanquished foot the bill. Were it only fine September weather we might be induced to "pitch in" for a bout or two with the crowned [k]night—when he *is* crowned—but just at present all our philosophy and good nature are actively exerted to keep our body corporate as cool as circumstances will allow. Meanwhile, we advise our extensive friend, the aforenamed Public, to read Messrs. P. & E. for his own edification.

THE LITERARY WAR has crowded us to-day as closely as Gen. Taylor pushed the Mexicans at Reseca [*sic*] and while we ask the reader's indulgence we can assure them [*sic*] if they lose by the operation we gain an afternoon siesta that is not to be winked at these days of drowsy dullness and dearth of distressing news and refreshing breezes.

---

27. 13 July 1846: "A Card: In Reply to Mr. Poe's Rejoinder"
Thomas Dunn English

[*Three days after the publication of "Mr. Poe's Reply to Mr. English and Others" in the* Spirit of the Times, *the* Evening Mirror *published English's rejoinder. The tone of this answer, compared with English's original "Card," is remarkably decorous. English merely cited Poe's scurrilities and added that Poe admitted the most serious of his charges by silence, presumably his alleged vilification of Mrs. Elizabeth Ellet. As for Poe's threat to sue for libel, English said: "That is my full desire. Let him institute a suit, if he dare, and I pledge myself to make my charges good by the most ample and satisfactory evidence."*]

IN REPLY TO MR. POE'S REJOINDER.

Mr. Edgar A. Poe is not satisfied, it would seem. In the 'Times,' a Philadelphia journal of considerable circulation, there appears a communication, headed—'Mr. Poe's reply to Mr. English, and others.' As it is dated '27th of June,' and the newspaper containing it is dated 10th July; and as it appears in another city than this,—it is to be inferred that Mr. Poe had some difficulty in obtaining a respectable journal to give currency to his scurrilous article. The following words and phrases, taken at random from the production, will give the public some idea of its style and temper:

'Blackguard,' 'coward,' 'liar,' 'animalcula with moustaches for *antennal*' [*sic*], 'block-heads,' 'quartette of dunderheads,' '*brandy-nose*,' 'best-looking, but most unprincipled of Mr. Barnum's *baboons*,' 'filthy lips,' 'rascally carcase,' 'inconceivable amount of *brass*,' 'poor miserable *fool*,' '*hog-puddles* in which he has wallowed from infancy,' '*by Heaven!*' 'dock-loafers and wharf-rats, his cronies,' 'the *blatherskite's* attack,' 'hound,' 'malignant a villain,' 'wretch,' 'filthy sheet,' 'hasty pudding by way of brains.'

To such vulgar stuff as this, which is liberally distributed through three columns of what would be, otherwise, tame and spiritless, it is unnecessary to reply. It neither suits my inclination, nor habits, to use language, of which the words I quote make up the wit and ornament. I leave that to Mr. Poe and the ancient and honorable community of fishvenders.

Actuated by a desire for the public good, I charged Mr. Poe with the commission of certain misdemeanors, which prove him to be profligate in habits and depraved in mind. The most serious of these he admits by silence—the remainder he attempts to palliate; and winds up his tedious disquisition by a threat to resort to a legal prosecution. That is my full desire. Let him institute a suit, if he dare, and I pledge myself to make my charges good by the most ample and satisfactory evidence.

To the charlatanry of Mr. Poe's reply; his play upon my name; his proclamation of recent reform, when it is not a week since he was seen intoxicated in the streets of New York; his attempt to prove me devoid of literary attainments; his sneers at my lack of personal beauty; his ridiculous invention of quarrels between me and others, that never took place; his charges of plagiarism, unsupported by example; his absurd story of a challenge accepted and avoided; his attempt to excuse his drunkenness and meanness on the ground of insanity; in short, to the froth, fustian, and vulgarity of his three-column article, I have no reply to make. My character for honor and physical courage needs no defence from even the occasional slanderer—although, if the gentlemen whose names he mentions, will endorse his charges, I shall then reply to them—much less does it require a shield from one whose habit of uttering falsehoods is so inveterate, that he utters them to his own hurt, rather [than] not utter them at all; with whom drunkenness is the practice and sobriety the exception, and who, from the constant commission of acts of meanness and depravity, is incapable of appreciating the feelings which animate the man of honor.

THOMAS DUNN ENGLISH.

---

28. 14 July 1846: "The War still Raging"
Morning News

[*The New York* Morning News, *having commented on English's first "Card" and on Poe's "Reply to Mr. English and Others," now commented on English's "Reply to Mr. Poe's Rejoinder." With a libel suit threatening, the editor was more discreet than he had been before.*]

THE WAR STILL RAGING.—T. D. English replies to Poe's bulletin No. 2, in last evening's *Mirror*. He dares Poe to a legal battle, and threatens to prove all the assertions made in his first official dispatch. We shall see in what all this warm work will result.

---

29. 14 July 1846: "The War of the Literati"
Public Ledger

[*The Philadelphia* Public Ledger, *contemning "the war between the literati" but maintaining its neutrality to the combatants, now called for "a truce or treaty of peace," and read the "critics" and "all publishers of periodicals" a lecture on breeding, taste, and judgment.*]

This article, beginning with ". . . we suggest to critics a little better breeding and a little better taste and a little better judgment," was reprinted in the New York Morning News *on July 16 under the title "CRITICS AND PERSONALITIES." The editor of the* Morning News *introduced the passage as follows: "There is so much good sense—so correct a principle, or series of principles—and such a brief yet wholesome rebuke administered to those who deserve it—in the following, that we do not hesitate to transfer it to our columns."]*

THE WAR OF THE LITERATI.—The war between the literati increases in violence. Mr. Poe, whose "Sketches of the New York Literati" drew from Mr. English such a caustic attack, has replied in a manner equally biting and severe. We suggest a truce or treaty of peace among these ecclesiastics of the church literary; for Billingsgate is not the wide *gate* or the straight *gait* to Parnassus or Helicon, any more than to the White Mountains or Saratoga. And seriously we suggest to critics [a] little better breeding and a little better taste and a little better judgment, than is exhibited by vituperative personalities concerning authors. To invade the fireside, and drag men before the public in relations exclusively private, is not very consistent with that precept of the gentleman, derived from a high source, which says "Do as you would be done by." It therefore exhibits not the best breeding. It not only outrages the feelings of all connected with the parties assailed, by the ties of consanguinity, affinity or friendship, but shocks the sensibilities of all strangers to the parties, who are too refined to relish slander or vituperation. It therefore exhibits not the best taste. It exposes the assailant to the imputation of envy, malignity, falsehood, and other vices of the heart, and to that of having exhausted his whole stock in the literary trade, and consequently of being driven to slander for raw material. To this we may add that the public are interested in authors only through their works, and care nothing for their personal affairs.

And we would seriously suggest to all publishers of periodicals, that they would exhibit quite as much taste and judgment, by excluding from their pages all personal sketches of authors. The works of an author are public property. His personal and private affairs demand equal immunity with those of other persons. People do not put their firesides in issue by writing books; and therefore nobody should be permitted, under pretence of literary criticism, to raise false issues on such points.

[64]

30. 15 July 1846: *The New Orleans* Daily Picayune *Defends Poe*

[*As Poe had asked him to do (Document 9), Field exercised his influence upon the editor of the* Picayune, *whose European correspondent he had been in 1840; and about two weeks after Field's article on Poe appeared in the* Reveille, *the* Picayune *published its defense of Poe.*

Poe had reason to believe that the Picayune *would prove cooperative, for, as he remarked in his letter to Field, that newspaper "has always been friendly to me. . . ." As editor and, later, as owner of the* Broadway Journal, *he had "exchanged" with the* Picayune. *That paper had high respect for Poe's magazine, hailing it as "almost the only journal we receive with any decided claims to originality" (14 October 1845). For other notices of Poe in the* Daily Picayune, *see the issues of 18 July; 1, 4, and 18 October; 8 and 12 November 1845; 7 January and 14 May 1846.*]

Mr. Edgar A. Poe has recently been writing for one of the Philadelphia magazines a series of papers upon the New York *literati*. They are off-hand sketches, and the critical opinions expressed in them appear to be sincere, and in this respect, so far as we know, they are fair enough. But these sketches have involved their author in a series of personal differences of the most rancorous description. He has been assailed in terms of unmeasured severity, and not content with efforts to impugn his critical judgments and to ridicule his literary pretensions, his enemies have assailed his personal character, and dragged his private affairs before the eyes of the public. So long as literary men confine their controversies to subjects of general interest, the public may laugh at their exhibitions of idle rage; but with their private, personal differences the public has nothing to do. We have seen with extreme regret that the controversy aroused by Mr. Poe's stricture, has degenerated into a personal persecution of him. With this no right-minded man can sympathize. There are modes of redress for such wrongs, real or imaginary, as he may have committed besides an indiscriminate onslaught upon his character as a man. The public ought not and does not care to hear what may be the personal failings of those known to it but as authors.

It is moreover quite idle to attempt to depreciate the position which Mr. Poe has attained as an author. He has been one of the most successful contributors to our literary periodicals, and his tales have been extensively copied both here and in England. They are not only copied, but are read and remembered by thousands. They are written with such power, that you cannot forget them if you would. We might cite several of his stories, wrought with an art so consummate, that it costs you an effort of mind to feel that they are fictions, nor can you wholly divest yourself of the idea that they may be or must be truthful narrations. Yet more idle does it appear to us to ridicule the poetry of Mr. Poe. That production of his which critics and his personal enemies have most frequently endeavored to deride is "The Raven," but the oft repeated efforts have been entirely harmless. The Poem is written with extraordinary power, and it is impossible to read it unmoved. This single poem is a complete vindication of his possession of genius of the most sterling quality, and it were to be wished that it might be devoted to themes more worthy of its strength than ephemeral papers for the fashionable magazines.

---

31. 15 July, 24 July, 28 July, 25 August 1846: From Philadelphia
T. F. G.

[*The* Evening Mirror's *Philadelphia correspondent, who signed himself only by his initials, made passing reference to Poe's "Literati" series from time to time. These appear below.*]

. . . Mr. Poe is making many enemies here by his insane writings.

I know of a case of physical deformity which is laughably strange, paradoxical as the announcement may seem. It is that of a man in middle life, whose ears have been growing from childhood, until they have become so disproportionately and ridiculously large, as to attract universal attention and remark. You will appreciate the picture when I tell you that each ear reaches far above the crown of a tall hat, and—they are still in course of development! I do not remember the name of the unfortunate individual, but it has a very *Poet*ical sound when pronounced by *the* English [Thomas Dunn]. An impression is general that it will be necessary to crop these big ears; at least, such an opinion obtains among some of the most gifted in the land.

'Now Go(e)dy [*sic*] please to moderate,' &c.

. . . I would mention that there is nothing new in literature [here], but I know it will vex you, particularly in these days of *Poe* etical and nonsensical doings.

. . . One or two publishers in Philadelphia are quite out of temper with the impartial Magazine criticisms of the editor of the Mirror. Well—well—the truth ought to be heard sometimes, even if it is unpleasant.

---

32. 16 July 1846: Letter to Louis A. Godey
Edgar A. Poe

[*Six days after the Philadelphia* Spirit of the Times *published his "Reply to Mr. English and Others," Poe wrote to Godey, reproving him for not having "done as I requested—published it in the 'Book'."*

The articles in the Saint Louis Reveille *and the New Orleans* Daily Picayune *that Poe mentions at the end of his letter appear as Documents 9 and 30. My search through the* Charleston Courier *for this period uncovered no mention of Poe.*

This letter appears in Ostrom, II 323–4.]

New-York: July 16. 46.

My Dear Sir,

I regret that you published my Reply in "The Times". I should have found no difficulty in getting it printed here, in a *respectable* paper, and gratis. However—as I have the game in my own hands, I shall not stop to complain about trifles.

I am rather ashamed that, knowing me to be as poor as I am, you should have thought it advisable to make the demand *on me* of the $10. I confess that I thought better of you—but let it go—it is the way of the world.

The man, or men, who told you that there was anything wrong in *the tone* of my reply, were either my enemies, or your enemies, or asses. When you see them, tell them so from me. I have never written an article upon which I more confidently depend for *literary* reputation than that Reply. Its merit lay in being *precisely* adapted to its purpose. In this city I have had, upon it, the favorable judgments of the best men. All the error about it was yours. You should have done as I requested—published it in the "Book". It is of no use to conceive a plan if you have to depend upon another for its execution.

Please distribute 20 or 30 copies of the Reply in Phil. and send me the balance through Harnden.

What paper, or papers, have copied E's attack?

I have put this matter in the hands of a competent attorney, and you shall see the result. Your charge, $10, will of course be brought before the court, as an item, when I speak of damages.

In perfect good feeling
Yours truly
Poe.

. . . I enclose the Reveillé article. I presume that, ere this, you have seen the highly flattering notices of the "Picayune" and the "Charleston Courier".

---

33. 17 July 1846: Letter to John Bisco
Edgar A. Poe

[*In his letter to Godey (preceding document) Poe mentioned that he had referred English's libels to an attorney. No doubt he had, for on the following day he wrote to Bisco, the original owner of the* Broadway *Journal, asking him to call upon Enoch L. Fancher, the lawyer he had engaged, most likely through Mrs. Clemm's agency, to conduct his libel suit against Hiram Fuller and Augustus W. Clason, Jr., proprietors of the* Evening Mirror *and* Weekly Mirror, *in which journals English's libels had appeared (see headnote to Document 13).*

Again Poe shows no willingness to appear in the city, especially as Fancher's office, located at 33 John Street, was only four short blocks from City Hall and in the heart of New York's Grub Street.

This letter appears in Ostrom, II, 325.]

New-York July 17. 1846.

My Dear Mr Bisco,

You will confer a *very* great favor on me by stepping in, when you have leisure, at the office of E. L. Fancher, Attorney-at-Law, 33 John St.

Please mention to him that I requested you to call in relation to Mr English. He will, also, show you my Reply to some attacks lately made upon me by this gentleman.

> Cordially yours.
> Poe

Mr John Bisco.

---

34. 20 July 1846: "A Sad Sight"
Hiram Fuller

[*In the article below, the editor of the* Evening Mirror *protests that he can no longer feel harsh, contemptuous, or vengeful toward Poe, only sorry, since the man "was evidently committing a suicide upon his body, as he had already done upon his character." Yet, regardless of how much compassion Poe's "wretched imbecility," "evil living," and "radical obliquity of sense" induced in him, Fuller managed to smear "the poor creature" in his editorial.*

The "aged female relative" mentioned by Fuller is Maria Clemm. This visit by Poe to New York's editorial and publishing district was a rare one for him. Perhaps he had come to see his attorney. No doubt, as Fuller alleged, Poe had drunk himself into "a state of inebriation" to brace himself for the occasion. No doubt too, in that condition, he had gone to the Mirror Building on the corner of Ann and Nassau Streets to tell Fuller his opinion of him.

Editors were horsewhipped, cowhided, or caned for less provocative articles than this one, which also appeared in the Weekly Mirror *on July 25.*]

A SAD SIGHT.—It is melancholy enough to see a man maimed in his limbs, or deprived by nature of his due proportions; the blind, the deaf, the mute, the lame, the impotent are all subjects that touch our hearts, at least all whose hearts have not been indurated in the fiery furnace of sin; but sad, sadder, saddest of all, is the poor wretch whose want of moral rectitude has reduced his mind and person to a condition where indignation for his vices, and revenge for his insults are changed into compassion for the poor victim of himself. When a man has sunk so low that he has lost the power to provoke vengeance, he is the most pitiful of all pitiable objects. A poor creature of this description, called at our office the other day, in a condition of sad, wretched imbecility, bearing in his feeble body the evidences of evil living, and betraying by his talk, such radical obliquity of sense, that every spark of harsh feeling towards him was extinguished, and we could not even entertain a feeling of contempt for one who was evidently committing a suicide upon his body, as he had already done upon his character. Unhappy man! He was accompanied by an aged female relative, who was going a weary round in the hot streets, following his steps to prevent his indulging in a love of drink; but he had eluded her watchful eye by some means, and was already far gone in a state of inebriation. After listening awhile with painful feelings to his profane ribaldry, he left the office, accompanied by his good genius, to whom he owed the duties which she was discharging for him, and we muttered involuntarily, 'remote, unfriended, solitary alone,' &c. &c. And this is the poor man who has been hired by a mammon-worshipping publisher to do execution upon the gifted, noble-minded and pure-hearted men and women, whose works are cherished by their contemporaries as their dearest national treasure. It would be unreasonable to look to such a person for a just appreciation of the works of an upright intellect. But the only harm that such men can do is by praise, and we might well suspect the merits of those who are lauded by such persons, if we did not know that their seemingly good words were as sinister as their abuse.

A transient emotion may be created in the public mind by such criticisms, but it is sure to be succeeded by a contemptuous forgetfulness. The public can never be humbugged a second time by the same operator. Charlatans should estimate their profits very closely before they embark in a speculation upon the credulity of the public, for if they fail in the first attempt they lose all. Dr. Brandreth could never get up another pill, if he were to spend all he has made by his first one, in the attempt. If the publisher and his critic fail to reap a sufficient reward from their exertions this time, they can never stir up the curiosity of a wonder-loving public again. They will find, we think, that they have killed their gold-laying goose, in their impatience to get *rich*.

---

35. 21 July 1846: "Mr. Poe"
Morning News

[With Poe being treated to Fuller's "backwoods vituperation," as in the preceding document, the Morning News now pleaded for decency ("let public opinion condemn him"—Poe—"but do not let us make the press a vehicle of personal abuse and revengeful cant").

The exhortations of the Morning News had little effect upon the editor of the Mirror and despite its condemnation of the article in question, Lewis Clark felt no compunction in reprinting portions of that "most inexcusable and vindictive editorial attack" in his Knickerbocker (Document 50). For good reason Clark did not identify his source except to say it was "one of our most respectable daily journals." Even this allusion was evasive, for there were many daily journals published in New York at the time but only one evening paper, the Evening Mirror.]

MR. POE.—There is no excuse more miserable than that which is used to palliate a wrong by a wrong. The man who picks a neighbor's pocket because that neighbor has picked his is none the less a criminal on the ground of retributive justice. We are pained by having read a most inexcusable and vindictive editorial attack upon Mr. Poe and his personal, ay! his domestic relations. That gentleman may have discoursed coarsely of others, but that furnishes no reason for those that have been attacked to make blackguards of themselves, and to offend the public by a wanton display of backwoods vituperation. Mr. Poe is a man of talent but he is, notwithstanding, flesh, and possesses frailties with which a great portion of the human family is afflicted.

If *he* has invaded domestic privacy, let public opinion condemn him, but do not let us make the press a vehicle of personal abuse and revengeful cant. We hope the press was instituted for worthier purposes. It is a melancholy fact that the literary profession is divided against itself. Instead of being a fraternity, it is like the athlete of old.—Gladiator like, we meet that we may destroy. There is no feeling in common among us— no *esprit de corps*; no brotherly sympathy. And yet, with all their necessities, the literary workies, or drudges, have greater need for mutual aid than any other class of men in the country.

36. 22 July 1846: Letter to Thomas Holley Chivers
   Edgar A. Poe

[*However much the letter below may be discounted for its "being pre-cisely adapted to its purpose," to use Poe's words about his "Reply to Mr. English and Others," it suggests what is true enough, that most of Poe's friends had deserted him, that he was ill, impoverished, and in de-spair, and that his literary enemies were attempting his ruin.*

   Twice moved, the Poe cottage, which came into possession of New York City in 1913, is now located in Poe Park at 194th Street and Kings-bridge Road in the Bronx, where, badly neglected, it has deteriorated from "a snug little cottage" into a shack. The "slip" from the Saint Louis Reveille that Poe says he enclosed in this letter appears as Document 9.

   Chivers, though a warm admirer of Poe during his lifetime (he even begged him to "come to the South to live" where "I will take care of you as long as you live"), charged after Poe's death that "The Raven" and "Ulalume" were plagiarized from two of his poems.

   Poe's reference to his being "done forever with drink" has to do with the fact that Chivers, according to the manuscript biography of Poe he left behind (since edited by Richard Beale Davis), saw Poe "as drunk as an Indian" in New York, where he had gone to see his Lost Pleiad and Other Poems through the press.

   The full version of this letter appears in Ostrom, II, 325–7.]

New-York, July 22 / 46.

My Dear Friend,
   I had long given you up (thinking that, after the fashion of numerous other *friends*, you had made up your mind to desert me at the first breath of what seemed to be trouble) when this morning I received no less than 6 letters from you, all of them addressed 195 East Broadway. Did you not know that I merely boarded at this house? . . . . I am living out of town about 13 miles, at a village called Fordham, on the rail-road leading north. We are in a snug little cottage, keeping house, and would be very comfortable, but that I have been for a long time dreadfully ill. I am getting better, however, although slowly, and shall get *well*. In the mean-time the flocks of little birds of prey that always take the opportunity of illness to peck at a sick fowl of larger dimensions, have been endeavoring with all their power to effect my ruin. My dreadful poverty, also, has

given them every advantage. In fact, my dear friend, I have been driven to the very gates of death and a despair more dreadful than death, and I had not even *one* friend, out of my family, with whom to advise. . . .

It is with the greatest difficulty that I write you this letter—as you may perceive, indeed, by the M.S. I have not been able to write *one line* for the Magazines for more than 5 months—you can then form some idea of the dreadful extremity to which I have been reduced. The articles [on the New York literati] lately published in "Godey's Book" were written and paid for a long while ago. . . .

There is one thing you will be glad to learn: . . . . I am done forever with drink—depend upon that—but there is much more in this matter than meets the eye.

Do not let anything in this letter impress you with the belief that I *despair* even of worldly prosperity. On the contrary although I feel ill, and am ground into the very dust with poverty, there is a sweet *hope* in the bottom of my soul. . . .

I enclose you a slip from the "Reveilée" [*sic*]. You will be pleased to see how they appreciate me in England. . . .

God Bless You.

Ever Your friend,
Edgar A Poe

DURING THE LAWSUIT

37. 23 July 1846: N.Y. Superior Court: Edgar A. Poe vs. Hiram Fuller and Augustus W. Clason, Jr.: Declaration of Grievances

[On 20 July 1846, after "Mr. English's Reply to Poe" appeared in the Evening Mirror (23 June 1846) and the Weekly Mirror (27 June 1846), Poe through his attorney, Enoch L. Fancher, wrote out his Declaration of Grievances, which was filed in New York Superior Court on July 23. (The New York Superior Court was merged with two other courts sometime in the 1870s to form the present-day New York Supreme Court.) The declaration contains two counts of libel based upon English's accusations that Poe had committed forgery and that he had taken money from him under false pretenses. Poe sued Fuller and Clason, owners of the Mirror, for publishing English's "Card" and thereby contriving, "wickedly and maliciously, . . . to injure the plaintiff in his good . . . name, fame and credit, and to bring him into public scandal, infamy and disgrace . . . ; to vex, harass, oppress, impoverish, and wholly ruin him," and asked damages of five thousand dollars.

Why Poe sued the owners of the Mirror and not English, or why he didn't sue the owners of the Mirror and English, can only be conjectured. There were personal reasons, of course, for his wanting to avenge himself upon Fuller; he had obviously been angered at Fuller's gratuitous and damaging editorial comments. Very likely his attorney had advised him that the proprietors of the Mirror had incurred a greater degree of culpability than English by giving circulation to English's libels and that typically one always sued the deeper pocket, advice that no doubt coincided with Poe's wishes. Perhaps, too, Poe wanted to be vindicated more than he wanted to avenge himself upon everyone implicated in the libel. If he could achieve this clearly by a legal victory in one case, there would be no point in bringing concurrent, consolidated, or subsequent suits against English and, for that matter, the owners of the Morning Telegraph who first published English's reply. As he no doubt had the sense to realize, bringing multiple suits would only damage his reputation still more, a reputation he was at pains to clear, by making him seem merely mercenary.

In any event, the first formal complaint was made against the Evening Mirror; the second, against the Weekly Mirror. Apart from modifications in the respective names and dates of the Mirrors involved in the complaints, the two statements are almost identical. The preliminary hearing was to be held in New York City Hall on 4 August 1846.

The entire Judgment Record is presented here episodically, as it was taken, so that the reader may follow the unfolding of events as Poe followed it. The reader who wishes to consult the entire court record at once can refer to the Index. No editorial liberties have been taken with this record except for some changes in punctuation, capitalization, spelling, and an occasional transposition of a phrase in order to gain clarity. The source of this and the other legal documents reproduced in this book are the records in the Hall of Records, Office of the County Clerk, New York County, New York.

Some scholars, having taken Poe's word that English's charges were "criminal" and that he could "have them investigated before a criminal tribunal," have assumed that Poe initiated a criminal suit. This is incorrect. To initiate a criminal prosecution requires haling a person before a magistrate, who must decide upon the testimony heard whether to hold the person for the action of the Grand Jury. If the Grand Jury finds there is sufficient prima facie evidence to warrant an indictment, the defendant is then brought before a court to plead. At the time the magistrate holds the defendant for the action of the Grand Jury, the defendant must post bail to assure his appearance. Moreover, before the matter is brought to the magistrate, the aggrieved individual has to submit his charge to the Office of the District Attorney, at which time all subsequent legal actions are taken by the district attorney. The proceeding in this case would be introduced in the name of the People of the State of New York, on the complaint of Edgar A. Poe; there would be a statement of charges, which would specify the breach of peace that had occurred on account of the libel, and the criminal statutes allegedly violated would be cited. Lastly, the information would call for the imposition of the punishment provided in the criminal statutes violated, not damages to the witness Poe in a sum of money.

Poe's declaration, then, initiated a civil suit for libel, which has the advantage that a far lesser degree of certainty of guilt is required to be established than in a criminal prosecution for libel. As one lawyer put it, it takes 99 per cent certainty of guilt to be established in a criminal prosecution, since a prison sentence and a fine may be the result, and only 51 per cent certainty of guilt in a civil action, since only money is involved.

On the grounds of the charges made, Poe claimed that he had been *damaged in his good name and reputation and demanded five thousand dollars in compensation. If Poe, believing that English's charges were criminal, had presented the matter to the Office of the District Attorney, the district attorney would have it within his discretion to determine whether to proceed for a violation of the pertinent criminal statutes or to advise him to find recourse in the civil court. Whatever Poe may have done, the records unmistakably attest that Poe's was a civil suit, not a criminal prosecution.]*

N. Y. Superior Court. Pleas before the Justices of the Superior Court of the City of New York, at the City Hall in the City of New York. Of July term, to wit, the twentieth day of July in the term of July, in the year one thousand eight hundred and forty-six.

City and County of New York, fs [*scilicet;* i.e., that is to say]: Edgar A. Poe, plaintiff in this suit, by Enoch L. Fancher, his attorney, comes into this Court, according to the form of the statute, authorizing the commencement of suits by declaration, and complains of Hiram Fuller and Augustus W. Clason, Junr, defendants in this suit, of a plea of trespass on the case [*a plea of trespass* is one of the general forms of pleading].

For that whereas the said plaintiff now is a good, true, honest, just and faithful citizen of this State, and as such hath always behaved and conducted himself, and until the committing of the several grievances by the said defendants, as hereinafter mentioned, was always reputed, esteemed and accepted by and amongst all his neighbors, and other good and worthy citizens of this State, to whom he was in anywise known, to be a person of good name, fame and credit, to wit, at the City and in the County of New York aforesaid and within the jurisdiction of this Court; and whereas also the said plaintiff hath not ever been guilty, and until the time of the committing of the said several grievances by the said defendants as hereinafter mentioned, been suspected to have been guilty of obtaining money under false pretences, [n]or of the offences and misconduct hereinafter mentioned to have been charged and imputed to the said plaintiff, [n]or of any other such offences and misconduct; by means of which said premises he, the said plaintiff, before the committing of the said several grievances by the said defendants, as hereinafter mentioned, had deservedly obtained the good opinion and credit of all his neighbors and other good and worthy citizens of this State to whom he was in anywise known, to wit, in the City and in the County of New York aforesaid and within the jurisdiction of this Court; yet the said defendants, well knowing the premises and greatly envying the happy state and condition of the said plaintiff, and contriving and wickedly and maliciously intending to injure the said plaintiff in his good name, fame and credit and to bring him into public scandal, infamy and disgrace with and amongst all his neighbors and other good and worthy citizens of this State, and to cause it to be suspected and believed by those neighbors and citizens that he, the said plaintiff, had been guilty of obtaining money under false pretences, and of the offences and misconduct hereinafter mentioned to have been imputed to him, and to subject him to the pains and penalties of the laws of this State made and provided against and inflicted upon persons guilty thereof, and to vex, harass, oppress, impoverish and wholly ruin him, the said plaintiff, heretofore, to wit, on the twenty-third day of June, in the year one thousand eight hundred and forty-six, at the City and in the County of New York aforesaid and within the jurisdiction of this Court, falsely, wickedly and maliciously did print and publish and cause and procure to be printed and published of and concerning the said plaintiff, in a certain newspaper called the "Evening Mirror," a certain false, scandalous, malicious and defamatory libel over the name of one Thomas Dunn English, containing amongst other things the false, scandalous, malicious, defamatory and libellous matter following of and concerning the said plaintiff, that is to say: "I" (meaning one Thomas Dunn English) "hold Mr Poe's acknowledgment" (meaning the acknowledgment of the said plaintiff)"for a sum of money which he" (meaning the said plaintiff) "obtained of me" (meaning said Thomas Dunn English) "under false pretences," thereby then and there meaning that the said plaintiff had obtained money under false pretences from the said Thomas Dunn English.

And the said plaintiff further saith that the said defendants further contriving and intending as aforesaid, heretofore, to wit, on the day and year last aforesaid, at the place last aforesaid, falsely, wickedly and maliciously did print and publish, and cause and procure to be printed and published, over the name of one Thomas Dunn English, a certain other false, scandalous, malicious and defamatory libel of and concerning the said plaintiff in a certain newspaper called the "Evening Mirror," containing amongst other things the false, scandalous, malicious, defamatory and libellous matter following of and concerning the said plaintiff, that is to say:—"I" (meaning one Thomas Dunn English) "know Mr Poe" (meaning the said plaintiff) "by a succession of his acts" (meaning the acts of said plaintiff) "one of which is rather costly. I" (meaning said Thomas Dunn English) "hold Mr Poe's acknowledgment" (meaning the acknowledgment of said plaintiff) "for a sum of money which he" (meaning the said plaintiff) "obtained of me" (meaning said Thomas Dunn English) "under false pretences" (meaning that said plaintiff had obtained money from said Thomas Dunn English by the false pretences of said plaintiff). "Another act of his" (meaning another act of the said plaintiff) "gave me" (meaning the said Thomas Dunn English) "some knowledge of him" (meaning said plaintiff). "A merchant of this City" (meaning a merchant of the City of New York) "had accused him" (meaning the said plaintiff) "of committing forgery. He" (meaning the said plaintiff) "consulted me" (meaning the said Thomas Dunn English) "on the mode of punishing his accuser" (meaning the said merchant) "and as he" (meaning the said plaintiff) "was afraid to challenge him" (meaning said merchant) "to the field or chastise him" (meaning said merchant) "personally, I" (meaning the said Thomas Dunn English) "suggested a legal prosecution as his sole remedy" (meaning the sole remedy of the said plaintiff). "At his request" (meaning the request of the said plaintiff) "I" (meaning the said Thomas Dunn English) "obtained a counsellor who was willing as a compliment to me" (meaning the said English) "to conduct his suit" (meaning the suit of the said plaintiff) "without the customary retaining fee. But though so eager at first to commence proceedings, he" (meaning the said plaintiff) "dropped the matter altogether when the time came for him" (meaning the said plaintiff) "to act—thus virtually admitting the truth of the charge." And thereby then and there meaning that he, the said plaintiff, had been accused of forgery, and had been charged with the crime of forgery by a merchant of the City of New York, and that the said plaintiff had virtually admitted the truth of such charge, by means of the committing of which said several grievances by the said defendants as aforesaid, he, the said plaintiff, hath been and is greatly injured in his said good name, fame and credit and brought into public scandal, infamy and disgrace with and amongst all his neighbors, and other good and worthy citizens of this State, insomuch that divers of these neighbors and citizens, to whom the innocence and integrity of the said plaintiff in the premises were unknown, have, on occasion of the committing of the said grievances by the said defendants as aforesaid, from thence hitherto suspected and believe and still do suspect and believe the said plaintiff to have been a person guilty of obtaining money under false pretences, and of the offences and misconduct as aforesaid charged upon and imputed to the said plaintiff, and have, by reason of the committing of the said grievances by the said defendants as aforesaid, from thence hitherto wholly refused and still do refuse to have any transaction, acquaintance or discourse with him, the said plaintiff, as they were before used and accustomed to have and otherwise would have had; and the said plaintiff hath been and is by means of the premises otherwise greatly injured, to wit, at the City and in the County of New York aforesaid and within the jurisdiction of this Court aforesaid.

And whereas also the said plaintiff now is a good, true, honest, just and faithful citizen, and as such hath always behaved and conducted himself, and until the committing of the several grievances by the said defendants, as hereinafter mentioned, was always reputed, esteemed and accepted by and amongst all his neighbors, and other good and worthy citizens of this State to whom he was in anywise know[n], to be a person of good name, fame and credit, to wit, at the City and in the County of New York aforesaid and within the jurisdiction of this Court; and whereas also the said plaintiff hath not ever been guilty or until the time of the committing of the said several grievances by the said defendants, as hereinafter mentioned, been suspected to have been guilty of obtaining money under false pretences or of the offences and misconduct hereinafter mentioned to have been charged and imputed to the said plaintiff or of any other such offences and misconduct, by means of which said premises, he, the said plaintiff, before the committing of the said several grievances by the said defendants, as hereinafter mentioned, had deservedly obtained the good opinion of all his neighbors and other good and worthy citizens to whom he was in anywise known, to wit, at the City and in the County of New York aforesaid and within the jurisdiction of this Court. Yet the said defendants, well knowing the premises but greatly envying the happy state and condition of the said plaintiff, and contriving and wickedly and maliciously intending to injure the said plaintiff in his said good name, fame and credit, and to bring him into public scandal, infamy and disgrace with and amongst all his neighbors and other good and worthy citizens of this State, and to cause it to be suspected and believed by those neighbors and citizens that he, the said plaintiff, had been guilty of

[82]

obtaining money under false pretences, and of the offences and misconduct hereinafter mentioned to have been imputed to him, and to subject him to the pains and penalties of the laws of this State made and provided against and inflicted upon persons guilty thereof, and to vex, harass, oppress, impoverish and wholly ruin him, the said plaintiff, heretofore, to wit, on the twenty-seventh day of June in the year one thousand eight hundred and forty-six, at the City and in the County of New York aforesaid, and within the jurisdiction of this Court, falsely, wickedly and maliciously did print and publish and cause and procure to be printed and published of and concerning the said plaintiff in a certain newspaper called the "Weekly Mirror" over the name of one Thomas Dunn English a certain other false, scandalous, malicious and defamatory libel concerning amongst other things the false, scandalous, malicious, defamatory and libellous matter following of and concerning the said plaintiff, that is to say: "I" (meaning one Thomas Dunn English) "hold Mr Poe's acknowledgment" (meaning the acknowledgment of the said plaintiff) "for a sum of money which he" (meaning the said plaintiff) "obtained of me" (meaning said Thomas Dunn English) "under false pretences," thereby then and there meaning that the said plaintiff had obtained money under false pretences from the said Thomas Dunn English.

And the said plaintiff further saith that the said defendants further contriving and intending as aforesaid, heretofore, to wit, on the day and year last aforesaid, at the place last aforesaid, falsely, wickedly and maliciously did print and publish and cause and procure to be printed and published over the name of one Thomas Dunn English a certain other false, scandalous, malicious and defamatory libel of and concerning the said plaintiff in a certain newspaper called the "Weekly Mirror," containing amongst other things the false, scandalous, malicious, defamatory and libellous matter of and concerning the said plaintiff, that is to say: "I" (meaning one Thomas Dunn English) "know Mr Poe" (meaning the said plaintiff) "by a succession of his acts" (meaning the acts of said plaintiff) "one of which is rather costly: I" (meaning said Thomas Dunn English) "hold Mr Poe's acknowledgment" (meaning the acknowledgment of said plaintiff) "for a sum of money which he" (meaning the said plaintiff) "obtained of me" (meaning said Thomas Dunn English) "under false pretences" (meaning that said plaintiff had obtained money from said Thomas Dunn English by the false pretences of said plaintiff). "Another act of his" (meaning another act of the said plaintiff) "gave me" (meaning the said Thomas Dunn English) "some knowledge of him" (meaning the said plaintiff). "A merchant of this City" (meaning a merchant of the City of New York) "had accused him" (meaning the said plaintiff) "of committing forgery. He" (meaning the said plaintiff) "consulted me" (meaning the said Thomas Dunn English) "on the mode of punishing his accuser" (meaning the said merchant) "and as he" (meaning the said plaintiff) "was afraid to challenge him" (meaning said merchant) "to the field or chastise him" (meaning said merchant) "personally, I" (meaning the said Thomas Dunn English) "obtained a counsellor who was willing as a compliment to me" (meaning the said English) "to conduct his suit" (meaning the suit of the said plaintiff) "without the customary retaining fee. But though so eager at first to commence proceedings, he" (meaning the said plaintiff) "dropped the matter altogether when the time came for him" (meaning the said plaintiff) "to act—thus virtually admitting the truth of the charge," and thereby then and there meaning that he, the said plaintiff, had been accused of forgery, and had been charged with the crime of forgery, by a merchant of the City of New York, and that the said plaintiff had virtually admitted the truth of such charge, by means of the committing of which said several grievances by the said defendants as aforesaid, he, the said plaintiff, hath been and is greatly injured in his said good name, fame and credit and brought into public scandal, infamy and disgrace with and amongst all his neighbors, and other good and worthy citizens of this State, insomuch that divers of these neighbors and citizens, to whom the innocence and integrity of the said plaintiff in the premises were unknown, have, on occasion of the committing of the said grievances by the said defendants as aforesaid, from thence hitherto suspected and believed and still do suspect and believe the said plaintiff to have been a person guilty of obtaining money under false pretences and of the offences and misconduct as aforesaid charged upon and imputed to the said plaintiff, and have by reason of the committing of the said grievances by the said defendants as aforesaid, from thence hitherto wholly refused and still do refuse to have any transaction, acquaintance or discourse with him, the said plaintiff, as they were used and accustomed to have and otherwise would have; and the said plaintiff hath been and is by means of the premises otherwise greatly injured, to wit, at the City and in the County of New York aforesaid and within the jurisdiction of this Court aforesaid, to the damage of the said plaintiff of five thousand dollars, and therefore he brings suit, &c.

[struck out]   [E. L. Fancher
                         [plaintiff's attorney

---

38. *23 July 1846*: "Godey's Magazine *for August*"
Hiram Fuller

[*The evening of the day Poe's Declaration of Grievances was filed in court, Fuller vituperated Poe again. Among other things, he asserted that Poe's "habit of misrepresentation is . . . confirmed, and malignity . . . is a part of his nature. . . ."*

Miss Fuller, of course, is Margaret Fuller, whom Poe treated generously in a "Literati" sketch. General Wetmore is Prosper M. Wetmore, whose Lexington and Other Fugitive Poems *had "considerable merit," according to Poe. Mrs. Kirkland is Caroline M. Kirkland, well known for her narratives of the frontier,* A New Home—Who'll Follow?, Forest Life, *and* Western Clearings. *If only because she was the wife of William Kirkland (see headnote to Document 8), Fuller was bound to be pleased with Poe's gracious treatment of her, just as he was bound as an adversary to say that Poe had "stumbled upon the truth" of her merits "by some fortunate accident. . . ."*

Poe, in lauding Margaret Fuller's review of Longfellow's Poems *in the* Daily Tribune *of 10 December 1845—which he correctly said was "frank, candid, independent, . . . giving honor only where honor was due"—made the remarks that Fuller attributes to him. But Poe did not insinuate, as Fuller asserts, that Longfellow's* Poems *(1845) was published at his own expense. Poe only "insinuated" that Longfellow had recently published collections of other people's poems, namely,* The Waif: A Collection of Poems *(1844, dated 1845),* Poets and Poetry of Europe *(1845), and* The Estray: A Collection of Poems *(1846).*

Fuller singled out Poe for condemnation this time rather than the bulk of the contents of Godey's Lady's Book *because, according to the report in the* Home Journal *of July 25, the August number was "beyond all dispute . . . a brilliant one."*

The article below also appeared in the Weekly Mirror *on August 1.*]

[85]

GODEY'S MAGAZINE FOR AUGUST.—. . . Mr Poe continues his Honest Opinions of the New York Literati in this number. In serving up Miss Fuller of the Tribune, and General Wetmore of the Navy Department, he has followed the recipe for preserving plums and quinces, and has 'done them up' in their own weight of sugar, although it is not exactly double refined. He has stumbled upon the truth by some fortunate accident, and spoken of Mrs. Kirkland in a manner to which her merits entitle her. The other articles in Mr. Godey's Magazine we will notice hereafter if we should ever read them. . . .

Mr. Poe's habit of misrepresentation is so confirmed, and malignity is so much a part of his nature, that he continually goes out of his way to do ill-natured things, when nothing can be gained by it. In his essay upon Miss F., he has the following lying insinuations about Mr. Longfellow:—

'Mr Longfellow is entitled to a certain and very distinguished rank among the poets of his country, but that country is disgraced by the evident toadyism which would award to his social position and influence, to his fine paper and large type, to his morocco binding and gilt edges, to his flattering portraits of himself, and to the illustrations of his poems by Huntingdon, that amount of indiscriminate approbation which neither could nor would have been given to the poems themselves.'

He also speaks of 'Professor Longfellow's magnificent edition of his own works, with a portrait,' meaning to insinuate that Carey & Hart's edition of Longfellow's Poems was published at the expense of the author.

For a man like Poe to talk of toadyism while penning such transparent adulations as are contained in this number of Godey's Lady's Book, is a very amusing spectacle to say the least of it. What does he mean by Professor Longfellow's portrait of himself?

---

39. *24 July 1846: "Edgar A. Poe"*
Hiram Fuller

[*The day after Poe's attorney filed Poe's Declaration of Grievances in court, Fuller announced the fact that Poe "has commenced a suit against us for a libel" and suggested dire exposure should the case come to trial, as well as the possibility of his bringing countersuits "against some of Mr. Poe's publishers for his scurrillous libels on us." The only time Poe had mentioned Fuller in print was in his "Reply to Mr. English and Others." The worst thing he said of him was that he had "prostituted his filthy sheet" to the circulation of English's calumny, hardly a libelous statement or one that involved more publishers than John S. Du Solle who had printed "Poe's Reply" in his Spirit of the Times. Moreover, as was established in court, Fuller did not print English's "Reply to Mr. Poe" "as an advertisement," as he alleges here. Though he had assigned the word "Card" to the article as a way of designating an advertisement, he had not charged English to have his reply printed.*

Fuller seemed not to be averse to libel suits in principle. Only recently he had challenged James Gordon Bennett of the New York Herald to "state in his paper that the Editor of the Evening Mirror was ever concerned in any 'black mail transaction,'" in which case Fuller would "bring an action for libel, and allow Bennett an opportunity to prove his charges" (Weekly Mirror, 30 May 1846).]

EDGAR A. POE has commenced a suit against us for a libel contained in a Card of *Thomas Dunn English*, which was copied from the *Morning Telegraph*, and published in the Mirror as an advertisement. We do not hold ourselves responsible for Mr. English's charges against Mr. Poe, but if the latter gentleman chooses to take the matter into Court, we shall not shrink from the trial. We are confident that his attorney cannot be aware of the testimony he will have to meet in the progress of the suit. In the meantime we may be compelled in self-defence to instigate counter proceedings against some of Mr. Poe's publishers for his scurrillous libels on us. We have hitherto deemed it best to treat him as one morally irresponsible.

---

40. *25 July 1846: "A new Chesterfield"*
Hiram Fuller

[*Fuller took a satirical tack in the article reprinted below. He attributed to Poe an unsigned two-page filler in Godey's Lady's Book entitled "A Few Words on Etiquette" and proceeded to quote its various banalities.*

"Innocent women" is an allusion to Mrs. Elizabeth Ellet; the "friend"
is Thomas Dunn English.]

A NEW CHESTERFIELD.—The August number of Mr. Godey's Magazine
contains a paper on etiquette, by Mr. Poe. It does not bear his signature,
but it was written by him, and is almost equal to . . . Chesterfield. Some
of the maxims in this essay are quite up to Rochefoucauld—for instance:
'A visit should always be returned; an insult never overlooked.' 'The style
of your conversation should always be in keeping with the character of
your visit.' 'Familiarity of manner is the greatest vice of society.' 'Never
use the term genteel.' 'Never ask a lady any question about anything
whatever.' . . . .

These maxims are excellent, and as they say in the Bowery, hard to
beat. . . . These new hints on etiquette should be immediately stereo-
typed, and hung up in all our primary schools and seminaries for young
gentlemen. Think of the enormity of wearing white trowsers of a Sunday!
or green spectacles on any day, or of touching any part of a lady but her
fingers! But to use the word genteel, Good gracious! We didn't know before that that was such a profane word. To get drunk, to curse and swear,
to slander innocent women, to betray your friend, are trifles, in comparison with such an offence.

---

41. 30 July 1846: Letter to Poe
William Gilmore Simms

[*Simms, the South Carolina novelist who was a literary ally of Poe rather
than his friend, was in New York during June and July 1846 to see a book
through the press. Poe recognized that he desperately needed help in
what was coming to be a life-or-death struggle for him in the jungle of
journalism. As he acknowledged in his Declaration of Grievances, a declaration that should be discounted somewhat for its exaggerations: those
"to whom the innocence and integrity of the . . . plaintiff . . . were unknown" have "refused and still do refuse to have any transaction, acquaintance or discourse with him . . . as they were before used and accustomed to have and otherwise would have. . . ." Poe therefore wrote to
Simms, knowing that the novelist resented the New York literary clique*

*as much as himself. Simms had been of help to him in the previous year.
When Boston editors were harassing him because of his alleged hoax at
the Boston Lyceum, Simms came to his aid in a long defense in the
Charleston Southern Patriot of 10 November 1845, a defense that Poe
quoted in full in the Broadway Journal of 22 November 1845.*

*Though Poe's letters to Simms are lost, the help he wanted at this time
is easy to infer from Simms's response. Poe wanted the novelist to offset
the abusive comments of Lewis Clark, Hiram Fuller, and Thomas Dunn
English by writing a flattering notice of "The Literati" sketches and of
their author, especially in regard to his personal appearance. Moreover,
as before, he wanted permission to quote Simms's remarks, this time by
Godey. Simms, however, obeying "a law of my own nature," could not
accede to Poe's wishes with a clear conscience. Instead, he read Poe a
lecture on his conduct and character. Furthermore, being a "Southern
man," he did not wish the "intolerable grievance" of "being mixed up in
a squabble with persons whom he does not know, and does not care to
know,—and from whom no Alexandrine process of cutting loose, would
be permitted. . . ." Poe did not publish any of Simms's remarks; in fact, he
seems to have been offended by them, for there is no evidence that he
wrote to Simms again.*

*Simms's advice that Poe cherish his wife and "trample those tempta-
tions underfoot, which degrade your person, and make it familiar to the
mouth of vulgar jest," has to do with Poe's romantic involvement with
Mrs. Osgood, which had become common gossip in the small literary
world of New York, especially as the malicious Mrs. Ellet was devoting
her energies to vilifying both of them.*

*Poe obviously did not attempt to see Simms in downtown New York.
Pleading illness as usual, he probably asked the novelist to visit him in
Fordham, as Simms's postscript suggests.*

*This letter, printed here with all its original errors, appears in Oliphant
et al., II, 174-7.]*

New York July 30. 1846

Edgar A Poe, Esq.

Dear Sir

I recieved your note a week ago, and proceeded at once to answer it,
but being in daily expectation of a newspaper from the South, to which,
in a Letter, I had communicated a paragraph concerning the matter

which you had suggested in a previous letter, I determined to wait until I could enclose it to you. It has been delayed somewhat longer than I had anticipated, and has in part caused my delay to answer you. I now send it you, and trust that it will answer the desired purpose; though I must frankly say that I scarcely see the necessity of noticing the sort of scandal to which you refer.—I note with regret the very desponding character of your last letter. I surely need not tell you how deeply & sincerely I deplore the misfortunes which attend you—the more so as I see no process for your relief and, extrication but such as must result from your own decision and resolve. No friend can well help you in the struggle which is before you. Money, no doubt, can be procured; but this is not altogether what you require. Sympathy may soothe the hurts of Self-Esteem, and make a man temporarily forgetful of his assailants;—but in what degree will this avail, and for how long, in the protracted warfare of twenty or thirty years. You are still a very young man, and one too largely & too variously endowed, not to entertain the conviction—as your friends entertain it—of a long & manful struggle with, and a final victory over, fortune. But this warfare, the world requires you to carry on with your own unassisted powers. It is only in your manly resolution to use these powers, after a legitimate fashion, that it will countenance your claims to its regards & sympathy; and I need not tell you how rigid & exacting it has ever been in the case of the poetical genius, or, indeed, the genius of any order. Suffer me to tell you frankly, taking the privilege of a true friend, that you are now perhaps in the most perilous period of your career—just in that position—just at that time of life—when a false step becomes a capital error—when a single leading mistake is fatal in its consequences. You are no longer a boy. "At thirty wise or never!" You must subdue your impulses; &, in particular, let me exhort you to discard all associations with men, whatever their talents, whom you cannot esteem as men. Pardon me for presuming thus to counsel one whose great natural & acquired resources should make him rather the teacher of others. But I obey a law of my own nature, and it is because of my sympathies that I speak. Do not suppose yourself abandoned by the worthy and honorable among your friends. They will be glad to give you welcome *if you will suffer them*. They will rejoice—I know their feelings and hear their language—to countenance your return to that community—that moral province in society—of which, let me say to you, respectfully and regretfully,—you have been, according to all reports but too heedlessly and, perhaps, too scornfully indifferent. Remain in obscurity for awhile. You have a young wife—I am told a suffering & interesting one,—let me entreat you to cherish her, and to cast away those pleasures which are not worthy of your mind, and to trample those temptations underfoot, which degrade your person, and make it familiar to the mouth of vulgar jest. You may [do] all this, by a little circumspection. It is still within your power. Your resources from literature are probably much greater than mine. I am sure they are quite as great. You can increase them, so that they shall be ample for all your legitimate desires; but you must learn the worldling's lesson of prudence;—a lesson, let me add, which the literary world has but too frequently & unwisely disparaged. It may seem to you very impertinent,—in most cases it is impertinent—that he who gives nothing else, should presume to give counsel. But one gives that which he can most spare, and you must not esteem me indifferent to a condition which I can in no other way assist. I have never been regardless of your genius, even when I knew nothing of your person. It is some years, since I counseled Mr. Godey to obtain the contributions of your pen. He will tell you this. I hear that you reproach him. But how can you expect a Magazine proprietor to encourage contributions which embroil him with all his neighbours. These broils do you no good—vex your temper, destroy your peace of mind, and hurt your reputation. You have abundant resources upon which to draw even were there no Grub Street in Gotham. Change your tactics & begin a new series of papers with your publisher.—The printed matter which I send you, might be quoted by Godey, and might be ascribed to me. But, surely, I need not say to you that, to a Southern man, the annoyance of being mixed up in a squabble with persons whom he does not know, and does not care to know,—and from whom no Alexandrine process of cutting loose, would be permitted by society—would be an intolerable grievance. I submit to frequent injuries & misrepresentations, content, though annoyed by the slaver, that the viper should amuse himself upon the file, at the expense of his own teeth. As a man, as a writer, I shall always be solicitous of your reputation & success. You have but to resolve on taking & asserting your position, equally in the social & the literary world, and your way is clear, your path is easy, and you will find true friends enough to sympathize in your triumphs. Very Sincerely though Sorrowfully, Yr frd & Servt.

W Gilmore Simms

P.S. If I could I should have been to see you. But I have been & am still drudging in the hands of the printers, kept busily employed night and day. Besides, my arrangements are to hurry back to the South where I have a sick family. A very few days will turn my feet in that direction.

---

42. 20 July 1846: "From our Correspondent"
William Gilmore Simms

[*In the foregoing letter to Poe, Simms remarked that he was enclosing some "printed matter," a paragraph of which had been suggested by Poe "in a previous letter. . . ." The "printed matter" had appeared anonymously in the Charleston* Southern Patriot *on July 20, though it was dated July 15, the time when Simms had sent the article to the newspaper. The paragraph on Poe, buried among other literary gossip, was neither an endorsement of "The Literati" sketches nor of their author. Poe must have been badly disappointed at what he probably regarded as Simms's squeamishness or cowardice and, of course, was hardly tempted to have Godey use the material.*

Simms's remark that Poe was suffering from "brain fever" had been widely circulated in New York. As early as 12 April 1846 the Saint Louis Reveille *wrote: "A rumor is in circulation in New York, to the effect that Mr. Edgar A. Poe, the poet and author, has become deranged, and his friends are about to place him under the charge of Dr. Brigham, of the Insane Retreat at Utica. We sincerely hope that this is not true; indeed we feel assured that it is altogether an invention." Similarly, the New Orleans* Daily Picayune *of 14 May 1846 noticed that Poe "is sojourning in a retired part of Long Island, where he is still suffering from an attack of brain fever. So says the correspondent of the North American." Simms himself in a letter dated 15 May 1846 reported: ". . . I see by one of the papers that it was gravely thought to send P. to Bedlam" (Oliphant et al., II, 163). And the New York* Morning News *as late as 24 July 1846 noted: "Poe is ill, we hear, of a brain fever." The basis for this rumor was that Poe had had Dr. John W. Francis certify him as temporarily insane in order to provide him with an alibi for having asserted that Mrs. Elizabeth Ellet had written compromising letters to him (see headnote to Docu-*

ment 89) and that he had moved to Fordham. Needless to say, Poe had never been committed to an insane asylum.

Simms's entire article is presented here to indicate how he managed to introduce his comments on one of the "petty excitements" of the New York literary scene.]

NEW YORK, July 15.

FROM OUR CORRESPONDENT.—I do not know that there is any thing in the literary world to interest you. At this moment, every thing in letters is particularly dull. Some personal items may give you pleasure. Washington Irving is expected daily from Europe. It is not understood that he has been doing any thing lately. He has it is said, had a work on hand for some time, but delays its publication to more auspicious seasons. Miss J. [*sic*] Margaret Fuller, the author of "Woman in the Nineteenth Century," and several other works of contemplative morality—a woman of real ability and thought—is about to sail on a two years tour in Europe. Wiley & Putnam have in preparation, two pretty volumes from her pen, the subjects of which are chiefly drawn from art and literature [*Papers on Literature and Art*, 1846]. She was a writer for the "Dial," one of those Boston Periodicals which our world styled transcendental, and the aim of which seems to have been spiritual progress. Mr. Cooper appears in a few days with a novel called "The Red Skins"—a title the taste of which seems very questionable. He is just now, we believe, at Philadelphia. His biographies of our naval heroes, of which two volumes have been published, have been quite successful, and deserved to be so. Mr. N. P. Willis, who is undoubtedly one of our most happy Magazine writers, is rusticating, we are told, in most unwonted obscurity. His chief literary employment seems to be in contributing in the form of correspondence, to one of the London Newspapers. His letters, which I have not seen, are said to be of the same staple with his well known productions of the same class and character, and to be equally worthy with them of the reader and himself. Fitz Greene Halleck is still banking, and likely to be so till the end of the chapter. The story of his getting up a newspaper was, to those who know, mere nonsense. His poems, however, are about to undergo illustrations like those of Bryant and Longfellow. His publishers are Appleton & Co. Bryant is looking well, but doing nothing for poetry. He works all the week at the Evening Post, and hurries down on Saturday to his delightful farm, Spring Bank, Long Island. Goodwin [Parke Godwin], his son-in-law, is busy preparing the Autobiography of Goethe,—a work which is due, at once, to the claims of the author, and the desires of the public. It is for Wiley & Putnam's Library. Goodwin will give us a good translation. Among the petty excitements common to authorship is that which Mr. Edgar A. Poe is producing by his pencil sketches of the New York Literati in Godey's Ladies Magazine. He has succeeded most happily (if such was the object), in fluttering the pigeons of this dove cote. His sketches, of which we have seen but a few, are given to a delineation as well of the persons as of the performances of his subjects. Some of them are amusing enough. I am not prepared to say how true are his sketches, but they have caused no little rattling among the dry bones of our Grub street. Of Poe, as a writer, we know something. He is undoubtedly a man of very peculiar and very considerable genius—but is irregular and exceedingly mercurial in his temperament. He is fond of mystifying in his stories, and they tell me, practises upon this plan even in his sketches; more solicitous, as they assert, of a striking picture than a likeness. Poe, himself, is a very good looking fellow. I have seen him on two or three occasions, and have enjoyed a good opportunity of examining him carefully. He is probably thirty three or four years old, some five, feet eight inches in height, of rather slender person, with a good eye, and a broad intelligent forehead. He is a man, clearly, of sudden and uneven impulses[,] of great nervous susceptibility, and one whose chief misfortune it is not to have been caught young and trained carefully. The efforts of his mind seem wholly spasmodic. He lacks habitual industry, I take it, which, in the case of the library [*sic*] man who must look to his daily wits for his daily bread, is something of a deficiency. He, also, is in obscurity, somewhere in the country, and sick, according to a report which reached me yesterday, of brain fever. By the way, the news from the West is that Henry R. Schoolcraft, the well known writer and Indian Agent has been murdered by a drunken savage at Sault de St. Marie. I trust that this report will turn out false. Schoolcraft's Algic Researches are of great value, and will rise in value as the aborignies [*sic*] disappear. He was for thirty years an Indian Agent under Government, married an Indian wife, and was admitted to all their mysteries. He was a gentleman of very respectable researches, considerable merit as a writer and of great industry. He had but just completed an elaborate report upon the Indian tribes of the State of New York. His most elaborate and valuable works are "Algic Researches" and "Oneota." We are pleased to see that Nathaniel

Hawthorne, one of our most original writers, has been permitted to dip his spoon into the treasury dishes—having received some appointment in the Customs in New England. This is as it should be. Hawthorne's volume just published by Wiley & Putnam, "The Mosses from an old Manse," is full of fresh and pleasant reading. The "Pictures of Italy," by Dickens, do not afford me pleasure. They seem laborious and strained. But they will be read on trust,—a sort of reading which never burdens the memory. A less artistical, but more readable book, is that just issued by Harper & Brothers, called "The Shores of the Mediterranean," by Francis Schroeder. It is light and sketchy, and if it taxes no thought, it at least provokes no dullness. It is a pleasant feature of these two volumes, the pictures which illustrate the most striking objects, from the pencil of the author. To those who travel there is no companion or auxiliary more commendable than the art of sketching. The *on dit* here is that a new "Punch" [*Yankee Doodle*] is about to be started in this city. We have heard something of the plan and the parties, but are permitted to say no more at present. They tell also of a new Monthly Magazine, to be sent forth from Manhatten, which is to confound and delight the natives. If it appears under the management named for it, and with the designated list of contributors, it will not improbably effect this object.

---

43. *4 August 1846: Preliminary Hearing in New York City Hall of the Case of Edgar A. Poe vs. Hiram Fuller and Augustus W. Clason, Jr.*

[*At this hearing Fuller and Clason, represented by their attorney William H. Paine, pleaded not guilty to the charge of libel on the grounds that the statements they had printed in the* Mirror *were true. Poe's attorney for his part argued that those statements were false and therefore libelous. In consequence, the Court ordered the trial set for the "first Monday of September next," which was September 7.*]

And now at this day, that is to say, on the fourth day of August, of August term in the year one thousand eight hundred and forty-six, to which day the said defendants had leave to imparle to the declaration aforesaid, and then to answer the same before the Justices aforesaid at the City Hall in the City of New York; comes as well the said plaintiff by his attorney aforesaid, as the aforesaid defendants by William H. Paine, their attorney.

And the said defendants, Hiram Fuller and Augustus W. Clason, Junior, by their attorney, William H. Paine, come and defend the wrong and injury, when, &c:

And say that they are not nor is either of them guilty of the premises above laid to their charge, in manner and form as the said plaintiff in this suit hath above thereof complained against them; and of this they put themselves upon the Country, and the said plaintiff likewise, &c.

And for a further plea in this behalf, the said defendants, by leave of the Court here for this purpose first had and obtained, according to the form of the statute in such case made and provided, say that the said plaintiff ought not to have or maintain his aforesaid action thereof against them, the said defendants, because they say that the said plaintiff, before the printing and publishing or causing to be printed and published in a certain newspaper called the "Evening Mirror," the said several words concerning the said plaintiff, as is said [in the] first count of said declaration mentioned, did obtain of one Thomas Dunn English a certain sum of money under false pretences; and that the said plaintiff was accused of forgery by a gentleman of the City of New York, and that the said plaintiff was advised by one Thomas Dunn English to commence a suit for the injury sustained thereby, and that the said plaintiff did commence a suit and abandon the same, thereby virtually admitting the truth of said charge of forgery.

And as to the second plea count in the said declaration mentioned, the said defendants say that the said plaintiff ought not to have or maintain his said action against the said defendants because they say that the said plaintiff, before the printing and publishing, or causing to be printed and published in a certain newspaper published in the City of New York, called the "Weekly Mirror," the said several words of and concerning the said plaintiff, as in said second count of said declaration mentioned, did obtain of one Thomas Dunn English a certain sum of money under false pretences, and that the said plaintiff was accused of forgery by a gentleman in the City of New York, and that the said plaintiff, by the advice and with the aid of one Thomas Dunn English, did commence a legal prosecution for the damage by said plaintiff thereby sustained; and that the said plaintiff did abandon the said suit, thereby virtually admitting the truth of said charge of forgery.

[96]

Wherefore the said defendants afterwards, to wit, at the City and within the County of New York, did print and publish and cause to be printed and published the said words in said several counts of said declaration mentioned, of and concerning the said plaintiff, as they lawfully might, for cause aforesaid, and this they are ready to verify.

Wherefore they pray judgment that the said plaintiff ought [not] to have or maintain his aforesaid action thereof against them, &c &c.

And the said plaintiff, as to the said plea of the said defendants by them secondly above pleaded, saith that the said plaintiff by reason of anything by the said defendants in that plea alleged ought not to be barred from having or maintaining his aforesaid action thereof against the said defendants, because he saith that the said plaintiff, before the printing or causing to be printed and published in a certain newspaper called the "Evening Mirror" the said several words concerning the said plaintiff, as in said first count of said declaration mentioned, did not obtain of one Thomas Dunn English a certain or any sum of money under false pretences; nor was the said plaintiff accused of forgery by a gentleman of the City of New York or advised by one Thomas Dunn English to commence a suit for the injury sustained thereby; [n]or commence suit and abandon the same; nor did the said plaintiff thereby or otherwise virtually admit the truth of said charge of forgery in manner and form as the said defendants hath above, in their said second plea in that behalf, alleged; and this, the said plaintiff prays, may be enquired of by the Country; and the said defendants likewise, &c.

And the said plaintiff, as to the said plea of the said defendants by them thirdly above pleaded, that the said plaintiff by reason of anything by the said defendants in that plea alleged ought not to be barred from having and maintaining his aforesaid action thereof against the said defendants, because he saith that the said plaintiff, before the printing and publishing in a certain newspaper published in the City of New York called the "Weekly Mirror" the said several words of and concerning the said plaintiff, as in said second count of said declaration mentioned, did not obtain of one Thomas Dunn English a certain or any sum of money under false pretences; nor was the said plaintiff accused of forgery by a gentleman in the City of New York; nor did the said plaintiff by the advice or with the aid of one Thomas Dunn English commence a legal prosecution for the damage thereby sustained by said plaintiff or abandon the suit; nor did the said plaintiff thereby or otherwise virtually admit the truth of said charge of forgery, in manner and form as the said defendants in this said third plea have above in that behalf alleged; and this the said plaintiff prays may be inquired of by the Country and the said defendants likewise, &c.

Therefore the issue above joined is ordered by the said Superior Court of the City of New York to be tried at the term of the said Court appointed to be held at the City Hall in the City of New York before the Justices aforesaid on the first Monday of September next. The same day is given to the parties aforesaid at the same place.

---

44. 27 August 1846: "Godey's Magazine, for September"
Hiram Fuller

[*Fuller continued to be critical of* Godey's Lady's Book *inasmuch as Poe's "Literati" sketches were still appearing in its pages. His squib, that Poe in "scanning the verse of Mrs. Osgood . . . is quite at home," is a double entendre. For Poe's sarcastic remarks about Lewis Clark, see the headnote to Document 50.*

The article below also appeared in the Weekly Mirror *on September 5.*]

Godey's Magazine, for September, is very much of a muchness with the past numbers; the proprietor will still persist in Americanising the Paris fashions, and Mr. Poe will go on with his pedantic sketches of our literati. His remarks on Mrs. [*sic*] Gould are evidently well intended. He describes her personal appearance with a flippant inaccuracy: it is possible that he has never seen her. In scanning the verses of Mrs. Osgood he is quite at home. His remarks about Mr. Clark of the *Knickerbocker* are probably intended to be sarcastic, but sarcasm is Mr. Poe's weakness. . . .

---

45. 5 September 1846: An Installment of 1844; or, The Power of the "S.F."
Thomas Dunn English

[*At this juncture Hiram Fuller began to serialize on the front pages of both the* Evening Mirror *and* Weekly Mirror *an anonymous novel en-*

titled 1844; *or, The Power of the* "S.F." *The authorship of the novel was a well-kept secret even at a time when literary secrets were all but impossible to keep among the New York literati.* According to Godey's Lady's Book *of July* 1847, *"the authorship was attributed to many celebrated authors" during the time* 1844 *ran in the* Mirrors. *Only when the novel appeared in book form in* 1847 *did its author become known. It was, of course, Thomas Dunn English.*

"S.F." *stands for "Startled Falcon," a secret organization whose purpose was to swing the election of* 1844 *to the Democrats. (*Yankee Doodle, *a weekly journal edited by the Duyckinck circle, alleged that "Poh" wanted to know if "S.F." stood for "Stupid Fiction.") The locale is New York City, and the multitudinous episodes are concerned with crime, political intrigue, and love. English at times introduced satirical sketches of the well known and the not so well known. Among the lesser lights are Mrs. Elizabeth Ellet, who is called Mrs. Grodenap and hails from South Carolina, and Mrs. Frances Osgood disguised as Mrs. Flighty and described as "one of our poetesses . . . and the best imitator of Mother Goose." Among the better known persons satirized are Margaret Fuller and Horace Greeley. Miss Fuller appears briefly as the authoress of* Women in the Present Day (*the real title of her book is* Woman in the Nineteenth Century). *Of this book one character remarks: It is "a work which, to understand properly, you must commence at the middle, and read backwards to the beginning, then jump to the end and read backwards to the middle. In that way I managed to explain to myself a great deal of what was otherwise inexplicable." Greeley of the* Tribune *appears as Satisfaction Sawdust, "editor of the 'Sly Coon.'" Apart from being portrayed as ineffably ugly, the head of Sawdust is said to be "filled with crotchets of every description"—philanthropy, Transcendentalism, hydropathy, Fourierism, worship of the* Dial, *opposition to the annexation of Texas, and compulsions to abolish the death penalty, slavery, and land titles; in short, the portrait of a man who "could swallow all the 'isms' that might arise, and after having bolted his meal, pick his teeth with the 'ologies.'"*

The person most sustainedly and savagely treated is Poe, who appears under the sobriquet of Marmaduke Hammerhead. All the episodes but one in which he appears are digressive to the rambling plot and the relevance of that one is questionable since almost any other character could have revealed the true identity of Hercules, one of the criminals featured in the work.

Both editions of the Mirror *carried large advertisements of the serial with fair regularity, though the serial itself appeared irregularly; and in 1847 the novel was the first to be published in the Mirror Library. No doubt, as the* Literary World *of 6 June 1847 pointed out, the serial "attracted no little attention as a* feuilleton *in the New York Mirror"; no doubt too, in book form, it was, to quote the* Literary World *again, "probably destined to still more general circulation," a circulation that damaged Poe's reputation still more.*

My collation of the three versions discloses only slight and infrequent variants. For the curious reader, references to the passages involving Hammerhead-Poe as they occur in these versions are given below. Since, as regards the Hammerhead episodes, there is only one major discrepancy between the Weekly Mirror *and book versions, a discrepancy noted in its proper place, I have chosen to reprint the book version here.*

The Appearance of Marmaduke Hammerhead in the
Three Versions of 1844; or, The Power of the "S.F."

As a serial in the Weekly Mirror	As a serial in the un-paginated Evening Mirror	As a book
With authorship withheld, the serial began on 25 July 1846 (Vol. IV) and ended on 7 Nov. 1846 (Vol. V).	*With authorship withheld, the serial began on 27 July 1846 (Vol. IV) and ended 6 Nov. 1846 (Vol. V).*	*With authorship identified, it appeared in the Mirror Library in late May or early June 1847.*
5 Sept. 1846, pp. 339–40.	*8 and 9 Sept. 1846.*	*Part of chap. xvi, pp. 120–4.*
19 Sept. 1846, pp. 371–2.	*23, 26, 28 Sept. 1846.*	*Parts of chap. xxiii, pp. 161–4, and of chap. xxiv, p. 170.*
3 Oct. 1846, p. 403.	*8 and 9 Oct. 1846.*	*Part of chap. xxix, pp. 206–8.*
24 Oct. 1846, p. 36.	*31 Oct. 1846.*	*Part of chap. xli, pp. 268–9.*
31 Oct. 1846, pp. 49–50.	*2 Nov. 1846.*	*Part of chap. lxi, pp. 273–6.*
7 Nov. 1846, p. 66.	*6 Nov. 1846.*	*Part of "Chapter the Last," p. 299.*

Some scholars, Willard Thorp and William Henry Gravely, Jr., among them, are convinced that English had earlier written a satirical sketch of Poe in a temperance tract called Walter Woolfe; or, The Doom of the Drinker *(1847), a work that had originally appeared in the* Cold Water Magazine *in 1843. Like Poe's Fortunato, however, I have my doubts, for no single detail in the sketch nor the sketch as a whole points infallibly to Poe. There were, after all, critics other than Poe, a number of whom might have sat for that portrait. (See* Princeton University Library Chronicle, *1943 and 1944, for the 1843 and 1847 versions of the sketch.)*

If Walter Woolfe *was really English's first satirical portrait of Poe, 1844 was not his last. In the* John-Donkey, *a humor magazine that English and* George G. Foster *edited from 1 January to 21 October 1848, English, among other editorial attacks on Poe, published another satirical portrait of the man in a fragmentary work called "The Untranslated Don Quixotte: The Adventures of Don Key Haughty." The references to the "roll of manuscript," "the minstrel of the Raven," and the poem as "the rhythmical creation of beauty," all point uneqivocally to Poe.]*

"I'm nothing if not critical."—*Othello.*

"TALKING of boots reminds me of a fish story," says some prating gentleman, when about to inflict a tedious narrative upon an unfortunate victim. Our transition is not less abrupt—from a dance-house at Pete Williams', in the Five Points, to a *conversazione* in one of our fashionable avenues. Yet it is necessary, or we should not make the change; and be it understood by all persons, little or great, that we intend telling our story in our own way, and snap our fingers in the face of the critics.

The Misses Veryblue were four young ladies, who possessed an intense admiration of all men and women who had acquired notoriety in literature, science, or the arts. Their weekly conversazione was a kind of *jardin des plantes* within whose bounds roared, frisked and gambolled various lions, old and young, collected from all parts of the Union, with not a few from other quarters of the globe. The beasts were exhibited weekly—not to be fed—since to gorge them were to prevent their roaring—but to be caressed and petted exceedingly by hosts of admiring young ladies. As this happy country produces lions in great abundance, who can either tear and rage in right royal fashion, or roar you like Nick Bottom's, "as gently as a sucking dove," of course the Misses Veryblue had no difficulty whatever in obtaining tenants to their menagerie.

On one evening in the latter part of September—we will not be particular as to dates, however, (our organ of time being rated by Mr. Fowler at "1")—a number of visiters were collected at the house of the Misses Veryblue. They were divided into groups, and the women (we bless them, dear little toads, as a widower should,) outnumbered the sterner sex in the proportion of two to one. Among the latter were Danby, Blair, the two O'Conors, John Melton, and Ivory. The latter acted as a kind of *cicerone* to Danby, and after a general introduction, informed him of the name, character, and quality of those around him. As it may save us considerable trouble, we may as well report a part of his information, and adopt it as our own.

"Do you see that man standing by the smiling little woman in black, engaged, by his manner, in laying down some proposition, which he conceives it would be madness to doubt, yet believes it to be known only by himself?"

"Him with the broad, low, receding, and deformed forehead, and a peculiar expression of conceit in his face?"

"The same."

"That is Marmaduke Hammerhead—a very well known writer for the sixpenny periodicals, who aspires to be a critic, but never presumes himself a gentleman. He is the author of a poem, called the 'Black Crow,' now making some stir in the literary circles."

"What kind of man is he?"

"Oh! you have nothing to do with his kind; you only want to know his character as an author."

"I beg your pardon, but you are wrong. I can form my own judgment of his authorship by his works, if I chance to read them; but before I make his personal acquaintance, I must fully understand his character as a man. How stands that?"

"Oh! passable; he never gets drunk more than five days out of the seven; tells the truth sometimes by mistake; has moral courage sufficient to flog his wife, when he thinks she deserves it, and occasionally without any thought upon the subject, merely to keep his hand in; and has never, that I know of, been convicted of petit larceny. He has been horsewhipped occasionally, and has had his nose pulled so often as to considerably lengthen that prominent and necessary appendage to the human face. For the rest, an anecdote they tell of him, may give you a better idea than any portraiture of mine."

"Oh the story, by all means."

"It appears, that when Miss Gloomy was flourishing here some years since, as a writer of melo-dramas, Hammerhead was very much smitten by her charms of mind and person. So he posted one day to her lodgings, and falling upon his marrow-bones, made her a formal proffer of his hand, with his heart in it. Not having the same admiration of him that he possessed of himself, from her rather indifferent powers of perception, Miss Gloomy had the undoubted bad taste to refuse the liberal proffer, and rejected him without hesitation. After renewing again and again his important proposition, and finding his pathetic appeals to be unavailing, he rose from his knees, and exclaimed, in heart-rending accents, 'Well, Miss Gloomy, if you won't marry me, won't you loan me ten dollars?'"

Danby laughed, and said—"That will do for him; but pray who is the lady with whom he is conversing?"

"That is Mrs. Grodenap. She belongs to South Carolina, and is merely here on a visit. She possesses much ability, and is quite a linguist withal. Shall I introduce her to you?"

"No—I have no desire, though I think she is pretty. But who is that languishing would-be-juvenile lady, who is now approaching the two? By Jove! what laughable affectation of manner!"

"That is Mrs. Flighty, one of our poetesses and all that sort of thing, and the best imitator of Mother Goose. Her poetry is remarkable for its simplicity. As a general rule, the verses of most female writers may be described by the words—'milk and water;' but her's resemble a large quantity of water, with a homœopathical addition of milk."

"You don't seem to have a high idea of female writers, Cloudsdale;" for this was the real name of Ivory. "Are you not aware that the writings of women are supposed to be exempt from criticism, and are to be praised *ad nauseam?*"

"Such is indeed the general impression, and it arises somewhat from the chivalry of man's nature. He connects insensibly the womanhood of the writer with her work, and will not attack the one lest the other should suffer. The reason is a weak one. The critic has his duty to per-form—he must assign a precedence to claimants, according to their quality —and not according to their sex. If he goes beyond the line of his duty, there are fathers, brothers, and husbands, to avenge mere personalities. The true critic speaks without fear or favoritism; he analyzes boldly and skilfully, and if he do not, he is no true critic."

"Well conceived, and properly delivered, to be sure. But what would the female writers present say, were they to hear your opinions?"

"I do not know, but they are welcome to name any atonement for my heresy—except it be to read their works, or swear by the intense indigo blue of their stockings. The Constitution of the United States provides that cruel and unusual punishments shall not be inflicted upon the citizen."

"You are in a sneering mood to-night, Cloudsdale; but since you seem to be *au fait* in these matters, I will ask your opinion, contrary to my custom, of the merits of Mr. Hammerhead yonder, as a writer."

"His pursuit after an idea always reminds me of a kitten hunting after its tail. He sees the end of it wagging at his side; he turns to snap at it— it turns with him; he snaps at it again, and it does as it did before. Thus he goes on, making continual efforts to seize that which eludes his grasp, until tired of spinning round—like a dancing dervish—through so many pages, he leaves the idea in a state of quiet, and settles down, in the last paragraph, into a profound sleep!"

"Has he not wit and humor, then?"

"Umph! that depends upon your definition of the terms. Hazlitt, I think it is, says that 'lying is a species of wit and humor—to charge a man with something of which he is not guilty shows spirit and invention, and the more incredible the effrontery, the more pointed the joke.' If that be the case, Hammerhead is a paragon of wit and humor—a perfect Joe Miller's jest-book among the critics. There is an immense deal of charlatanry, however, in all his productions. He affects ignorance in general of the author's real name, and seems to think that sarcasm and scurrility are identical."

"Is he an educated man?"

"After a fashion. He has a knowledge of no language except his own, and that to a very limited extent; and of course interlards his works with an abundance of quotations, obtained from the works of other authors. As he does not understand the meaning of these, he occasionally commits some rather ludicrous errors."

---

46. *7 September 1846: The Case of Edgar A. Poe vs. Hiram Fuller and Augustus W. Clason, Jr., Postponed*

[*Because the court's calendar was full, the trial for libel, scheduled for 7 September 1846, was postponed until the "first Monday of February," which was 1 February 1847. The Judgment Record, continued in a different hand at this juncture, is hurried and abrupt.*]

At which day before the Justices aforesaid at the City Hall aforesaid, cometh parties aforesaid by their respective attorneys aforesaid. And because the aforesaid issue, as above joined in this cause between the parties aforesaid, was not tried at the term of the said Court, held at the time and place last aforesaid, therefore the process aforesaid between the parties aforesaid is continued until the term of the said Court appointed to be held at the City Hall in the City of New York, on the first Monday of February in the year one thousand eight hundred and forty-seven.

---

47. *9 September 1846: "Epigram on an Indigent Poet"*
Weekly Mirror

[*The fact that Poe persisted in prosecuting his case earned him a piece of doggerel in the* Mirror.]

EPIGRAM
ON AN INDIGENT POET
P— money wants to 'buy a bed,'—
   His case is surely trying;
   It must be hard to want a bed,
   For one so used to *lying*.

---

48. *19 September 1846: "More Plagiarism"*
Hiram Fuller

[*On this date, which also marked the publication of the second episode in 1844 featuring Hammerhead-Poe (see next document), Fuller printed the following squib on Poe in the* Weekly Mirror.]

MORE PLAGIARISM.—Somebody out in the extreme back part of Missouri, has discovered that Tom Moore, like other great poets, has been filching the ideas of another, and altering them to suit himself. He cites the following instance, which is perfectly unanswerable—the critical acumen of a Poe could no further go.

'The minstrel boy to the war is gone,
In the ranks of death you'll find him;
His father's sword he has girded on,
And his wild harp slung behind him.'

'Little Bo-Peep has lost his sheep,
And does not know where to find 'em;
Let 'em alone, and they'll come home,
Bringing their tails behind 'em.'

---

49. *19 September 1846: The Second Episode in 1844 Depicting Hammerhead-Poe*
Thomas Dunn English

[*In this passage that appeared in the* Weekly Mirror, *Poe is shown as a panhandling, pugnacious, bragging, and drunken critic. It is the only passage that has the slightest relation to the plot. For a fuller discussion of* 1844, *see the headnote to Document 45.*]

"A most drunken monster."—*Tempest.*

MARMADUKE HAMMERHEAD was making his way along Broadway, by a peculiar progression, which has been called "worm-fence," by the vulgar, since it enables the performer to go over a great deal of ground without making much headway. He had an indistinct notion in his head that he was about to do something—what, he could not tell—but something of importance, nevertheless. That he could perform it, and admirably at that, was his firm self-conviction; but he could not imagine what was necessary to be done. So he staggered back and forth, swaying his body unsteadily, and setting his hat on his head with a fierce cock, and looking daggers at every passer who dared to bestow a glance at the disgusting object before him.

The truth is that Hammerhead was drunk—though that was no wonder, for he was never sober over twenty-four hours at a time; but he was in a most beastly state of intoxication. His cups had given him a kind of courage; and though naturally the most abject poltroon in existence, he felt an irresistible inclination to fight with some one. Such a propensity can always be gratified in the city of New York, which is blessed with as pugnacious a population as any other city in the world. True to his purpose, Hammerhead accosted the first comer, and taking him by the button, said—

"Did—did—did you ever read my review of L—L—Longfellow?"

"No!" said the one addressed—a quiet, sober-looking personage—"I dare say it's very severe, but I never read it."

"Well," said Hammerhead, "you lost a gr—gr—eat pleasure. You're an ass!"

"Oh! not quite so bad as that, surely," said the puzzled man, endeavoring to free himself from detention.

"Yes you are, damn you!—I'll kill you!" exclaimed Hammerhead.

The stranger saw but one course to pursue—the controversy was exciting a crowd—so he knocked Hammerhead down, and quietly went on his way.

Hammerhead lay on the pavement for a moment or so, when one of the by-standers helped him up, and, replacing his hat on his head, endeavored to lead him away. Hammerhead refused to budge—offered to fight the whole crowd, six at a time—entered into a disquisition on English metre, to the amusement of the by-standers, and finally begged some one in the crowd for God's sake to lend him sixpence.

The elder O'Conor, attracted by the crowd, had stopped to note its cause; and, on looking at the face of Hammerhead, felt there was something familiar in those features. So he pushed the crowd aside, and said—

"I'll loan you a sixpence, if you'll come with me, my friend."

"You will!" cried Hammerhead. "Damn it if I don't follow you to the end of the earth for half the money. As I said in my review of Longfellow, says I——"

"Yes, yes—I know all that. Here, let us get in this coming omnibus."

The drunkard suffered himself to be assisted into the omnibus, in which there were, luckily, no other passengers; and O'Conor having followed him, the omnibus drove on.

As soon as they were seated, O'Conor commenced questioning Hammerhead—for he discovered one who had met Catesby abroad at one time, and he judged he might obtain some information. He inquired concerning the one whom he sought.

"Catesby," said Hammerhead, "d——d good fellow—yes, I saw him when—did you ever see my review of Longfellow?"

"Yes—very good thing it is—but when did you see Catesby last?"

"When—oh—yes—'in the bleak December, when each'—did you see my re—review?"

"Of course I did; and when do you expect to see him again?"

"Quoth the raven—never more! Did you ever read my——"

"Certainly; he is dead, then?"

"Dead, yes, 'the lost Lenore.' But I used up Longfellow—he's dead; yes, dead!"

"Oh, curse Longfellow! Is Catesby alive?"

"Cates—Catesby—oh! I saw him once—he—oh, Hercules can tell you—Hercules is a d——d clever fellow; but he hasn't read my review of——"

"And who is Hercules?"

"Hercules isn't at all. He was. Understand that. Hercules was a Grecian and a gentleman. He slew the hydra. I am Hercules—Longfellow is hydra—hydra, hydros—water—I hate water. It can't be defined by the calculus of probabilities. Did you ever read my re——"

"Yes, yes; but where shall I find Hercules?"

"Stranger," said Hammerhead, "you're an ass—understand me—you're an ass. Longfellow has endeavored to give us some English hexameters. Now, they're not hexameters, because there is not a pure spondee in—did you ever read my review of Longfellow?"

O'Conor found it was useless to attempt to gain anything further from Hammerhead: he was entirely too drunk for the purpose. After ineffectual questioning to discover Hammerhead's residence, a new passenger having entered, O'Conor paid for his companion and himself, and left the stage.

As he walked up Broadway, he met Frederick, to whom he communicated the result of his interview with Hammerhead. Frederick laughed, and said—

"Why, father, he *has* given you information, probably. There *is* a man named Hercules, who can give you information of Catesby, provided Catesby has ever been reduced to the necessity of resorting to the Five Points, as his wife has. This Hercules is a noted burglar, whose plundering has always escaped punishment, from the secrecy with which he has conducted it."

"But how does Hammerhead know Hercules? The writer is not a burglar, I hope."

"No; but he frequents low grog-shops, and is likely at such places to pick up acquaintances. At all events, it is worth search; and if you desire it, I will go in quest of this Hercules, and sound him."

* * * *

While he [O'Conor] spoke, Hammerhead came staggering up, and accosted Hercules.

"How do you do?" said he, "you don't know me, perhaps—my name's Ham—ha—ha—ammerhead. I met you abroad—you're Catesby—Ca—Ca—Catesby."

Frederick started, as if seized with a sudden pang. Hercules saw and was amused by his consternation.

"You see," said Hercules, "this drunken fool calls me Catesby. Singular, is it not?"

He turned on his heel, as he said it, and walked up Centre street, leaving Frederick standing, gazing after him, with feelings of intense and angry mortification.

Hammerhead laid his hand on the arm of Frederick, saying:

"Your friend is a queer kind of fellow—eh! He used to be so. Did you see my re—re—view upon L—L—L—ongfellow?"

"No!" said Frederick, walking away, "nor do I desire to."

"You d—don't! you miserable reptile! You're d—d—runk! You haven't the common elements of an English education! You'd b—b—etter take care. I'll write you down! I'll use you up! I—I—you—you haven't got such a thing as a shilling, have you?"

There was no withstanding this. Frederick, laughing in despite of his vexation, handed Hammerhead the required coin, and went in one way, as the drunken poet staggered the other.

---

50. *October 1846: Poe Discussed in the* Knickerbocker
Lewis Gaylord Clark

[*Poe's "Literati" sketch of Lewis Clark appeared in September 1846 even as Godey had promised in his Card (Document 5). Poe spoke of the* "editorial scraps" to be found at the back of each number of the Knicker-bocker—a reference to Clark's "Editor's Table," a famous feature of the magazine—as "the joint composition of a great variety of gentlemen," which it was in the sense that Clark habitually quoted items from news-papers, magazines, and correspondents. "Were a little more pains taken in elevating the tone of this 'Editors' Table,' (which its best friends are forced to admit is at present a little Boweryish)," Poe went on, deliberate-ly misplacing the apostrophe and at the same time alluding to such vulgar attacks as those represented by "The Literary Snob" (Document 1), "I should have no hesitation in commending it . . . as a specimen of . . . easy writing and hard reading."

When Poe turned to the Knickerbocker itself, he said that it seemed

to have in it some important elements of success. . . . Still some in-comprehensible incubus has seemed always to sit heavily upon it. . . . On account of the manner in which it is necessarily edited, the work is deficient in that absolutely indispensable element, individuality. As the editor has no precise character, the magazine, as a matter of course, can have none. When I say "no precise character," I mean that Mr. C., as a literary man, has about him no determinateness, no distinctiveness, no saliency of point;—an apple, in fact, or a pumpkin, has more angles. He is . . . noticeable for nothing in the world except for the markedness by which he is noticeable for nothing.

Poe then mischievously speculated about the circulation of the Knicker-bocker and arrived at the figure of "some fifteen hundred copies," though its circulation was greater than five thousand. In a final paragraph, Poe offered a description of Clark, his characteristic way of ending these sketches. In doing this, he overstated Clark's age by four or five years, said that his "forehead is, phrenologically, bad . . . [and that] the smile is too constant and lacks expression. . . ."

Clark's response appears below. Lest readers of the Knickerbocker should regard these views of Poe as aroused and distorted by rancor, Clark corroborated them by citing apparently impartial opinions to indi-cate that his views were universally held. He alluded to an unnamed correspondent, "J. G. H." of Springfield, Massachusetts, very likely Josiah Gilbert Holland who was an anonymous contributor to the Knickerbocker and who became a close friend of Emily Dickinson. He quoted from a newspaper identified only as "one of our most respectable daily journals,"

which chanced to be the Evening Mirror *(Document 34) whose editor
was conducting his own war on Poe. In addition he cited the London*
Athenaeum *of 28 February 1846. Thus J. G. H.'s view of Poe is by impli-
cation so much harsher than Clark's own and even perhaps so obscene
that "man! you can't expect us to publish it." Thus from Fuller of the*
Mirror *there are more defamations: "evil living," "imbecility," "radical
obliquity of sense," and "suicide upon body and character." And thus in
the third source there appear to be further heinous charges, but ones
which only assert that Poe was pretentious at times or obscure or absurd
in his stories, though Clark fobbed off these adjectives, not in relation to
Poe's tales or poems as the* Athenaeum *had, but to his "literary" opinions."*

Thus wrote, quoted, and commented the editor of the Knickerbocker
*whose complacency, he averred, was not ruffled for a moment. He even
added a footnote to his remarks, obviously to assign a discreditable motive to Poe's attack on him, that of vengeance for Clark's having rejected
a number of his manuscripts, though Poe never attempted to contribute
to the* Knickerbocker. *That many of Clark's fabrications were baseless or
exaggerated, his readers could not know, and the article no doubt had the
effect it was intended to have.*]

Our thanks are due to 'J. G. H.,' of Springfield, (Mass.,) for his communication touching the course and the capabilities of the wretched in-
ebriate whose personalities disgrace a certain Milliner's Magazine in
Philadelphia; but bless your heart, man! you can't expect us to publish
it. The jaded hack who runs a broken pace for common hire, upon whom
you have wasted powder, might revel in his congenial abuse of this
Magazine and its EDITOR from now till next October without disturbing
our complacency for a single moment. He is too mean for hate, and
hardly worthy scorn. In fact there are but two classes of persons who
regard him in *any* light—those who despise and those who pity him; the
first for his utter lack of principle, the latter for the infirmities which have
overcome and ruined him. Here is a faithful picture, for which he but
recently sat. We take it from one of our most respectable daily journals:

'It is melancholy enough to see a man maimed in his limbs, or
deprived by nature of his due proportions; the blind, the deaf, the
mute, the lame, the impotent, are all subjects that touch our hearts,
at least all whose hearts have not been indurated in the fiery furnace
of sin; but sad, sadder, saddest of all, is the poor wretch whose want

of moral rectitude has reduced his mind and person to a condition where indignation for his vices and revenge for his insults are changed into compassion for the poor victim of himself. When a man has sunk so low that he has lost the power to provoke vengeance, he is the most pitiful of all pitiable objects. A poor creature of this description called at our office the other day, in a condition of sad imbecility, bearing in his feeble body the evidences of evil living, and betraying by his talk such radical obliquity of sense, that every spark of harsh feeling toward him was extinguished, and we could not even entertain a feeling of contempt for one who was evidently committing a suicide upon his body, as he had already done upon his character. Unhappy man! He was accompanied by an aged female relative, who was going a weary round in the hot streets, following his steps to prevent his indulging in a love of drink; but he had eluded her watchful eye by some means, and was already far gone in a state of inebriation. After listening awhile with painful feelings to his profane ribaldry, he left the office, accompanied by his good genius, to whom he owed the duties which she was discharging for him.'

Now what can one gain by a victory over a person such as this? If there are some men whose enemies are to be pitied much, there are others whose alleged friends are to be pitied more. One whom this 'critic' has covered with what *he* deems praise, describes him as 'a literary person of unfortunate peculiarities, who professes to know many to whom he is altogether unknown.'* Can it then be a matter of the least moment to us, when the *quo animo* of such a writer is made palpable even to his own readers, that he should underrate our circulation by thousands, overrate our age by years, or assign to other pens the departments of this Magazine which we have alone sustained, with such humble ability as we

* He is equally unknown to those whom he abuses. The EDITOR hereof has no remembrance of ever having seen him save on two occasions. In the one case, we met him in the street with a gentleman [Thomas Holley Chivers?], who apologized the next day, in a note now before us, for having been seen in his company while he was laboring under such an '*excitement;*' in the other, we caught a view of his retiring skirts as he wended his 'winding way,' like a furtive puppy with a considerable kettle to his tail, from the publication-office, whence—having left no other record of his tempestuous visit upon the publisher's mind than the recollection of a coagulum of maudlin and abusive jargon—he had just emerged, bearing with him one of his little narrow rolls of manuscript, which had been previously submitted for insertion in our 'excellent Magazine,' but which, unhappily for his peace, had shared the fate of its equally attractive predecessors [Clark's note].

possessed, through nearly twenty-six out of its twenty-eight volumes? As well might CARLYLE lament that he had called him an 'unmitigated ass,' or LONGFELLOW grieve at being denounced by him as 'a man of no genius, and an inveterate literary thief.' And as to his literary *opinions*, who would regard *them* as of any importance?—a pen-and-ink writer, whose only 'art' is correctly described by the '*London Athenæum*' to 'consist in conveying plain things after a fashion which makes them hard to be understood, and commonplaces in a sort of mysterious form, which causes them to sound oracular.' 'There are times,' continues the able critical journal from which we quote, 'when he probably desires to go no farther than the obscure; when the utmost extent of his ambition is to be unintelligible; that he approaches the verge of the childish, and wanders on the confines of the absurd!' We put it to our Massachusetts correspondent, whether such a writer's idea of style is at all satire-worthy? And are we not excused from declining our friend's kindly-meant but quite unnecessary communication?

---

51. 3 October 1846: The Third Episode in 1844 Depicting Hammerhead-Poe

Thomas Dunn English

[*Sawdust in this episode is Horace Greeley. Boltanbar, the author of the "Moon Hoax," is Richard Adams Locke, whom Poe had sketched in "The Literati" (October 1846). The "anecdote" concerning Poe and Locke seems to have been inserted in reaction to Poe's essay on Locke. The "coincidence" of Poe and English discussing Locke within the same week or two seems much too fortuitous, especially as the entire episode is irrelevant to the narrative and as English was clearly bent on discrediting the author of "The Literati."*

Here again Hammerhead-Poe is shown to have a reputation for meanness and folly, a reputation that even the foolish Sawdust recognizes to be just. Again, too, Hammerhead is depicted as a sponger and as a critic who threatens to use criticism for personal vengeance.]

"Well, I suppose you're satisfied now?" said Sawdust. "Eh! there's some one calling to me through the speaking-pipe. "Well?" he cried, putting his mouth to one aperture, and immediately after applied his ear to another.

"Mr. Hammerhead wants to see you," said the man in the lower story.

"I'll be there presently," replied Sawdust, through the tube. "I wonder," continued he, to Pump, "what the fool wants with me—the shortest way is to ask him; I am going to Wall street, at all events."

"A fool! he's a man of great parts. His Tales display a deal of ingenuity."

"Yet he is a fool, nevertheless—since he prostitutes his talents to base use, and commits acts of meanness which, unless you admit him to be radically bad, must be ranked as folly. Did you hear of the trick he served Boltanbar, the author of the 'Moon Hoax?'"

"No!"

"Some days since, Hammerhead called on Boltanbar, who is in the custom-house, and insisted on his accompanying him to a tavern and taking some liquid fire, in the shape of a whiskey punch. Boltanbar, to get rid of him peaceably, consented. He took him to a house where the latter was unacquainted, and while there insisted on treating the company—supplying whiskey punch to every one in the room. This he did. When it came to settling-up time, Hammerhead had no money, and the bar-keeper, after a torrent of abuse, which his victim stood without flinching, seized the hat of the debtor. Boltanbar, not expecting this catastrophe, was not provided with money, but went home immediately, obtained it, and relieved Hammerhead's hat."

"Oh! well, that's nothing. A drunken man's freak."

"Stop! Boltanbar insisted that Hammerhead should go home. The latter promised he would, if Boltanbar would accompany him. The latter agreed to this; and the two were passing the Carlton House, when Hammerhead insisted on going in. As his companion had provided himself with money, he thought the best way of getting him safely housed was to humor him, and yielded. Hammerhead called for something to drink, and drew out a roll of bank-bills to pay for it, to the utter astonishment of his companion."

Pump laughed immoderately, and said:

"What has he to do with you—*you* are a temperance man."

"He wants to borrow money, I suppose."

On reaching the office below stairs, they met Hammerhead, who, if not so drunk as when we last introduced him, had drank sufficiently to make him quarrelsome. He took Sawdust by the button-hole, and drawing him aside, requested, as the latter had predicted, the loan of some money. This was denied, and Hammerhead waxed indignant.

"You're a fool, Sawdust," said he, "and don't understand the elements of the English language. You haven't the rudiments of an English education."

"I admit the charge to its fullest extent," said Sawdust.

"You're a transcendentalist, and eat brown bread," said Hammerhead.

"I confess to both of these enormities."

"D——n you! I made you. You owe all your reputation to me. I wrote you up. I'll criticise you; I'll extinguish you—you ungrateful eater of bran pudding—you—you—galvanized squash."

"Undoubtedly," replied Sawdust, "and now let me go."

He disengaged his coat from Hammerhead's grasp, as he spoke, and the poet, fastening on a stranger, informed him that he was the great critic, Hammerhead, at that moment in want of a loan—of a shilling. Sawdust and Pump separated—the latter crossing to the Park, and the former going down Nassau street.

---

52. 21 October 1846: "Godey's Lady's Book, for November"
Hiram Fuller

[*The October 1846 number of* Godey's Lady's Book *saw the last of Poe's "Literati of New York City" in its pages. Fuller, who had censured Godey for running the series (Document 8) and who had derided all but the May number of the* Lady's Book *containing the sketches (Documents 22, 38, 44), now in his* Evening Mirror *praised Godey and the November number of his magazine, obviously because of the "absence of the rigmarole papers on the literati of New York city. . . ."*]

Godey's Lady's Book, for November.—This magazine makes its appearance in a very beautiful new cover, of a delicate tint, and with the prettiest border we have seen of a similar work. If the design is original, we congratulate Mr. Godey on the discovery of an artist worth knowing. The illustrations in this number are of the usual order; but the literary department is much better than usual. What adds particularly to the value of the magazine, is the absence of the rigmarole papers on the literati of New York city, which, we are happy to hear, for his own sake, Mr. Godey has determined to discontinue. . . .

---

53. *24 October 1846: The Fourth Episode in 1844 Depicting Hammer-head-Poe*
Thomas Dunn English

[*In this installment of 1844 that appeared in the* Weekly Mirror, *we see how the "course of drunkenness" leads to Hammerhead-Poe's physical and mental collapse. He becomes paranoiac and thinks himself the "object of persecution on the part of the combined literati of the country. . . ." In this wreck of "his fine abilities," we are told, he wrote "The Literati" papers. But perhaps "mania-a-potu"—craziness from drink—was not the sole cause of his degeneration: there may have "been a taint of insanity in the blood," for "his acts, during the previous part of his life," would seem to suggest as much.*]

> "*Fool.*—Prythee, nuncle, tell me whether a madman be a gentleman,
> or a yeoman?
> *Lear.*—A King! A King!"—KING LEAR.

THE course of drunkenness pursued by Hammerhead had its effect upon his physical and mental constitution. The former began to present evidences of decay and degradation. The bloated face—blood-shotten eyes—trembling figure, and attenuated frame, showed how rapidly he was sinking into a drunkard's grave; and the drivelling smile, and meaningless nonsense, he constantly uttered, showed the approaching wreck of his fine abilities. Although constantly watched by his near relatives, he would manage frequently to escape their control, and seeking some acquaintance, from whom he could beg a few shillings, he would soon be seen staggering through the streets in a filthy state of intoxication.

At length, before this constant stimulation, the brain gave way, and the mind manifested its operations, through a disordered and imbecile medium. Mania-a-potu, under which he had nearly sunk, supervened, and this was succeeded by confirmed insanity, or rather monomania. He deemed himself the object of persecution on the part of the combined literati of the country, and commenced writing criticisms upon their character, as writers, and their peculiarities, as men. In this he gave the first inkling of his insanity, by discovering that there were over eighty eminent writers, in the city of New York, when no sensible man would have dared to assert that the whole country ever produced one-fourth of that number, since it had commenced its existence as a nation. This promise of coming mental disorder was fulfilled in the end; for no sooner had the writer finished the first volume of his essays—he promised ten more—containing notices of about two hundred writers, than the disease broke out in its full extent, and he became an unmistakeable madman. There had, most probably, been a taint of insanity in the blood of the Hammerheads; and his acts, during the previous part of his life, showed a tendency to the distressing malady.

Mr. and Mrs. John Melton—for Melton and Mary Blair had now married—were on the customary tour, and were staying for a few days at Utica. Among the few lions of the place, was the Lunatic Asylum, which Mary was anxious to visit, and though John was averse to such sights, he thought it unnecessary to oppose her wishes. So they obtained an order, from one of the directors, and started to view the place. . . .

---

54. 31 October 1846: The Fifth Episode in 1844 Depicting Hammerhead-Poe

Thomas Dunn English

[In the preceding installment of 1844, the Meltons had obtained permission to visit the Lunatic Asylum in Utica, New York. In the course of visiting various cells, they are introduced to Hammerhead "who was an author in a small way," but who is now a confirmed madman, though never thought by Melton and Quipp, the attendant, "to be very sane" before. Hammerhead reflexively begs a shilling from Melton and brags that he is "using up" Carlyle and the Transcendentalists, as he had earlier "used up" Alexander Pope, Robert Burns, Longfellow, and Cornelius Mathews.

English made some telling thrusts in this installment. In a critique on William Ellery Channing, the Transcendentalist poet (Graham's Magazine, August 1843) Poe had remarked about Thomas Carlyle: If a man "write a book which he means to be understood, and in this book be at all possible pains to prevent us from understanding it, we can only say he is an ass—and this, to be brief, is our private opinion of Mr. Carlyle. . . ." Similarly, Poe had reversed his previous and considered judgment of Mathews and had recently praised him, if weakly and ambiguously (Godey's Lady's Book, November 1845). (The complicated reasons for this critical shift are explained by Moss, Poe's Literary Battles, pages 104 ff.) Likewise, Poe's judgments of Pope, Burns, and Emerson are represented without significant distortion.

R. H. Horne, mentioned in this episode, was the English poet best known for his long poem Orion, which Poe extolled with his usual reservations in Graham's Magazine (March 1844). Poe wrote at least two letters to Horne, none of them extant, in one of which he enclosed his review, but there is no indication that he asked Horne to "notice my works favorably." Horne answered that he could "derive advantage in the way of revision" from Poe's comments, "which is more," he added, "than I can say of any of the critiques written on this side of the waters" (Harrison, XVII, 168). Despite this evidence of mutual respect, the "London Correspondent" of the Weekly Mirror, namely Charles F. Briggs who signed himself F. M. Pinto, published the following item on 12 September 1846 in his gossipy report: "Horne enquired after Mr. Poe, and said that he had received from him a review of 'Orion' in some wishy-washy Magazine—the name of which he had forgotten. I asked what he thought of Poe as a critic? He replied, 'He is a very good critic for a lady's magazine.'"

For Elizabeth Barrett, also mentioned in this episode, see Documents 9 and 10. Poe wrote an extensive review of her Drama of Exile and Other Poems (Broadway Journal, 4 and 11 January 1845) and dedicated his Raven volume to her. In addition, he sent her a copy of his compound book (the book made up of The Raven volume and the Tales) inscribed "To Miss Elizabeth Barrett Barrett, With the Respects of Edgar A. Poe," which she received on 20 March 1846. Perhaps Poe also sent her a covering letter; if so, it is not extant. There is no evidence that Poe wrote to Carlyle.]

After showing them various cells, and allowing an opportunity of conversing with the inmates, the assistant took them to see the various departments of labor and recreation, used to divert and amuse the patients.

When they had exhausted their admiration, they crossed over the quad-
rangle, in the centre of the building, and came to a part which, he informed them, was the department assigned to the confirmed madmen.

"We have a new man," said the assistant, "a Mr. Hammerhead, who
was an author in a small way, but whose constant intemperance has
driven him mad."

"Hammerhead!" said Melton, "why, I have met him. Has he gone mad?
Though, by-the-bye, it is a matter of little wonder. I never thought him to
be very sane."

They entered the cell. Hammerhead was sitting at a table, writing.
He raised his head, and seeing Melton, recognised him, and rose.

"Ah!" said the poet, "how are you? Come to see me? I am staying
here a little while, to get rid of the bustle of the town. But I'm glad to
see you, really. Pleasant quarters, these."

"Very, indeed," replied Melton, "let me present you to Mrs. Melton—
Mary, my dear, this is Mr. Hammerhead, the celebrated writer of the
'Black Crow,' a poem—'The Humbug, and other Tales,' with various pop-
ular works."

Hammerhead bowed, and went on to say—"Pray, take a seat, madam.
Melton, my dear fellow, I am really glad to see you, indeed I am." Here
he took Melton aside, and said, confidentially—"You haven't such a thing
as a shilling about you, have you? The fact is, I'm devilish hard up, till
I get some money for the article I'm writing."

Melton produced the required small coin, and Hammerhead continued—

"I'm engaged on a critique on Carlyle, and the transcendentalists. I'll
read a little to you, in order to show you how I use the fellows up." Here
he read in a sing-song tone of voice—"The fact is, that Mr. Carlyle is an
ass—yet it is not in the calculus of probabilities to explain why he has
not discovered what the whole world long since knew. Perhaps—and for
this suggestion, I am indebted to the wit of my friend, M. Dupin, with
whose fine powers the whole world, thanks to my friendship, are acquainted—perhaps, I say, it could not be beaten into his noddle. He is
a pitiable dunderhead, with a plentiful lack of brains. All that he is
capable of—in sober truth he is capable of nothing—is to demonstrate his
own lamentable absurdity. He is a rhapsodist and a noodle. He forgets
the advice of Moulineau—'Belier, mon ami, commencez au commencement.' Carlyle, my friend, begins at the beginning—and goes into his sub-

ject about four feet from the tail end. He is, in short, a gigantic water-melon. So are all his admirers. So are all his imitators, except Ralph Waldo Emerson, who, being a Yankee, may be considered a squash."

Melton laughed very much at the extract, which he thought, bating its Billingsgate, contained a deal of truth, and was not like the writing of an insane man; while Hammerhead, delighted at this appreciation of his wit and humor, went on—

"Now, what does Mr. Carlyle mean by 'hero-worship?' Has he any definite idea attached to it at all, or is it only a bubble kicked up on the surface, after he has stirred the mud-puddle of his brain, with a stout stick? He reminds me of that fellow, Robert Burns, who has been extra-vagantly and unjustly praised—but who never wrote anything which would live a week, if published in the present day. In sober truth, and I say it with a just and proper appreciation of my own powers—he never wrote anything equal to my 'Black Crow'—nothing, so to speak, with that sonorous and musical rhythm, which marks it from its commencement to its close. But the difference is equally plain. I am a man of genius, and Burns was not. My productions will live, and his are rapidly passing away. The truth is, Burns *could* not be a great man. I can. He drank brandy—I drink small-beer. Now brandy is a mischievous and pernicious thing, according to the observations of Herodotus—Lib. I., Cap. V., who says—'Brandiarum est pernicium et abominalibus'—Brandy is pernicious and abominable—Horace says, in his fourth ode—'Topus not Brandiarum' —Drink not brandy. But small-beer is the fabled nectar of the gods. There can be but little doubt that Jupiter, Juno, and the rest, drank small-beer. So do I. It suits my style, and suits me. I am small-beer. I was small-beer. I will be small-beer. This same small-beer made me what I am. Now there is no small-beer about Carlyle; therefore I pitch into him, as Shak-speare, who, by-the-bye, was no poet, says, in 'Measure for Measure'— 'like a thousand of brick.' "

Hammerhead grew excited—his eyes seemed starting from their sockets —the fit was on him, and though Melton desired to leave, he thought it best to humor him. So he sat still, and listened as the poet read.

"That Mr. Barlyle, or Tarlyle, or Farlyle—or whatever the man's name may be, is not a man of genius, is undoubtedly true—although his ad-mirers may think this heresy. I am prepared to prove that in less than ten pages of his book, I have discovered no less than one hundred and ten dashes, instead of parentheses. Can any man who uses the dash instead of the mark of parenthesis, be considered a man of genius? Certainly not. The dash is a straight line, the parenthesis a curved one. To admirers and lovers of beauty, the superiority of a curved line is apparent. No worshipper of beauty admires a straight line—Mr. Carlyle admires a straight line; therefore, he is not a worshipper of beauty. He who is not a worshipper of beauty, cannot be great. Mr. Carlyle is not a worshipper of beauty. Therefore, Mr. Carlyle is not a great man. That is logically put. It is as plain as that part of a game of marbles, vulgarly called 'knuckle from baste!' Let us, therefore, hear no more of Mr. Carlyle. We *shall* hear no more of him. I have settled that—I have settled him, as I have settled Pope and Burns, and Longfellow—and such like small potatoes. I once settled Cornelius Mathews; and the proof that I did it well, is to be found in the fact, that I have tried to restore him to life by puffing, ever since, but have failed. No one can withstand me. I am the great mogul of all the critics. My *ipse dixit* is law, my assertion gospel—my commandments, the whole five books of Moses, with a considerable slice of the Revelations of St. John. As Homer makes Ajax say '*Keepme soberos, aniamthe scrougeron ki.*' Keep me sober, and I am *the* scrouger!

"There, what do you think of that? can Carlyle survive that? Damn it, it's so severe, that I'm afraid it will kill all his readers. However, it serves Carlyle right. I wrote him a letter as I did Horne, and Miss Barrett, requesting them to notice my works favorably. Horne and Miss Barrett did—Carlyle never noticed them, nor me. See what follows. I puff them, and abuse him. This teaches a great moral lesson—that 'virtue is its own reward!' "

"Well," said Melton, "we must leave you. Come, Mary—Good-day, Mr. Hammerhead."

"Good-day, Melton—you're a smart fellow, and a great writer."

"Well, Mary,["] inquired Melton, "what do you think of him?"

"Why, his language is very queer, to be sure—but all that he wrote before he came here, was of the same character. I don't see why they confine him as a lunatic."

"Oh, Madam,["] said Quipp, "he is quite rational to-day, but sometimes he goes on dreadfully, and threatens to kill every one. To be sure he is quite harmless—you have only to offer to pull his nose, he'll settle down immediately, and cry most piteously; but he makes a great noise till coercive measures are used."

55. *November 1846: "Epitaph on a Modern 'Critic': 'P'oh' Pudor!"*
Lewis Gaylord Clark

[*Still unhappy with Poe's sketch of himself in "The Literati," Clark in his*
Knickerbocker *magazine published an epitaph on Poe somewhat reminis-
cent of the doggerel that appeared in the* Weekly Mirror *(Document 47),
at least in respect to the pun on lies.*

*This verse is attributed to Clark because he had often referred to Poe
as Aristarchus and Poh in many of his diatribes. "Aristarchus" was a common epithet of the times for a captious critic. " 'P'oh' Pudor" of the subtitle seems to be a strained pun on Poe, pooh, and pro in the expression*
pro pudor *(for shame).*]

Epitaph on a Modern 'Critic.'
'P'oh' Pudor!

'Here Aristarchus lies!' (a pregnant phrase,
And greatly hackneyed, in his early days,
By those who saw him in his maudlin scenes,
And those who read him in the magazines.)
Here Aristarchus lies, (nay, never smile,)
Cold as his muse, and stiffer than his style;
But whether Bacchus or Minerva claims
The crusty critic, all conjecture shames;
Nor shall the world know which the mortal sin,
Excessive genius or excessive gin!

---

56. *7 November 1846: The Final Episode in 1844 Depicting Hammerhead-Poe*
Thomas Dunn English

[*In the last chapter of his novel, English took one final fling at the two
major figures he had chosen to satirize, Sawdust-Greeley and Hammerhead-Poe.*]

"*Walter* (rising)—The story's told.—*Hunchback.*

IT is time that we sum up the history of those we have introduced.
O'Sycophant, Phumby, Bang and Sawdust still survive. The latter

only remains as editor—and is as full of crotchets as ever. He has lately taken the morals of the community under his protection, and is engaged in advocating the creation of Magdalen societies in every ward of the city.

Hammerhead is still in the mad-house, writing as vigorously as ever.

---

57. 23 November 1846: "Godey's Lady's Book for December"
Hiram Fuller

[*Fuller's esteem for* Godey's *was almost fulsome now that the installments of Poe's "Literati of New York City" would no longer "blemish" its pages, and Fuller praised the magazine again in his* Evening Mirror, *as he had on October 21 (Document 52).*]

GODEY'S LADY'S BOOK FOR DECEMBER.—This is really a beautiful number, surpassing all its predecessors. The embellishments are exquisitely done, and the literary matter is unusually attractive. . . . The fashion plate, the art of making lace, and the music of the *Redowa* waltz, with instructions how to dance it, will be fully appreciated by the ladies. We are glad to learn that no more personalities under the head of 'honest opinions of the New York Literati' will hereafter blemish the pages of Godey's handsome Lady's Book.

---

58. 15 December 1846: Letter to George W. Eveleth
Edgar A. Poe

[*The last installment of "The Literati" appeared in the October 1846 number of* Godey's Lady's Book, *apparently at Godey's injunction. The series had aroused harsh criticism in Philadelphia, Boston, and especially Manhattan, which reflected upon Godey and his magazine; Poe's libel suit was pending and the charges and revelations to be made at the trial were likely to be discreditable to the parties involved; and Godey, despite the temptation of great sales, was not inclined to let his genteel "Lady's Book" be long associated with anything disreputable. (See Document 6 and its headnote for Godey's protestations of innocence in the matter.) In the letter below, however, Poe led his young admirer Eveleth to believe that the discontinuance of the series was the result of his own decision, not Godey's.*

Eveleth, a student at Maine Medical School in Brunswick, had introduced himself to Poe in a letter dated 21 December 1845 in the hope that Mr. Poe, "selected from all the writers of whom I know any thing, for my especial favorite," would "'stoop so low' as to address by letter a rustic youngster of the backwoods of Maine" (Mabbott, page 173). Despite the self-disparagement, Eveleth was shrewd and forthright. Even in this letter of introduction, while lauding the writer, he found the man "rather graceless—rather egotistical; rather irreverent towards his fellows. . . ." Notwithstanding, Poe was surprisingly gentle and patient in answering Eveleth's queries, which were sometimes captious and annoying. Yet he tended to assume a role with him, rather that of the grand old man of letters, somewhat under a cloud to be sure, but pretty much in charge of his destiny.

The "book on American Letters" that Poe speaks of and that he provisionally titled Literary America: Some Honest Opinions about our Autorial Merits and Demerits with Occasional Words of Personality *resulted in revised versions of his "Literati" articles on Richard Adams Locke, Thomas Dunn English, and Christopher Pearse Cranch. Both the original and revised versions of his articles on English, which are representative, appear as Documents 11 and 12 and are indication enough that it was just as well that he abandoned the work, for "haste, inaccuracy, or prejudice," not to speak of other limitations, still mark the revisions.*

The full version of this letter appears in Ostrom, II, 331–3.]

New-York : Dec. 15 / 46.

My Dear Sir,

. . . You will see that I have discontinued the "Literati" in Godey's Mag. I was forced to do so, because I found that people insisted on considering them elaborate criticisms when I had no other design than critical *gossip*. The unexpected circulation of the series, also, suggested to me that I might make a hit and some profit, as well as proper fame, by extending the plan into that of *a book* on American Letters generally, and keeping the publication in my own hands. I am now *at* this—body & soul. . . .

Do not trust, in making up your library, to the "opinions" in the Godey series. I *meant* "honest"—but my meaning is not as fully made out as I could wish. I thought too little of the series myself to guard sufficiently against haste, inaccuracy, or prejudice. The book will be *true—according* to the best of my abilities. . . . .

Truly Your Friend
Edgar A Poe

---

59. *15 December 1846: "Illness of Edgar A. Poe"*
Morning Express

[*By winter of 1846 the Poes were in a desperate state. Virginia Poe was dying of tuberculosis—her death would occur on 30 January 1847—and her husband continually complained in his letters of the period that he had "been for a long time dreadfully ill." Maria Clemm, Poe's widowed aunt and mother-in-law who was living with them at Fordham, had to beg help of friends, the family was so impoverished. When Mary Gove, a literary friend, first visited the Poes, she found the "little cottage at the top of a hill" very attractive. She reported, however, that when autumn came*

> *Mrs. Poe sank rapidly in consumption. . . . The weather was cold, and the sick lady had the dreadful chills that accompany the hectic fever of consumption. She lay on the straw bed, wrapped in her husband's great-coat, with a large tortoise-shell cat on her bosom. . . . The coat and the cat were the sufferer's only means of warmth, except as her husband held her hands, and her mother her feet. . . . As soon as I was made aware of these painful facts, I came to New York and enlisted the sympathies and services of a lady whose heart and hand were open to the poor and the miserable. . . . The lady headed a subscription, and carried them sixty dollars the next week. (Mary Gove Nichols, "Reminiscences of Edgar Allan Poe.")*

The lady whose sympathies and services she enlisted was Mary Hewitt. Reporting to Mrs. Frances Osgood, another friend of the Poes, Mary Hewitt wrote:

*The Poes are in the same state of physical and pecuniary suffering—
indeed worse, than they were last summer, for now the cold weather
is added to their accumulation of ills. I went to enquire of Mr.
[Israel] Post [publisher of the* Columbian Magazine] *about them. He
confirmed all that I had previously heard of their condition. Although
he says Mrs. Clemm has never told him that they were in want, yet
she borrows a shilling often,* to get a letter from the [post]office—*but
Mrs. Gove had been to see the Poes and found them living in the
greatest wretchedness. I am endeavoring to get up a contribution for
them among the editors, and the matter has got into print—very much
to my regret, as I fear it will hurt Poe's pride to have his affairs made
so public. . . . (Harrison, XVII, 272, n. 1.)*

So far as I can determine, the New York Morning Express *was the
first newspaper to announce the illness and poverty of the Poes. Wiley
and Putnam, mentioned in the article, had recently published Poe's* Tales
(June 1845) and The Raven and Other Poems *(November 1845), as well
as the compound book made of these two volumes (February 1846).]*

ILLNESS OF EDGAR A. POE.—We regret to learn that this gentleman and
his wife are both dangerously ill with the consumption, and that the
hand of misfortune lies heavy upon their temporal affairs. We are sorry
to mention the fact that they are so far reduced as to be barely able to
obtain the necessaries of life. This is, indeed, a hard lot, and we do hope
that the friends and admirers of Mr. Poe will come promptly to his assistance in his bitterest hour of need. Mr. Poe is the author of several tales
and poems, of which Messrs. Wiley & Putnam are the publishers, and, it
is believed, the profitable publishers. At least, his friends say that the
publishers ought to start a movement in his behalf.

---

60. *26 December 1846: "Edgar A. Poe"*
Bostonian

[*In addition to some New York papers, the* Bostonian *announced the
sickness and impoverishment of the Poes, though one would hardly have
expected a Boston newspaper to do so. Poe had alienated many Bos-*

tonians the previous year by his attacks upon Longfellow and Henry Norman Hudson, the Boston lecturer on Shakespeare; by the "hoax" he played at the Boston Lyceum (he had attempted to pass off "Al Aaraaf" as a new poem under the title "The Messenger Star"); and by the nasty exchange between him and many of the Bostonian newspaper editors when his deception was exposed.

Clarke, mentioned in the article, is McDonald Clarke (1798–1842), who was called the "Mad Poet," his own sobriquet. He died in a cell of the asylum on Blackwell's, now Welfare, Island. His tomb, whose cost was paid by friends, is on the edge of Sylvan Lake in Greenwood. The fact that Clarke wrote inferior poetry and was deranged makes the linking his name with Poe's less than flattering, despite the writer's good intentions.]

EDGAR A. POE.—Great God! is it possible, that the literary people of the Union, will let poor Poe perish by starvation and lean faced beggary in New York? For so we are led to believe, from frequent notices in the papers, stating that Poe and his wife are both down upon a bed of misery, death and disease, with not a ducat in the world, nor a charitable hand to minister a crumb to their crying necessities. This is really too bad to be looked for in a christian land, where *millions!* are wasted in a heathenish war, in rum, in toasting and feasting swindlers, robbers of the public purse and squandering thousands for dress and parade, in ungodly finery, jewelry and such profanity, while a poor and suffering man, and a splendid genius, is left with the dying partner of his misfortunes *to perish with hunger! Christians* for shame. Poor Clarke, the poet, while *living* wandered around the streets of New York without a meal or a home; when he was *dead* his marrowless bones were honored with a *magnificent* sepulture at Mt. Auburn.

---

61. 26 December 1846: "Hospital for Disabled Labourers with the Brain" and Covering Letter to Poe
Nathaniel P. Willis

[*Willis was one of the most popular writers and successful editors of his time. Before he and George Pope Morris had purchased and edited the*

New York Home Journal, *they had jointly owned and edited the* Evening Mirror *and* Weekly Mirror. *(The* Evening Mirror *appeared six times a week; the* Weekly Mirror, *consisting largely of items published in the* Evening Mirror, *appeared on Saturday.) Given Willis's literary production, the task of running the* Mirrors *had probably become too onerous, which may account for Willis and Morris allowing Hiram Fuller, a former school principal and bookseller from Providence, to become a partner and junior editor in the firm. The editorial work was divided as follows: Willis ran the* Evening Mirror, *in which capacity he hired Poe as an assistant; Morris and Fuller ran the* Weekly Mirror. *As Fuller remarked in the* Weekly Mirror *of 18 January 1845: "For the opinions of the Daily paper, Mr. Willis is alone the gate-keeper, and by himself or by his direction, all its principal articles are written." (Fuller, of course, with the help of his brother-in-law, Augustus W. Clason, Jr., eventually bought both* Mirrors *and became the sole editor of them.)*

The Weekly Mirror *of 12 October 1844 contained Willis's first allusion to Poe's connection with the paper: "We wish to light beacons for an authors' crusade and we have no leisure to be more than its Peter the Hermit. We solemnly summon Edgar Poe to do the devoir of Coeur de Lion—no man's weapon half so trenchant!" Aside from doing the series on authors and authors' pay and the need for an international copyright law, Poe performed other services, all of which earned Willis's approbation, including the two-installment review of Longfellow's* The Waif, *which launched what Poe came to call the "Little Longfellow War" and which induced Charles F. Briggs ("Harry Franco") to lure Poe away from the* Mirror *in March 1845 with the offer of a co-editorship of the* Broadway Journal.

Having recently become aware of Poe's financial and physical difficulties through the Morning Express *(Document 59), Willis decided to do his friend a good turn by proposing a hospital for disabled writers. His proposal was not too wild a notion for the period. A philanthropic epoch in America, there were "societies," "institutions," "homes," and "missions" of all kinds, including a Society for Destitute Roman Catholic Children and a Home for Aged Hebrews, an Association for the Relief of Respectable Aged Indigent Females and a Home for Friendless Women. Willis devoted a great part of his editorial in the* Home Journal *to Poe's problems, pointing out his poverty and sickness and offering to forward donations of money to him. Less discreetly, he attempted to gain forgiveness for Poe's erratic behavior by explaining that a "single glass of wine" made him behave in a way "neither sane nor responsible." (Some three years later, however, in the "Death of Edgar Poe"—Home Journal of 20 October 1849—Willis insisted, contrary to the report here, that he knew about this condition of Poe's only through "hearsay": "we repeat, it was never our chance to see him" in this condition.)*

Uneasy at taking liberties in such a public way with a proud man's private life, Willis was apologetic both in the editorial and in his covering letter to Poe. In the letter he makes a point that he did not make in the editorial; namely, that his statements in the Home Journal *"will have a good bearing . . . on your law case," though what bearing he had in mind I cannot guess. The letter, dated merely Wednesday, was no doubt written on 23 December 1846 when the* Home Journal *containing Willis's editorial was ready for distribution.*

Griswold, in the "Memoir of the Author" that he prefixed to his edition of Poe's Literati, *said of Willis's editorial that it "was an ingenious apology for Mr. Poe's infirmities," which he identified as his "habits of frequent intoxication and his inattention to the means of support."*

The letter appears in Harrison, XVII, 272.]

Wednesday.

My dear Poe,—The enclosed speaks for itself—the letter, that is to say. Have I done right or wrong in the enclosed editorial? It was a kind of thing I could *only* do *without asking* you, & you *may express anger about it if you like in print.* It will have a good bearing, I think, on your law case. Please write me whether you are suffering or not, & if so, let us do something systematically for you.

In haste
Yours faithfully
N.P. Willis.

Kindest remembrance to Mrs Clemm.

HOSPITAL FOR DISABLED LABOURERS
WITH THE BRAIN.

IF pity, felt more for a stab than for a bruise—more for an operation on the brain than for one on the arm—more for a man broken on the wheel than for one in prison—if this pity, greater in proportion as the suffering is keener, were answered to by correspondent Institutions for its relief, there would have been, long ago, in this or any other city, a *Retreat for disabled labourers with the brain.* We have long wished for the handle of this subject to come round. Obvious as its merit is, even with the simple statement we have just made—ready as any one will be to acknowledge, that the poverty of the diseasedly sensitive author must be ten-fold harder to bear as well as ten-fold more hopeless of self-relief, than the mere flesh and blood pauper's—the subject is difficult of mention, the relief difficult of application, and the lesser sufferer is consequently provided for, while the greater is set aside and forgotten. *Twenty-six thousand* visits of sympathy are mentioned in a late Report as having been made "to the poor" of this city, by one society; and what one of these visits was in search of sufferers whose first apprehension, even, of want, is a mental agony not many removes from madness?

The feeling we have long entertained on this subject, has been freshened by a recent paragraph in the *Express* announcing that Mr. EDGAR A. POE, and his wife, were both dangerously ill and suffering for want of the common necessaries of life. Here is one of the finest scholars, one of the most original men of genius, and one of the most industrious of the literary profession of our country, whose temporary suspension of labour, from bodily illness, drops him immediately to a level with the common objects of public charity. There was no intermediate stopping-place—no respectful shelter where, with the delicacy due to genius and culture, he might secure aid, unadvertised, till, with returning health, he could resume his labours and his unmortified sense of independence. He must either apply to individual friends—(a resource to which death is sometimes almost preferable)—or *suffer down* to the level where Charity receives claimants, but where Rags and Humiliation are the only recognised Ushers to her presence. Is this right? Should there not be, in all highly civilized communities, an Institution designed expressly for educated and refined objects of charity,—a hospital, a retreat, a home of seclusion and comfort, the sufficient claims to which would be such susceptibilities as are violated by the above mentioned appeal in a daily newspaper.

Mr. Poe lives out of the city, and we cannot ascertain before this goes to press, how far this report of his extreme necessity is true. We received yesterday a letter from an *anonymous hand*, mentioning the paragraph in question, expressing high admiration for Mr. Poe's genius, and enclosing a sum of money, with a request that we would forward it to him.

We think it very possible that this, and other aid, may be timely and welcome, though we know, that, on Mr. Poe's recovery from former illnesses, he has been deeply mortified and distressed by the discovery that his friends had been called upon for assistance. The highly cultivated women who share his lot, his wife and mother, are, we also know, the prey of constant anxiety for him; and though he vigorously resumes the labours of his poorly paid profession with the first symptoms of returning strength, we have little doubt that a generous gift could hardly be better applied than to him, however unwilling he may be to have received it. We venture, therefore, while we acknowledge the delicate generosity of the letter of yesterday, to offer to forward any other similar tribute of sympathy with genius.

In connection with this public mention of Mr. Poe's personal matters, perhaps it will not be thought inopportune, if we put on its proper footing, a public impression, which does him some injustice. We have not seen nor corresponded with Mr. Poe for two years, and we hazard this delicate service without his leave, of course, and simply because we have seen him suffer for the lack of such vindication, when his name has been brought injuriously before the public, and have then wished for some such occasion to speak for him. We refer to conduct and language charged against him, which, were he, at the time, in sane mind, were an undeniable forfeiture of character and good feeling. To blame, in some degree, still, perhaps he is. But let charity for the failings of human nature judge of the degree. Mr. Poe was engaged with us in the editorship of a daily paper [*Evening Mirror*], we think, for about six months. A more considerate, quiet, talented, and gentlemanlike associate than he was for the whole of that time, we could not have wished. Not liking the unstudent-like necessity of coming every day into the city, however, he left us, by his own wish alone, and it was one day soon after, that we first saw him in the state to which we refer. He came into our office with his usual gait and manner, and with no symptom of ordinary intoxication, he talked like a man insane. Perfectly self-possessed in all other respects, his brain and tongue were evidently beyond his control. We learned afterwards that the least stimulus—a single glass of wine—would produce this effect upon Mr. Poe, and that, rarely as these instances of easy aberration of caution and mind occurred, he was liable to them, and while under the influence, voluble and personally self-possessed, but neither sane nor responsible. Now, very possibly, Mr. Poe may not be willing to consent to even this admission of any infirmity. He has little or no memory of them afterwards, we understand. But public opinion unqualifiedly holds him blameable for what he has said and done under such excitements; and while a call is made in a public paper for aid, it looks like doing him a timely service . . . [at] least partially to exonerate him. We run the risk of being deemed officious.

The subject of a *Retreat for disabled labourers with the brain*, we shall resume hereafter.

---

62. 26 December 1846: A Comment on Nathaniel P. Willis's "Hospital for Disabled Labourers with the Brain"
Hiram Fuller

[Fuller commented on Willis's editorial almost at once. His allusions to Poe, though Poe's name does not appear in Fuller's statement, are quite apparent, as are Fuller's reasons for suppressing his name: the libel suit was still pending. This, by the way, was not to be the last time Fuller would refer to Willis's editorial (see Document 94).

Fuller was not alone in commenting humorously on Willis's proposal. Peculiarly enough, Yankee Doodle, which was edited by the Duyckinck circle (see headnote to Document 72) and to which Willis himself contributed at times, used the occasion on 9 January 1847 to feature an article entitled "Hospital for Disabled Authors." Among its various remarks was the following: "More forcibly to illustrate the necessity for the institution we are advocating, we present beneath a full-length view of the destitute and suffering condition to which even one of the most popular of American authors is reduced." The "full-length view" is of Willis himself, famous for his dandyism, attired in patent-leather shoes, a Leary top hat, and an overcoat cut in the latest Regent Street style. "Any contributions for the above 'object,'" the article concluded, "may be left with YANKEE DOODLE *or sent to Mr.* WILLIS, *at the office of the* Home Journal.*"]*

N.P. *Willis* proposes to build a 'hospital for disabled laborers with the brain.' This is all very well; we approve of charity in any shape. But we propose to add to the building, an asylum for those who have been ruined by the diddlers of the quill. We think it quite possible that *this* apartment might be soonest filled, as we cannot now call to mind a single instance of a man of real literary ability suffering from poverty, who has always lived an industrious, honest and honorable life; while of the other class of indigents, we know of numerous melancholy specimens, of both sexes.

---

63. 27 December 1846: "Edgar A. Poe"
Joseph M. Field

[*The editor of the* Saint Louis Daily Reveille *had proved sympathetic to Poe on various occasions (see Document 9 and its headnote). Now, apprised of Poe's misfortunes, he made the following brief but sensitive statement. The item in the* Morning Express, *part of which Field quotes, appears as Document 59.*]

EDGAR A. POE.—If Poe has made enemies, his misfortunes, unhappily, have afforded them ample revenge; and not all of them have had magnanimity enough to forego it. We still see his infirmities alluded to uncharitably. The New York [Morning] Express has the following painful announcement—enough, we think, to sweeten the bitterest disposition:

> We regret to learn that this gentleman and his wife are both dangerously ill with the consumption, and that the hand of misfortune lies heavy upon their temporal affairs. We are sorry to mention the fact that they are so far reduced as to be barely able to obtain the necessaries of life.

---

64. 29 December 1846: A Notice of the "Plea in Behalf of Mr. Poe"
Horace Greeley

[*Much as Greeley respected Poe's genius, he had no reason to like him as a man. Among other reasons, Poe had antagonized Margaret Fuller, though he had treated her generously enough in a "Literati" sketch, and Miss Fuller, as an intimate family friend, not only shared the Greeleys' house but had served as the* Tribune *book reviewer until she went abroad in August 1846. Poe had also been unkind to another friend of Greeley, George Ripley, the major founder of Brook Farm. Poe had called it "Snook Farm" and dubbed the* Harbinger, *which Ripley was then editing in quarters provided by Greeley in the Tribune Building, the "organ of the Crazyites." To make their relations still worse, Poe had borrowed fifty dollars from Greeley to help buy the* Broadway Journal—*Greeley, generous to a fault, had helped to launch many a journal, even competitive ones—and this debt Poe was unable to repay. Greeley's single anecdote about Poe in his autobiography is that he replied to a searcher after Poe's autograph that he had one: "It is his note of hand for fifty dollars . . . and you may have it for half the amount." If this were not enough, Poe had derided the Transcendentalist and Fourieristic schemes which Greeley was advocating. It hardly helped matters for Poe to write in "Fifty Suggestions" (Graham's Magazine, 1845) that the "High Priest in the East" of a "new sect of philosophers is Charles Fourier—in the West, Horace Greeley," and that the "only common bond among them is Credulity:—let us call it Insanity at once, and be done with it." Finally, Greeley may have resented being featured with Poe in English's 1844 and wished to dissociate himself from the man. Whatever the reasons, it was no accident that Greeley allowed Rufus Griswold's infamous "Ludwig" obituary of Poe to be printed in his paper (9 October 1849).*

At all events, the Daily Tribune *carried Greeley's unfriendly notice of Poe printed below, which begins by quoting an item from the* Morning Express *commenting on Willis's editorial (Document 61). How Greeley knew, if he in fact did know, that Poe was "steadily, though slowly, recovering his health" has to be conjectured. The publishing and editorial world of New York—and New York was the literary capital of America at this time—was concentrated in an area of less than eight short square blocks near City Hall and gossip quickly spread from office to office. Any of the literary ladies who visited the Poes in Fordham at this time (see headnote to Document 59) could have quoted Poe to the effect, "I am getting better, and may add—if it be any comfort to my enemies—that I have little fear of getting worse" (Document 70). Greeley may have made his premature announcement to put an end to the contributions Willis was collecting for Poe. The thrust in the last phrase of his notice—Poe "is engaged at his usual literary avocations"—seems suggestive of ill will.]*

A Plea in Behalf of Mr. Poe.—The Home Journal of this week contains an article about Mr. Poe, suggested by the paragraph in our paper, and to which we would like to call the attention of the public. It would appear from the article in question, that what we said of Mr. Poe's condition was strictly true; and it also appears that Mr. Willis has received certain monies for his benefit, and that he is willing to act as agent in receiving more. We trust that the admirers of genius will remember the unfortunate but gifted author.

[Express.

We are glad to be able to state that the distressing accounts regarding Mr. Poe, if they have not been from the first greatly exaggerated, are no longer applicable to his situation. He is steadily, though slowly, recovering his health, and is engaged at his usual literary avocations.

---

65. 31 December 1846: "Edgar A. Poe"
Cornelia Wells Walter

[*Miss Walter, editress of the Boston* Daily Evening Transcript, *had reasons to be unhappy with Poe. Resentful of his treatment of Longfellow and of Boston and Bostonians in general, she had in 1845 pronounced his performance at the Boston Lyceum "A Failure" and exposed him as a humbug in trying to pass off a juvenile poem ("Al Aaraaf") as an "original" before a "literary association of adults. . . ." Poe held his fire, no doubt wishing that the event might be forgotten, but Miss Walter, not to mention other editors, kept squibbing him. Besides alluding to his reputation for drunkenness and suggesting that his performance was a swindle, Miss Walter called him a "poe-ser" and said that, like the "immortal Barabelle, the 'Broadway poet of Rome,'" he should be "crowned with cabbage." Having waited two weeks without seeing the least abatement of this needling, Poe responded to Miss Walter, as well as other Boston editors. In a reply blustering and crude, Poe called her a "little old lady" who had "been telling a parcel of fibs about us," but whose heart was in the right place—would that the same might be said of her wig. (For a full discussion of this episode, see Moss,* Poe's Literary Battles, *pages 190–207.)*

Miss Walter, as is evident from Document 1, was not inclined to be sympathetic when she read the news that Poe was sick and impoverished. She suggested that much of his trouble was owing to "improvidence"; she quoted the Tribune *(Document 64) as evidence that the report of his illness and poverty was exaggerated and, in any case, no longer applicable to his "present condition"; and she read him a lecture which concluded that he should with a "thankful spirit mark out for himself a new career...."]*

EDGAR A. POE. The papers have told us in various ways, of the sufferings of this writer, who has been reduced to beg for sustenance owing to improvidence and sickness. The *"Bostonian"* has opened a subscription for the relief of Mr. Poe, and so has the *Home Journal* of New York. This is all very proper; no object of humanity should be permitted to die of hunger, or to lay upon the couch of sickness without some ministering angel to relieve distress. With respect to the *present* condition of Mr Poe, however, we copy from the N. Y. Tribune the following paragraph:

We are glad to be able to state that the distressing accounts regarding Mr Poe, if they have not been from the first greatly exaggerated, are no longer applicable to his situation. He is steadily, though slowly, recovering his health, and is engaged at his usual literary avocations.

If the burthen of this information be correct, and Mr Poe be recovering his health sufficiently to engage in literary avocations, will he not remember his *duty to himself* as a man and as a writer? *Reformation of habits and proper principle exerted to others* is what is requisite to free him in future from the necessity of pity; and, having in his distresses found those who have relieved his wants, let him no longer *pervert* those faculties which God has given him for his ennoblement. Let him remember how much of his pecuniary distress he has brought on through the indulgence of is own *weaknesses.* Let him in a thankful spirit mark out for himself a new career for the future.

---

66. 5 January 1847: The Evening Mirror Hopes Poe Will Heed the Good Advice of the Boston Transcript
Hiram Fuller

[*Fuller was no doubt gratified that Poe, having become an object of char-ity, had also become an object of advice, a condition which, Poe's advisers assumed, privileged them to invade his privacy and to harangue him in public about reforming his habits, altering his principles, and changing his career. Fuller likewise used the opportunity to urge Poe to follow the* Transcript's *"good advice" and to refer self-justifyingly to Poe's pending libel suit against him.*

Despite his statement, Fuller did not pay Poe fifteen dollars a week; that salary was paid by all three partners in the Mirror *firm. Nor is it true that Poe assisted "Morris and Willis . . . in . . . editing the Evening Mirror." It was Fuller who assisted George P. Morris in putting out the* Weekly Mirror *and Poe who assisted Nathaniel P. Willis in putting out the* Evening Mirror *(see headnote to Document 61).*]

The Boston Transcript, in copying a paragraph from a New York paper, which announces that Mr. Poe is again able to resume his pen, very properly adds—

'If the burthen of this information be correct, and Mr. Poe be recovering his health sufficiently to engage in literary avocations, will he not remember his *duty to himself* as a man and as a writer? *Refor-mation of habits and proper principles exercised to others* is what is requisite to free him in future from the necessity of pity; and having, in his distresses, found those who have relieved his wants, let him no longer *pervert* those faculties which God has given him for his ennoblement. Let him remember how much of his pecuniary distress he has brought on through the indulgence of his own *weaknesses.* Let him in a thankful spirit mark out for himself a new career for the future.'

We sincerely hope this good advice will be heeded. Mr. Poe, after libelling half the literary men in the country, commenced a libel suit against us for publishing as an *advertisement* an article which originally appeared in a morning paper [the New York *Morning Telegraph*] in reply to one of his own coarse attacks. This suit was commenced *after* he had grossly abused us in a Philadelphia paper in one of the most scurrilous articles that we ever saw in print; and all this, too, after we had been paying him for some months a salary of $15 a week for *assisting* Morris and Willis, and two or three other 'able bodied men,' in the Herculean task of editing the Evening Mirror.

---

67. *30 December 1846: Letter to Evert A. Duyckinck*
Edgar A. Poe

[Poe's only means of support was his pen, and the irony is that "The Literati" series, the journalistic sensation of the year, cost him his livelihood (see headnotes to Document 1 and 102). The enmity he had aroused with "The Literati" and the illness that chronically beset him now, probably psychosomatic, discouraged him from going to the city. The task thus fell to Maria Clemm, now turning sixty, to make the thirteen-mile trip for him, which she frequently did, taking the Harlem Railroad that conveniently passed near their cottage. There were his messages and letters to convey; his manuscripts to deliver or peddle; the latest literary intelligence to be gathered; and the mail to be collected from the city post office, since Fordham had none.

Nathaniel Willis, one of Poe's abiding friends, recalled in the Home Journal *of 20 October 1849 that "winter after winter, for years, the most touching sight to us, in this whole city, has been that tireless minister to genius, thinly . . . clad, going from office to office with a poem, or an article on some literary subject to sell—sometimes simply pleading in a broken voice that he was ill, and begging for him." Mary Hewitt in a letter to Frances Osgood dated 20 December 1846 noted that Mrs. Clemm "borrows a shilling often, to get a letter from the [post] office." And Mrs. Clemm, without the pity for herself that others accorded her, wrote to Neilson Poe on 19 August 1860: "Oh, how supremely happy we were in our dear cottage home! We three lived only for each other. Eddie rarely left his beautiful home. I attended to his literary business." (These two letters appear in Harrison, XVII, 273 and 430, respectively.)*

On one such trip Mrs. Clemm heard from Evert Duyckinck, who in 1845 had published Poe's Tales *and the* Raven *volume in his* Library of American Books, *that Poe had gained sudden fame in France. A French*

adaptation of his "Murders in the Rue Morgue" had been published in
La Quotidienne. *(Neither Duyckinck nor Poe had heard that* La Revue
brittanique *had earlier published translations of "The Gold-Bug" and "A
Descent into the Maelström.") When a second Paris paper,* Le Commerce,
published another version of "The Murders," La Presse *accused the trans-
lator, E.-D. Forgues, of plagiarism from* La Quotidienne. *Forgues wrote
an explanation of the coincidence. Both versions, he said, derived from a
common source and were done independently. But the editor of* La
Presse, *who had never heard of Poe, refused to publish Forgues's statement because Forgues had himself once charged* La Presse *with plagiarism. To clear his name, Forgues sued the journal for libel, as Poe, coinci-
dentally, was suing the owners of the* Mirror. *Though the Frenchman lost
his case, the trial held in December 1846 became a* cause célèbre *that
brought Poe's name prominently before the French public.*

Nathaniel P. Willis reported these events in the Home Journal *of 30
January 1847 as follows:*

EDGAR A. POE AND THE PARISIAN FEUILLETONISTS.—*All lovers of
fiction have read Mr. Edgar A. Poe's famous story of "Valdemar,"
and will remember the excitement which it created not only in this
country but in Europe. We find, by the following, from a Parisian
correspondent of* Willmer and Smith's European Times, *that this excitement has not yet subsided:—"The name of Mr. Edgar A. Poe the
American novelist, has figured rather prominently of late before the
law courts. A newspaper, which, for the sake of clearness, I will call
No. 1, gave a* feuilleton, *in which one of Mr. Poe's tales of a horrible
murder in the United States was dressed up to suit the French palate;
but no acknowledgment was made of the story being taken from Mr.
Poe. Another newspaper, No. 2, stated that the said* feuilleton *was
stolen from one previously published in another journal. This led to
a squabble between the writer of* feuilleton *No. 1 and the editor of
the newspaper No. 2, that accused him of plagiary from newspaper
No. 3. This squabble resulted in a process [of litigation], in the course
of which the* feuilletoniste *No. 1 proved that he had stolen it from
Mr. Poe. It was proved, too, that No. 3 was himself an impudent
plagiarist, for he had filched Mr. Poe's tale without one word of acknowledgment; whilst, as to No. 2, he was forced to admit that not
only had he never read Mr. Poe, but had never heard of him in his*

life. All this, it will be perceived, is anything but creditable to the three newspapers in question."

In the meantime, to vindicate himself, Forgues, the "No. 1" of Willis's report, published his critique of Poe's Tales *in the prestigious* Revue des deux Mondes *on 15 October 1846, which turned what would only have been a succès de circonstance for Poe into a succès d'estime. Thus, at the very time Poe was being pilloried at home, he was coming into his own abroad. (For Forgues's essay see Document 69.)*

All that Mrs. Clemm seems to have remembered of her conversation with Duyckinck was that some Paris papers had been discussing "The Murders in the Rue Morgue." As Poe said, "She could not give me the details. . . . Sensing an opportunity to enlist Duyckinck's aid, as earlier he had enlisted Field's and Simms's (Documents 9 and 41), Poe wrote the letter below and provided Duyckinck with information for "a paragraph or two for some one of the city papers. . . ."

Poe's statement notwithstanding, no one has located a discussion of "The Murders in the Rue Morgue" in the Charivari. *The "letter from Stonehaven" that Poe enclosed was from Arch Ramsay, a druggist (reprinted in Harrison, XVII, 268–9). "Facts in the Case of M. Valdemar" did appear as a sixteen-page pamphlet with the title and publisher Poe ascribed to it. The tale also appeared, as Poe says, in the London Morning* Post *(5 January 1846) under the title "Mesmerism in America," and in the* Popular Record of Modern Science *(10 January 1846) under the title "Mesmerism in America. Death of M. Valdemar, of New York." The* Record *of 29 November 1845 carried Poe's "Mesmeric Revelation" under the title "The Last Conversation of a Somnambule." The letter from Miss Barrett appears as Document 10.*

This letter appears in Ostrom, II, 336.]

Dec. 30. 46.

Dear Duyckinck,

Mrs Clemm mentioned to me, this morning, that some of the Parisian papers had been speaking about my "Murders in the Rue Morgue". She could not give me the details—merely saying that you had told her. The "Murders in the R. M." was spoken of in the Paris "Charivari", soon after the first issue of the tale in Graham's Mag:—April 1841. By the enclosed letter from Stonehaven[,] Scotland, you will see that the "Valdemar Case" still makes a talk, and that a pamphlet edition of it has been published by

Short & co. of London under the title of "Mesmerism in Articulo Mortis." It has fairly gone the rounds of the London Press, commencing with "The Morning Post". The "Monthly Record of Science" &c gives it with the title "The Last Days of M. Valdemar. By the author of the Last Conversation of a Somnambule"—(Mesmeric Revelation).

My object in enclosing the Scotch letter and the one from Miss Barrett, is to ask you to do me a favor which (*just at this moment*) may be of great importance. It is, to make a paragraph or two for some one of the city papers, stating the facts here given, in connexion with what you know about the "Murders in the Rue Morgue". If this will not give you too much trouble, I will be deeply obliged. If you think it advisable, there is no objection to your copying any portion of Miss B's letter. Willis or Morris will put in anything you may be kind enough to write; but as "The Home Journal" has already said a good deal about me, some other paper would be preferable.

Truly yours
Poe.

---

68. 9 *January 1847*: "An Author['s Reputation] in Europe and America" Evert A. Duyckinck

[*Acting on Poe's request (see preceding document) Duyckinck wrote the article below, which appeared in the same number of the* Home Journal *as Poe's open letter to Willis (Document 70). Though Duyckinck used some of the information Poe provided, he seems not to have concerned himself with Poe's wish that he publish the article in a paper other than the* Home Journal.

Since Duyckinck's assessment of Poe's European and American reputation appeared anonymously and is here identified for the first time, a few words should be said about its authorship. In addition to Duyckinck's using some of the information Poe provided, Willis in printing Poe's open letter referred to a "communication" in "another column" respecting Poe's "literary position, kindly furnished by one of the best of our scholars and gentlemen." Poe explained to Eveleth that the scholar and gentleman Willis had reference to was Duyckinck (Ostrom, II, 348). Eveleth thanked Duyckinck "for this kindly speaking of my favorite one while 'pestered

*and annoyed by those penny-a-liners'" in your "kind notice of him pub-
lished in . . . the Home Journal for the ninth of last January–'An Author
in Europe and America'" (Mabbott, page 192). Duyckinck was evidently
touched by this compliment, for he kept Eveleth's letter until he be-
queathed it with the rest of his papers to the New York Public Library in
the 1870s.*

*If only as editor of the Library of American Books, Duyckinck had
reason to mention the* North American Review *contemptuously. In October 1846, the same month in which Forgues's article on Poe's* Tales
appeared in the Revue des deux Mondes *(next document), the* North
American *had taken occasion in reviewing Simms's* Wigwam and the
Cabin *and* Views and Reviews *to remark that they form a "part of Wiley
and Putnam's Library of American Books, a series, by the by, which, with
the exception of a few volumes, is not likely to do much honor to American literature." Among the works in the Library pointedly attacked–
those by Simms, J. T. Headley* (Letters from Italy), *and Cornelius
Mathews* (Big Abel and the Little Manhattan)–*was Poe's* Tales, *which
the reviewer said "belongs to the forcible-feeble and the shallow-pro-
found school" of literature.*]

An Author['s Reputation] in Europe and America. While Mr. Poe,
an author of understood merits, quite unique and apart from the rest of
the literary race in his literary productions, which are all his own, *paid
for by himself in actual experience of heart and brain*, is pestered and
annoyed at home by penny-a-liners whom his iron pen has cut into too
deeply, and denied all ability and morality whatever—it is curious to contrast this with his position abroad, where distance suffers only the prominent features of his genius to be visible, and see what is made of his
good qualities in Europe.

Why the American press should be so intolerant of the original authors of the country, and battle with them at every step, while the most
liberal good words are freely accorded to mediocrity, and imitative
talents, is one of those little problems of human nature, well enough for
Rochefoucault [sic] to pry into, but which we have too much of the wisdom of the serpent and the good feeling of the dove to meddle with. The
fact is, that our most neglected and best abused authors, are generally
our best authors.

The reception of Mr. Poe's tales in England is well known. The mystification of M. Valdemar was taken up by a mesmeric journal as a literal verity, and enquiries were sent on here, to be supplied (in case the historian of the event were not accessible) by personal solicitation of the poor victim's neighbours at Harlem, where the scene was laid. This story is still going the rounds of Great Britain. A London publisher has got it out, in pamphlet, under the title of "Mesmerism in Articulo Mortis," and a Scotchman in Stonehaven has recently paid a postage by steamer, in a letter to the author, to test the matter-of-factness of the affair. We can conceive of nothing more impressive in the way of curiosity. Miss Barrett, by the way, paid the author a handsome compliment on this story. After admiring the popular credulity, she say[s] "The certain thing in the tale in question, is the power of the writer, and the faculty he has of making horrible improbabilities seem near and familiar."

The tale of the "Murders in the Morgue," is giving rise to various editorial perplexities, in Paris. It has been translated in the feuilletons, local personal allusion discovered and the American authorship denied. One of the journals says "if there turn out to be such an American author, it will prove that America has at least one novelist besides Mr. Cooper"—and this, in France, is praise. The *Revue des deux Mondes*, in the meantime, has an elaborate review of the "Tales." The North American Review of the same date calls them trash.

Besides a peculiar vein of invention, Mr. Poe has a style, a clearness, cleanness and neatness of expression, which, together, will always make their way. They are unmistakeable classic elements. By them Mr. Poe will live. A writer so ready in *new resources* as Mr. Poe, should command his own terms and full employment from the trade. It is a duty they owe the world, to astonish it now and then by some clever performance, and a duty they owe their own families to put money in their pockets. An occasional book from Mr. Poe would unite these desirable conditions.

---

69. *15 October 1846: Studies of English and American Fiction: The Tales of Edgar A. Poe*
   E.-D. Forgues

[*The curious reader will want to read Forgues's critique of Poe, a condensed translation of which is made available below. A twenty-page article in the prestigious* Revue des deux Mondes, *it represents the first discussion of Poe to be published in France and, owing to its perspicacity and judgment, provides a very sharp contrast with Poe's general literary reputation at home. Hardly the least of its value was that it brought Poe to the attention of other French critics, translators, and literary figures, the most important of whom was, of course, Charles Baudelaire.*

The chief talent of Forgues, who had abandoned law for belles lettres, lay in discovering, translating, and discussing literary works that would interest his French public. Though he concentrated on English authors such as Thackeray, Dickens, and George Eliot, he devoted critiques to Holmes, Melville, and Hawthorne, among others, and even translated The Scarlet Letter, The House of the Seven Gables, *and* Uncle Tom's Cabin.

Forgues rendered Poe the ultimate critical courtesy by treating him as a serious writer. He knew Poe only through the Tales *of 1845, however; he did not know that Poe was also a poet and, like himself, a journalist and critic. What especially impressed him about the handful of stories was Poe's powers as a probabilist, powers, he felt, Poe was using "to explore the most difficult problems of speculative philosophy," and he paid him the highest compliment by placing him in the French mathematical tradition represented by Blaise Pascal, Pierre Fermat, and the Marquis de Laplace. Probability theory was first developed by Pascal (1623–1662) and Fermat (1601–1665) to analyze games of chance, and it remained limited to such amusements until Laplace (1749–1827), not to mention Karl Friedrich Gauss (1777–1855), discovered that the theory had wider application. Laplace saw no essential difference between calling observable outcomes "heads or tails" and calling them "life or death," from which observation emerged actuarial science and demography. By like logic Mendel's study of the "toss-ups" of genes in garden peas enabled him to formulate his famous laws concerning hereditary phenomena.*

Forgues (1813–1889), whose full given name was Paul Emile Daurand, was no trained probabilist and his firsthand knowledge of Laplace seems limited to his Essai philosophique sur les Probabilités, *a short popular version of his great* Théorie analytique des Probabilités. *For this reason he discussed probability in nonmathematical terms easily understood by the uninitiated. If Poe could have foreseen his French reception on these grounds, he might not have complained so often that Duyckinck's selection for the volume was too one-sided. "Duyckinck," he wrote to Philip*

Cooke on 9 August 1846, "has what he thinks [is] a taste for ratiocination, and has accordingly made up the book mostly of analytic stories," though he had about seventy to choose from. "But this is not representing my mind in its various phases" (Ostrom, II, 328).

Forgues considered all the stories in the Tales except two. His neglect of "Lionizing" is understandable; his disregard of "The Fall of the House of Usher" is puzzling.

The article below has been condensed to about a third of its original length and Forgues's notes, specifying the book under discussion or identifying Charles Brockden Brown, have been dropped as unnecessary. Minor deletions are indicated by ellipsis marks; the nature of large omissions is explained in brackets; and the footnotes are mine. For other information concerning Forgues, see the headnote to Document 67.]

Are you acquainted with the [Marquis de Laplace's] *Philosophical Essay on Probabilities?* It is one of the books in which the boldness of the human mind is best revealed at its most audacious. Since the venture of Prometheus . . . one has scarcely seen anything so daring as the urge of those men who want to make the mutable, uncertain, mysterious order of the destinies submit to their calculations, to penetrate the obscure realm of the future, to reduce the fortunes of chance to numbers. . . . For this reason Laplace's book exerts a real fascination on certain minds which the power of reason intoxicates, and on which a new truth acts like an opium pipe. . . . Such minds make probability their gospel; they devote themselves to propagating its theories. . . . The *Philosophical Essay* is not only an ambitious effort of the intellect . . . to know; the *Essay* has its moral aspect in that it brings men back to the practice of the good by observation of eternal principles.[1]

Without being of such an exalted order, without leading to such a noble end, without emanating from so vigorous a mind, the tales we are about to discuss have an evident kinship with the serious work of the learned Marquis. If the incoherent fictions of the common narrative have enough to attract and hold your interest, you will find nothing here to intrigue you. Poetry, invention, effects of style, logical dramatic sequence, all are subservient in these tales to a bizarre preoccupation. We might

1. Laplace considered in some detail what he called the "Application of the Calculus of Probabilities to the Moral Sciences." The last half of the *Essay* is devoted to such applications. Poe speaks of "the Calculus of Probabilities" in the opening of "The Mystery of Marie Roget," to cite only one instance.

almost call it an obsession of the author, who seems to have only one faculty of inspiration, reason; only one muse, logic; only one effect upon his readers, the creation of doubt. There are as many enigmas as there are tales and all of them take diverse forms and guises. Whether wearing the fantastic livery of Hoffmann or the grave and magisterial costume of Godwin renovated by Washington Irving or Dickens, it is always the same combination which sets Oedipus and the Sphinx by the ears—a protagonist and a puzzle; . . . an apparently impenetrable mystery and an intellect which irritated . . . by the veil stretched before it solves the enigma after incredible operations of the mind rendered in the most minute detail.

. . . Every narrative . . . implies a plot whose doubtful vicissitudes are . . . linked together by a bond of logic, according to the ability of the writer. The syllogism is at the bottom of the most moving situations, and the climax that arouses the reader's emotions is fundamentally only a development of a dramatically rendered logical sequence. In short, logic is the hidden pivot of the action. It is concealed in an infinite number of details which are designed to dazzle and bewilder our minds; and because the action moves so quickly from its starting point and rushes so headlong to its conclusion, we tend not to be conscious of the logic. To see that logic is concealed by the fiction, you have merely to separate the logical substratum from its brilliantly colored and ingeniously embellished envelope. You will then notice from what a thin argument, from what a tenuous thread, the magnificent fabric hangs.

In contrast, the unique tales that we wish to make known and that have just arrived from New York by the last packet boat have a logic that is unconcealed. It dominates everything; it is queen and mistress. Its office is not to hide itself; it is not a monument to exterior riches—it is its own monument; it borrows nothing or nearly nothing from the many resources of fiction. It no longer plays the role of the submissive slave which lends its robust shoulders to its master tottering with wine and conducts him, not without difficulty, to a door barely seen. Instead, it walks alone, strong in its own strength; it is the end and the way, the cause and the effect. Yesterday, in the hands of a philosopher, logic was used to explore the most difficult problems of speculative philosophy; today, it lodges in a fiction so as to put itself within reach of the greatest number, yet for all that departing as little as possible from philosophical dignity.

Exactly what was Laplace looking for in his analysis of chance and Buffon in his political arithmetic? Each of them . . . wanted to subdue an obstinate unknown quantity by the power of induction, to neutralize the resistance it offers to reason, and to gain mathematical certainty in regard to moral problems. For this reason Laplace weighs in the same balance the periodical reappearance of a comet, the chances of a lottery ticket, and the value of historical testimony. The same power of reasoning serves to assure him that the action of the moon on the ocean is more than twice as powerful as that of the sun, and that Pascal's niece, the young Perrier, was not cured of her fistula by the direct and miraculous intervention of divine Providence.[2] Thus whether in respect to the past, the present, or the future, he lays down a system of principles and establishes the general laws of probability.

In his own unique way, Mr. Poe is also concerned with probabilities, but he does not weigh them by rules but by intuition. . . . The fundamental idea of his tales seems to be borrowed from the first adventures of Zadig in which the young . . . philosopher displays marvelous perspicacity. The eccentric character who is Mr. Poe's favorite protagonist and whose subtle intelligence he puts to such difficult tests would also have inferred by merely inspecting their tracks that the Queen of Babylon's spaniel had just had a litter of puppies and that the King's horse . . . had twenty-three-caret gold bosses on his bit.[3] This protagonist is really Mr. Poe who hardly troubles to conceal himself, and in those tales in which he does not have a surrogate Mr. Poe appears in his own person.

Who other than this searcher after problems to solve would have imposed on himself the task of imagining what the posthumous sensations of a man, or rather of a body, might be, stretched out first on the funeral bed, then in a coffin under the damp earth, listening to himself dissolve and watching himself rot? To whose mind would it have occurred to relate in such a convincing way the final catastrophe which must reduce this terrestrial globe to nothingness? To touch on these great secrets of human and planetary death seems the business of the profoundest think-

2. Mlle Perrier had suffered for more than three years from a lachrymal fistula. When she touched her afflicted eye with a relic supposed to be one of the thorns on Christ's crown, she recovered instantaneously. Doctors attested to the remarkable cure and declared it was wrought supernaturally. This "miracle" occurred in 1656 and made a great sensation. See chap. xi of the *Essay on Probabilities* for Laplace's discussion of this event.

3. Zadig's inferences concerning the queen's spaniel and the king's horse are recounted in chap. iii of Voltaire's *Zadig*.

ers, the longest studies, and the most complete systems. For Mr. Poe it is only a question of assuming a hypothesis, of establishing a starting point, and letting the tale develop in the most plausible way among all its probable and possible consequences.

Monos has died. Una, his adored mistress, has followed him into the somber kingdom of death. They meet. Una wants to know of her beloved what he felt a while ago when, desolate, she contemplated him immobile, cold, disfigured, marked by the supreme wound. Had all thought disappeared with life? Is the divorce of soul and body so abrupt, . . . so complete, that with the last death-rattle the soul escapes entirely, leaving behind it only an inert lump? The common man answers yes. Hardly afraid of shocking everyone's judgment, our author denies the validity of this unprovable assumption and, supporting his denial by logic, he erects his narrative from beyond the grave.

It is not, to tell the truth, the first time that imagination has gone beyond the limits of life, those limits impassable to reason and before which all philosophy lowers its eyes, humbled; but I do not think that anyone has ever before in fiction given to the *recollections of a dead person* this character of exact definition and reasoned conviction. It is not a question here of fantastic adventures, of arbitrary complications, of dialogues . . . filled with fancy, but rather the matter of a veritable monograph patiently and methodically developed which seems to aspire to take its place among the other documents of humane philosophy. Mr. Poe has deduced from the phenomena of the dream the phenomena of the sensibility of the corpse; he has taken seriously the brotherhood of sleep and death of which so many poets have sung; and from this philosophical doctrine he has applied himself to drawing all the truths he could derive from it. One will agree that such work is not hackneyed. [Here follows a long quotation from "The Colloquy of Monos and Una" in which Monos describes his postmortem sensations.]

We shall not prolong this singular quotation which is indispensable for justifying what we said above of the unique character of Mr. Poe's work—in this instance, that of a dead man analyzing his posthumous sensations.

The final ruin of the globe, the destruction of our planet, is as methodically treated in the conversation of Eiros and Charmion as is the decomposition of the human being in that of Monos and Una. The principle is presented in the same way. Given the elementary fact that the breathable air is composed of twenty-one parts oxygen and seventy-nine parts nitrogen, . . . as well as the fact that the earth is surrounded by a thick atmosphere of nearly fifteen leagues, what would happen if the elliptical course around the sun taken by a comet led that comet into contact with the terrestrial globe? This is exactly the supposition Trissotin makes in *The Learned Ladies*,[4] but Mr. Poe does not adopt his way of viewing the problem. He sees the comet not as a massive and heavy body but as a whirlwind of impalpable material whose nucleus is of a density much less than that of our lightest gases. The imminent meeting does not present the same kind of danger as that of two locomotives rushing toward each other on the same rails; indeed, it even seems probable that the earth might pass through this enemy comet without difficulty. But what is likely to happen to us while we are in this peculiar situation? Oxygen, the principle of combustion, would become a hostile force, for nitrogen would be completely drawn out of our earthly atmosphere. And what would be the result of this double phenomenon? An irresistible combustion would devour all, would prevail over all. . . . On this fundamental idea, once conceded, the story develops with implacable logic, with inevitable deductions, with pitiless consequences. Challenge if you wish the major and minor premises which are the points of departure; the remainder is strictly unassailable.

[Here follows a detailed retelling of "The Conversation of Eiros and Charmion."]

You see, then, that this extraordinary story, this unprecedented freak of an imagination which nothing stops, has all the appearance, if not all the reality, of a severe logic. Few people will deny that a comet and the earth can meet in space. Granting this, one must recognize that the possibility of this conflagration of gas, this combustion of the atmosphere, and this horrible end of the entire human race, all of whom are reduced to breathing only fire, is at least very probable.

Having approached such problems, one takes pleasure in examining all those that philosophy seems eternally condemned to deny us the solution, reserved as they are to God. Mr. Poe is thus led to look for a plaus-

4. Trissotin in Molière's play, *Les Femmes savantes*, remarks: "Last night we had the narrowest escape! / A world passed just beside us, fell across / Our vortex; if in passing it had struck us, / We had been dashed to pieces just like glass." This allusion to Trissotin is odd, for Trissotin, meaning Triple Fool, is the name under which Molière satirized the Abbé Charles Cotin. A poet and member of the French Academy, Cotin had published a work entitled *Gallant Dissertation upon the Comet Which Appeared in December 1664 and January 1665.*

ible explanation of the human soul and of divinity. This is the subject of a third story entitled *Mesmeric Revelation*. The author imagines himself at the bedside of a skeptic who, arrived at the final stage of a fatal illness, has himself treated by mesmerism. Mr. Vankirk has all his life doubted the immortality of the soul. Now, troubled by the vague recollections that mesmeric trances have induced in him, he wonders if in this strange state a series of well-directed questions might not clarify . . . those metaphysical truths which philosophy has guessed but has badly explained because of the inadequacy of our ordinary resources. Indeed, granting that mesmeric action permits man to compensate for the imperfection of his finite organs and enables him while endowed with miraculous clairvoyance to be transported to that domain of creation which is beyond the senses, does it not follow that the mesmerized person is better qualified than others to explain to us the hidden realities of the invisible world? This prime point granted, do you trust the storyteller to give you by questions and answers a very probable theory of all that which is related to the division of soul and body, with the essence that constitutes . . . the superior order known under the name of God. . . ? It goes without saying that we do not take it upon ourselves to guarantee . . . the system expounded by the American storyteller. . . . [Here is explained Poe's conception of the unparticled materiality of God, to be found in "Mesmeric Revelation."]

We will not pursue this purely hypothetical revelation that reminds us of the inspirations or aspirations of those fiction writers of fourteen or fifteen years ago who found it fascinating to put into "madrigals" the visions of Jacob Boehm, of Saint Martin, of Swedenborg, and even of Mme Guyon. It must be said, however, that Mr. Poe's logic has a much more precise character. It is much more tenacious. . . . It is not satisfied with vague, grandiloquent words and with impenetrable formulas rendered with feigned rigor. Once the principles are posed, his logic deviates only rarely; it is always clear, always intelligible, and it takes possession of the reader in spite of himself.

It is time to return to earth and . . . follow this inexorable logic. . . .

In *The Gold-Bug* we can see all the ratiocinative faculties of man at grips with an apparently impenetrable cipher, upon the solution of which depends a rich pirate's treasure. . . . Later, in *A Descent into the Maelström*, Mr. Poe will tell us how a sound observation, a well-followed argument, will deliver safe and sound from the bottom of a Norwegian gulf an unfortunate fisherman carried away by a devouring whirlpool. We do not insist that ordinary verisimilitude be completely respected here—that a theory of gravity could be improvised by an uneducated countryman in a situation that would arrest the mental faculties . . . ; but if everything that is rigorously and strictly possible in the situation is conceived by the human mind, one must admit the possibility that extreme peril might induce in a man . . . a peculiar lucidity of intellect, a miraculous power of observation, and that is enough to make this story captivate you, as do the Anacandaïa [?] of ["Monk"] Lewis or the novel of *Frankenstein*, both of which are certainly not very probable.

Here is something easier to believe. [The power of Auguste Dupin is recounted, that of a man who is "first rate in all games in which success depends on the exact valuation of chances" and who is able to read his companion's mind from a few clues.]

Apply this astonishing perspicacity, the result of almost superhuman concentration of the mind and of a marvelous intuition, to a police operation and you have . . . an investigator whom nothing escapes. . . . Mr. Poe fastens upon this situation and with completely American tenacity develops the extraordinary events to their extreme limits.

Three or four stories rest on this very simple contrivance with very telling effect. We regret only that the foreign storyteller has thought to enhance the interest of these tales by locating them in Paris, of which he has not the least idea, and in our contemporary society, which is very badly known in the United States. . . . Mr. Poe was . . . not . . . unwise in removing his scenes to a distance in order to conceal the artifices of his painting and lend to it all the semblance of truth, but he should have foreseen that French readers, pausing before these canvases, would be astounded to find the capital of France completely overturned, the main quarters very suddenly dislodged—an Impasse Lamartine in the neighborhood of the Palais-Royal, a Rue Morgue in the Saint-Roch quarter, and the Barrière du Roule at the edge of the Seine "on the shore opposite the Rue Pavée-Saint-André." Neither should he have applied the ideas of a much more democratic country to our social structure by supposing that the prefect of police, at his wit's end and not knowing which way to turn to recover a mysterious letter . . . , would come one evening familiarly to smoke one or two cigars with the young observer of whom we have spoken, to ask his advice, to express his doubts, and to make a wager on the success of the measures proposed by this obliging counselor. Yet we do not cite all the blunders nor the most egregious ones that our red pencil has noted in the margin of these curious little fictions. These blunders are explained not only by their foreign origin but also by the method that the author adopts of transporting to our country some real chronicles chosen from among the crimes which have occupied the magistrates of New York or Boston. The story of Marie Roget . . . is a famous American case; the names alone have been changed to French ones; the incidents could not be. The Hudson becomes the Seine; Weehawken the Barrière du Roule: Nassau Street, the Rue Pavée-Saint-André, and so forth. Likewise, Marie Roget, the supposed young Parisian grisette, is no other than Mary Cecilia Rogers, the cigar girl whose mysterious murder terrified a few years ago the people of New York. Let us first tell the event as it was related in the *New York Mercury* or in *Brother Jonathan*. We will return to the fiction when we have an exact idea of the reality.

[Here is summarized the murder mystery of Mary Rogers as it was reported in the newspapers.]

Mr. Poe seizes upon this story in his turn and sets in the midst of all these conflicting newspaper accounts his unique character, this living syllogism of whom we have spoken. The Chevalier Dupin—such is the name he has fabricated for him, a truly characteristic name that has a very remarkable improbability and strangeness—the Chevalier Dupin, attentive to all the contradictory versions, discusses them rigorously and submits them to mathematical analysis. One sees that he has read in Laplace's *Philosophical Essay* the chapter devoted to *The Probability of the Judgments of Tribunals*. . . . His calculations of probability are striking and curious. That is all one must ask of them.

Novalis has this passage in his *Moral Ansichten:* "There are ideal series of events which run parallel with the real ones. They rarely coincide. Men and circumstances generally modify the ideal train of events, so that it seems imperfect, and its consequences are equally imperfect. Thus with the Reformation; instead of Protestantism came Lutheranism." In choosing this passage as the epigraph of his story, the American author explains to us his metaphysical design. When he exhibits the various hypotheses of the French (which is to say, American) journals on the subject of the murder committed in New York, when he exposes the gross errors of common logic, improvised as fodder for the unintelligent masses, his purpose is to prove that by virtue of certain principles an ideal series —one that is purely logical and consisting of mutually related facts—must lead, by an accumulation of mutually corroborative suppositions, to the nearest point of the real series or the truth. By an inexorable dialectic he thus destroys the false systems and, having thoroughly cleared the terrain, constructs a new edifice with all the pieces in place.

In the eyes of this remarkable thinker, the practice of the courts which restricts the admission of evidence to a few crucial facts is extremely erroneous. Modern science, which very often depends on the unexpected and proves the known by the unknown, understands better than the courts the importance of secondary incidents, of collateral evidence, which, above all, must be taken into consideration. There are seemingly inessential facts, apparent fortuities, which have become the foundation of the most complete and best-established systems. . . .

This principle once granted, the consequences are self-evident. By abandoning the main fact in order to concentrate on the details which seem insignificant, the Chevalier succeeds in establishing a number of circumstances that eventually serve to clarify the mystery.

[Here follows a retelling of "The Mystery of Marie Roget" which emphasizes Poe's power of logic.]

We do not give you—notice this well—a twentieth part of the reasonings which directly or indirectly corroborate this inference. . . .

Now that you have an idea of the American author in his favorite aspect, we should try to see him under another one. We have studied him as a logician, as a pursuer of abstract truths, and as a lover of the most eccentric hypotheses and the most difficult calculations. Now we should see him as a poet, as an inventor of objectless fantasies, of purely literary whims. We will confine ourselves to two tales we have expressly reserved for this purpose, *The Black Cat* and *The Man of the Crowd*.

The Black Cat reminds us of the gloomiest inspirations of Theodore Hoffmann. Never did the Sérapion Club listen to anything more fantastic than the story of this man, this unfortunate maniac, who harbors in his liquor-burned brain a monstrous hatred, the hatred of his poor cat. [Here follows a retelling of the story.]

The Man of the Crowd is not a story; it is a study, a simple idea vigorously rendered. [Here the tale is retold.]

We have already compared the talent of Mr. Poe with that of Washington Irving, the latter more cheerful, more varied, less ambitious, as well as to that of William Godwin, whose "sombre and unwholesome popularity" was so severely censured by Hazlitt. One must, however, recognize in the author of *St. Leon* and *Caleb Williams* more true philosophy and a tendency less pronounced toward purely literary paradox. If one wanted to show in America itself a predecessor of Mr. Edgar Poe, one could . . . compare him to Charles Brockden Brown who also searched in good faith, even in his most frivolous fictions, for the solution of some intellectual problem, taking pleasure as Mr. Poe does in describing those interior tortures, those obsessions of the soul, those maladies of the mind which offer so vast a field for observation and so many curious phenomena to the thoughtful makers of metaphysical systems.

Brockden Brown, it is true, wrote novels and we know of Poe only by very brief short stories, some no more than six to ten pages, but it would be unwise, it seems to us, to classify compositions of this genre by length. It is so easy to protract indefinitely a series of facts and so difficult, on the other hand, to condense . . . in the form of a tale a whole abstract theory with all the elements of an original concept. Today when the least scribbler appears with a melodrama in ten or twenty volumes, Richardson himself, if he returned to the world, would be . . . obliged to trim his characterizations, curtail his interminable dialogues, and reduce to finely wrought medallions the numerous figures of his vast canvases. Yesterday the victory was to large battalions; tomorrow it will belong to elite troops. From the great novels . . . one came to the stories of Voltaire and Diderot. . . . Tales like these of Mr. Poe's offer more substance to the mind, open newer horizons to the imagination, than twenty volumes like those of Courtilz de Sandras, de Baculard D'Arnaud, and de Lussan, precursors and prototypes of many contemporary story writers. . . .[5] Between such writers and the American author we will refrain from making comparisons. It will be opportune and useful to compare them when time has established the nascent reputation of the foreign storyteller and—who knows?—has shaken a little that of our prolific novelists.

5. Gatien Courtilz de Sandras (1644–1712) spent nine years in the Bastille for writing scandalous novels; Françoise-Thomas de Baculard D'Arnaud (1718–1803) and Marguerite de Lussan (1682–1758) were once popular novelists.

70. 9 *January 1847: Letter to Nathaniel P. Willis Published in the* Home
   Journal *(with Willis's Preface)*
   Edgar A. Poe

[*His "Reply to Mr. English and Others," his attempts to enlist Field,
Simms, and Duyckinck as allies (Documents 9, 41, 67), and his initiation
of a libel suit against the owners of the* Mirror *seem to have exhausted
Poe's possibilities for action against his persecutors. Even if he still had
the* Broadway Journal *at his disposal, he could hardly have defended
himself or assailed his enemies, for he was chronically ill, penniless, and
no doubt distraught at his wife's imminent death.*

*Now invited by Willis to "express anger . . . in print" about his edi-
torial "Disabled Labourers with the Brain," Poe wrote the letter below,
dated 30 December 1846, which Willis published on 9 January 1847, together with Duyckinck's article on Poe (Document 68). (Until now the
precise dating of the publication of this letter was impossible, for the
crucial issue of the* Home Journal *was unlocated and an undated clipping
in the Ingram Collection at the University of Virginia was all that was
available.)*

*One of the "anonymous letters" that Poe mentions was sent by Mrs.
Ellet (see Moss,* Poe's Literary Battles, *pages 207–21, for the reasons and
Poe's letters dated 18 October and 24 November 1848 in Ostrom, as well
as Ostrom's notes, for identification of her as the culprit). The "published
calumnies of Messrs _____," for which, Poe says, he yet hopes "to find
redress in a court of justice," were written, of course, by Hiram Fuller
and Thomas Dunn English. Poe said as much, almost to the very words,
in his October 18 letter, except that there he considered Mrs. Ellet to be
the manipulator of Fuller and English. There was, he wrote, "one instance, where the malignity of the accuser hurried her beyond her usual
caution, and thus the accusation was of such character that I could appeal
to a court of justice for redress. The tools employed in this instance were
Mr Hiram Fuller and Mr T. D. English." Poe may not have been so paranoiac as he sounds here, for Fuller on 8 July 1847 admitted: "There have
been actors behind the scenes in all this business, whom we may yet have
to call before the footlights" (Document 98). Moreover, we know for certain that Rufus Griswold was persecuted by Mrs. Ellet for three years
and that he found the situation intolerable. "From time to time during
. . . three years," he wrote,*

anonymous letters about me, made up of almost every species of slander and vituperation, were continually appearing in the public journals. If I was observed to be a visitor at the house of any gentleman of social or professional eminence, an anonymous letter against me was addressed to him. Gentlemen and ladies called at my own house at the peril of receiving communications of the same description. . . . All these communications, to individuals, or to the public, were easily traceable to the same circle, and the larger part of them to a single individual. . . .

The individual Griswold alluded to was, of course, Mrs. Ellet. (See Joy Bayless, Rufus Wilmot Griswold: Poe's Literary Executor, *especially page 229.)*

Mrs. Ellet's persecution of Griswold began in 1853. In 1850, however,. Griswold, still spared, made this statement about Poe's letter to Willis in his "Memoir of the Author": "This was written for effect. He had not been ill a great while, nor dangerously at all; there was no literary or personal abuse of him in the journals; and his friends in town had been applied to for money until their patience was nearly exhausted."

In a letter dated 10 March 1847 (it is a draft and may not have been sent), Poe explained to Mrs. Jane Locke why he denied having "ever materially suffered from privation": "a natural pride . . . impelled me to shrink from public charity, even at the cost of truth. Those necessities," he added, *"were but too real" (Ostrom, II, 347).]*

MR. POE.—We have received the following letter from this gentleman. It speaks for itself. What was the under-current of feeling in his mind while it was written, can be easily understood by the few; but it carries enough on its surface to be sufficiently understood. In another column, we give a communication respecting his literary position, kindly furnished by one of the best of our scholars and gentlemen.

MY DEAR WILLIS:—The paragraph which has been put in circulation respecting my wife's illness, my own, my poverty, etc., is now lying before me; together with the beautiful lines by Mrs. Locke and those by Mrs.——, to which the paragraph has given rise, as well as your kind and manly comments in "THE HOME JOURNAL."

The motive of the paragraph I leave to the conscience of him or her who wrote it or suggested it. Since the thing is done, however, and since the concerns of my family are thus pitilessly thrust before the public, I perceive no mode of escape from a public statement of what is true and what erroneous in the report alluded to.

That my wife is ill, then, is true; and you may imagine with what feeling I add that this illness, hopeless from the first, has been heightened and precipitated by her reception, at two different periods, of anonymous letters—one enclosing the paragraph now in question; the other, those published calumnies of Messrs——, for which I yet hope to find redress in a court of justice.

Of the facts, that I myself have been long and dangerously ill, and that my illness has been a well understood thing among my brethren of the press, the best evidence is afforded by the innumerable paragraphs of personal and of literary abuse with which I have been latterly assailed. This matter, however, will remedy itself. At the very first blush of my new prosperity, the gentlemen who toadied me in the old, will recollect themselves and toady me again. You, who know me, will comprehend that I speak of these things only as having served, in a measure, to lighten the gloom of unhappiness, by a gentle and not unpleasant sentiment of mingled pity, merriment and contempt.

That, as the inevitable consequence of so long an illness, I have been in want of money, it would be folly in me to deny—but that I have ever materially suffered from privation, beyond the extent of my capacity for suffering, is not altogether true. That I am "without friends" is a gross calumny, which I am sure *you* never could have believed, and which a thousand noble-hearted men would have good right never to forgive me for permitting to pass unnoticed and undenied. Even in the city of New York I could have no difficulty in naming a hundred persons, to each of whom—when the hour for speaking had arrived—I could and would have applied for aid and with unbounded confidence, and with absolutely *no* sense of humiliation.

I do not think, my dear Willis, that there is any need of my saying more. I am getting better, and may add—if it be any comfort to my enemies—that I have little fear of getting worse. The truth is, I have a great deal to do; and I have made up my mind not to die till it is done.

Sincerely yours,
EDGAR A. POE.

December 30th, 1846.

71. 8 January 1847: The Philadelphia Spirit of the Times Comments on Poe's Letter in the Home Journal
John S. Du Solle

[*Du Solle at Godey's direction had printed "Mr. Poe's Reply to Mr. English and Others" in his newspaper (Document 24), though the article had alleged that English's "primary thrashing . . . was bestowed upon him . . . by Mr. John S. Du Solle, the editor of 'The Spirit of the Times,' who could not very well get over acting with this indecorum on account of Mr. E's amiable weakness—a propensity for violating the privacy of a publisher's MSS." Now with the* Home Journal *of 9 January 1847 in his possession—the* Home Journal, *like other magazines, appeared earlier than its dateline indicates—Du Solle felt obliged to comment upon Poe's letter to Nathaniel P. Willis.*]

WE NEVER THINK OF MR. POE, the brilliant but bitter writer, but the Persian saying saturates the singular impression, viz: "The rose prayed for a gift, and the genius gave it thorns. The rose wept, until it saw the antelope eating lilies!" If Mr. P. had not been gifted with considerable gall, he would have been devoured long ago by the host of enemies his genius has created.

In the "Home Journal" of this week, we find a letter from Mr. P. full of this interesting mixture of acerbity and self-confidence. It is Poe-ish all over! In very truth we sincerely respect both the singular ability and fascinating diablerie that pervade all Mr. P's intellectual productions. When his celebrated M. Valdemar mystification appeared, it delighted us beyond expression. We were in London at the time, and its republication there as a grave statement of facts, compelled us to admit it one of the most triumphant imitations of reality, upon record. Mr. P. now says:

"I am getting better, and may add—if it be any comfort to my enemies—that I have little fear of getting worse. The truth is, I have a great deal to do; and I have made up my mind not to die till it is done."

72. 16 January 1847: "Editorial Delicacy"
Yankee Doodle

[Yankee Doodle, *a New York weekly modeled on* Punch, *was issued by members of the Duyckinck circle from October 1846 to October 1847. G. G. Foster, the original editor who had earlier been on the* Tribune *staff and who later became T. D. English's co-editor on the* John-Donkey, *another humor magazine, was succeeded by Duyckinck's closest friend, Cornelius Mathews. Herman Melville, Nathaniel P. Willis, and Horace Greeley were among those who published unsigned articles in the weekly.*

During its brief existence Yankee Doodle *engaged in a slanging match with the* Mirror, *its chief target, calling it the* "Mirror of Nighthood" *and the* "Evening Opiate." *It labeled English's* 1844; or, The Power of the "S.F.," *then appearing in both* Mirrors, "*an admirable sudorific (the smallest conceivable quantity acting immediately, emetically and otherwise),*" *and alleged that* "Poh" *wanted to know if* "S.F." *stood for* "Stupid Fiction." *It also ran such items as the following under the head* "To Scavengers Out of Work": "*Wanted, several fearless and unprincipled men to search a deep and filthy sewer for the little valuables which may perhaps have accidentally fallen into it—Apply to the Office of the* Evening Mirror."

Fuller, of course, responded in kind, referring to Yankee Doodle's "*usual running attack on the* Mirror." "*Its squibs at us,*" *Fuller remarked, are* "*prompted by revenge,*" *and he observed that* Yankee Doodle *had done its* "*best to imitate the London 'Punch,'*" *and had succeeded, "excepting the wit, humor, good-nature, philanthropy, fun, learning, didacticism, and embellishments."*

Yankee Doodle *had other targets than the* Mirror, *of course. One was the* "paralytic" North American Review, *which had recently (October 1846) attacked Poe, Simms, and Mathews, whose books had appeared in Duyckinck's* Library of American Books. *Another was Lewis Gaylord Clark of the* Knickerbocker *who was called* "A Lying Editor, A Busy-Body Editor, A Critical Editor Paid to Puff, A Jobby Editor, A Cockney Editor." *Another was Rufus Wilmot Griswold, the indefatigable anthologist.* "Let no one plunder you of your brains," Yankee Doodle *declared;* "*they are your own property; and let no one put his Griswold Hook into your jaws or nose.*" *Still another was Longfellow, typically called* "H. W. Briefbody" *or author of* "Noises of the Night," *whose* "Excelsior" *was par-*

odied. Even Poe was not spared. His "Haunted Palace" was travestied under the title, "The Haunted Pastry." Now with Poe helpless and his private affairs bandied about in print, Yankee Doodle carried a sympathetic article about him, though earlier it had found occasion for humor in Willis's editorial (see headnote to Document 62).

Apart from its role in the Poe-Fuller controversy, Yankee Doodle, like other American humor magazines of the period, was very dull. As James Russell Lowell remarked in his Fable for Critics:

> Petty thieves, kept from flagranter crimes by their fears,
> Shall peruse Yankee Doodle a blank term of years,—
> That American Punch, like the English, no doubt,—
> Just the sugar and lemons and spirit left out.]

EDITORIAL DELICACY.—We have been inexpressibly delighted with the the considerate delicacy and forbearance with which the temporary misfortunes of a distinguished author have been recently dragged before the public by the newspapers. Every mean-spirited cur, who dared not bark when his tormentor had strength, feeds fat his ancient grudge, now that he sees his enemy prostrate and powerless—with heart crushed and brain shattered by the sickness and suffering of those most dear to him in life. This shows in a just and flattering light the prudence and discrimination of the Press, and is a pregnant commentary on the blessings of type-metal.

---

73. 1 February 1847: Creation of a Commission To Obtain Thomas Dunn English's Deposition

[When the court convened as scheduled on February 1, English, the chief witness for the defense, was absent. Though he had pledged "to make my charges good by the most ample and satisfactory evidence" (Document 27), English in the previous month had gone to Washington, D.C., to avoid the trial. William H. Paine, attorney for the defense, urged the court to secure his deposition. Justice Aaron H. Vanderpoel of New York Superior Court acceded to his wishes and created a commission consisting of John Ross Browne, J. B. H. Smith, and John Lorimer Graham, Jr., to interrogate English in Washington. At the same time Justice Van-

derpoel postponed further proceedings in the case until the third Monday in February, which was February 15. (A harsh "Mirror Reflex" of the Judge appears in the Evening Mirror *of 21 June 1846 and in the* Weekly Mirror *of 4 July 1846.)*

John Ross Browne (1821–1875) was serving at this time as private secretary to Robert J. Walker, secretary of the treasury. Among other works, he wrote Etchings of a Whaling Cruise *(1846), which Herman Melville reviewed for the Duyckincks'* Literary World *on 6 March 1847. J. B. H. Smith was an attorney at law. As it turned out, he was the only commissioner to secure English's testimony. John Lorimer Graham (1835–1876) became the owner of Poe's personal copy of* The Raven and Other Poems *in which the poet had made revisions with an eye to republication. (A facsimile of the volume has been edited by Thomas O. Mabbott.) His position in Washington at this time cannot be determined, for the city directories for 1846, 1850, and 1853 do not list him and it seems there was no city directory published in 1847.*

The order creating the commission to receive English's deposition was a standard printed form. The information that was penned into this form is here put into brackets to distinguish it from the printed matter.]

The People *of the State of New-York, To* [J. Ross Browne, J. B. H. Smith & John Lorimer Graham, Junior]

> KNOW YE, That we, with full faith in your prudence and competency, have appointed you *Commisioner* and by these presents do authorize you, [or any one of you] to examine [Thomas Dunn English]

as *witness* in a cause pending in the [Superior Court of the City of New York, between Edgar A. Poe, plaintiff, & Hiram Fuller and Augustus W. Clason, Junior] *defendant*[s] on the part of the [defendants] on oath, upon the interrogatories annexed to this Commission, to take and certify the depositions of the *witness* and return the same according to the directions hereunto annexed.

WITNESS, [Samuel Jones, Esq., Chief Justice]
the [First Mon]day of [February] one thousand eight hundred and [forty-seven]

[J. Oakley
Clerk]

· · · · · · · · · · ·

This Commission, when executed, is to be returned [by mail to the Clerk of the Superior Court of the City and County of New York. Dated 8 February 1847.

A. Vanderpoel, Justice of Superior Court &c]
The execution of this Commission appears in certain schedules hereunto annexed.

Commissioner

. . . .

---

74. *8 February 1847: Direct and Cross-Interrogatories To Be Put to Thomas Dunn English*

[*More was needed than a commission to obtain testimony from English, who had gone to Washington, D.C. (see headnote to preceding document), and had found employment as a newspaper correspondent. Questions to be asked of English had to be prepared for the commission.*

Since English was the star witness for the defense, the defense attorney, William H. Paine, drew up the direct interrogatories, while Poe's attorney drew up the cross-interrogatories. These interrogatories were approved by Justice Aaron H. Vanderpoel of the Superior Court on February 8.]

Superior Court

Hiram Fuller and
Augustus W. Clason, Junior
            ads [*ad sectam*; i.e., at the suit of]
Edgar A. Poe

-- -- -- -- -- -- -- -- --

Order
[signed] Wm H. Paine
                        Atty fr Defts

$1.00

New York Superior Court: Interrogatories to be administered to Thomas Dunn English
            of the City of Washington in the District of Columbia, a witness to be produced. Sworn and examined under and by virtue of the an-

nexed Commission before J. Ross Browne, J. B. H. Smith, and John Lorimer Graham, Junior, of the City of Washington aforesaid, the Commissioners therein named, in a certain cause now pending and at issue in the Superior Court of the City and County of New York wherein Edgar A. Poe is plaintiff and Hiram Fuller and Augustus W. Clason, Junior, defendants: on the part and behalf of the said defendants.

First interrogatory: Do you know Edgar A. Poe? If yea, how long and how intimately have you known him?

Second interrogatory: What is the general character of said Poe?

Third interrogatory: Have you ever been connected with him as an editor? If yea, what is his character as an editor and critic?

Fourth interrogatory: State the particulars of a pecuniary transaction with Edgar A. Poe referred to in an article published in the Evening Mirror of the twenty-third day of June in the year one thousand eight hundred and forty-six, over the signature of Thomas Dunn English.

Fifth interrogatory: State what you know of the charge of forgery imputed to Edgar A. Poe in an article alluded to in last interrogatory.

General [sixth] interrogatory: State any thing further within your knowledge pertinent to the matter in issue.

[initialed] E.L.F [ancher].

> I allow the above interrogatories
> Dated 8 Feby 1847
> [signed] A Vanderpoel

N Y Superior Court

Edgar A. Poe	I allow these cross interrogatories
vs.	Dated 8 Feby 1847
Hiram Fuller and	[signed] A Vanderpoel
Augustus W. Clason, Jr.	

Cross-interrogatories in the above cause to be administered to Thomas Dunn English, a witness to be examined under and by virtue of the annexed Commission:

First cross-interrogatory: What is your present business or profession, and in what have you been engaged for the last two years?

Second cross-interrogatory: Do you know the defendants in this suit and how long have you known them?

Third cross-interrogatory: Are you acquainted with, or were you, in and about the month of June last, in the habit of seeing or reading a paper published in the City of New York called "The Evening Mirror"? If yea, do you know who at that time was the editor, and who the proprietor of that paper, and if so state.

Fourth cross-interrogatory: Did you see or read in the Evening Mirror, of the date of the 23^d day of June 1846, a card or article entitled "Mr English's Reply to Mr Poe," and signed "Thomas Dunn English"? If yea, are you the author and writer of that article? (The latter branch of interrogatories witness not obliged to answer, if by answering he may criminate himself.)

Fifth cross-interrogatory: Had you any and what agency in procuring the publication of that article in the Evening Mirror? To whom did you hand the manuscript, and what inducement or offer, if any, did you make for its publication? (Not obliged to answer, if it may criminate.)

Sixth cross-interrogatory: Supposing this suit to be an action for alleged libellous matter contained in that article, and that a recovery should be had against the defendants for such publication, are you in any manner obligated, or under promise to the defendants or either of them, to indemnify them from such recovery, or to share or pay the damages and costs? If so, state particularly.

Seventh cross-interrogatory: Did Edgar A. Poe personally ever receive from your hands any money for which you now hold or in June last held acknowledgements? If so, state when and where, and produce such acknowledgements and set forth a copy of it.

Eighth cross-interrogatory: Did not Mr John Bisco apply to you and receive the money alluded to when Mr Poe was not present, and what was the amount? And at the time you gave Mr Bisco such money, were you not indebted to Mr Poe for an article relating to American poetry published by you in a periodical called "The Aristidean"?

Ninth cross-interrogatory: Had you not, previous to Mr Bisco's calling on you, caused to be published in "The Aristidean" articles or an article or some portion thereof from Mr Poe's manuscript which had been written by him, and for which you had never paid him?

Tenth cross-interrogatory: Have you ever and how often paid Mr Poe for
  literary articles to be published by you, or which you had published?
  [initialed] E.L.F[ancher].

---

75. 6 February 1847: "Death of Mrs. Edgar A. Poe"
Nathaniel P. Willis

[*On January 30 Willis and George Pope Morris, his partner, went in
bitter-cold weather to Fordham to attend the funeral for Virginia Poe.
With the exception of Sarah Lewis of Brooklyn, whose poems Poe had
edited and praised for a fee, no other literary figures appeared. The literati
saw no occasion in Virginia's death to forgive Poe his derelictions.*

*In addition to Mrs. Lewis's husband, there were Mrs. Shew, a nurse,
who had come earlier to tend Poe's failing wife and who remained for the
funeral; Eliza Herring (Mrs. Smith), a relative; Mary Devereaux, an early
girl friend of Poe who had known Virginia when the deceased was a
child; and finally some neighbors, including the John Valentines whose
cottage Poe was renting. The Valentines, aware that Poe had no grave
plot or money to purchase one, put their family vault in Fordham's Dutch
Reformed Church cemetery at his disposal.*

Willis's statement, made in the Home Journal, *that Virginia's "loss is
mourned by a numerous circle of friends" was in the circumstances more
kind than accurate.*]

DEATH OF MRS. EDGAR A. POE.—Among the deaths, last week, we regret to notice that of Mrs. Poe, who fell a victim to pulmonary consumption. Mrs. Poe was an estimable woman and an excellent wife. Her loss
is mourned by a numerous circle of friends.

---

76. 11 February 1847: J. B. H. Smith Takes Thomas Dunn English's
Testimony

[*Smith, a Washington attorney and a member of the three-man commission appointed to take English's testimony, was the only one to examine*

English. John Ross Browne could not attend the examination because of his official duties, and John Lorimer Graham could not be located.

The direct and cross-interrogatories are interpolated in brackets to make this portion of the court record easier to read.]

Depositions of witness—produced, sworn and examined the eleventh day of February in the year one thousand eight hundred and forty-seven at the office of J. B. H. Smith in the City of Washington, D. C., under and by virtue of a commission issued out of the Superior Court of the City of New York in a certain cause therein depending and at issue between Edgar A. Poe, plaintiff, and Hiram Fuller and Augustus W. Clason, Junior, defendants, as follows.

Thomas Dunn English of the City of New York, at present in the City of Washington, by occupation an author, aged twenty-eight years, being duly and publickly sworn pursuant to the directions hereto annexed and examined on the part of the defendants, doth depose and say as follows.

To wit:

To the first interrogatory [Do you know Edgar A. Poe? If yea, how long and how intimately have you known him?] he saith: I know Edgar A. Poe; became acquainted with him shortly after he was first associated with Mr Wm E. Burton in the conduct of the Gentleman's Magazine. This was sometime previous to the year 1840. I cannot say in what year without I had the files of the Magazine by me to refresh my memory. Our acquaintanceship at portions of the time was very intimate.

To the 2^d interrogatory [What is the general character of said Poe?] he saith: The general character of said Poe is that of a notorious liar, a common drunkard and of one utterly lost to all the obligations of honor.

To the 3^d interrogatory [Have you ever been connected with him as an editor? If yea, what is his character as an editor and critic?] he saith: No.

To the 4th interrogatory [State the particulars of a pecuniary transaction with Edgar A. Poe referred to in an article published in the Evening Mirror of the twenty-third day of June in the year one thousand eight hundred and forty-six, over the signature of Thomas Dunn English] he saith: Mr Poe called upon me, I think in the early part of October 1845; stated that he had an opportunity to purchase the whole of the Broadway Journal, of which he said he was then part owner; that he lacked a part of the money necessary to effect the purchase; that if I would let him have the money which he desired he would let me have an interest in said journal; that the said journal would be profitable to those concerned in it, which consideration induced me to loan him the money he required, which was only $30, being aware that my only chance of re-payment would be from the profits of said journal. I had not the money by me & Mr Poe was to send for it the next day. Accordingly at the time appointed, Mr John Bisco, the person of whom Mr Poe had said the remaining interest in said journal had to be purchased, called on me with a written order from Mr Poe. I gave him the money & retained the order, which I have since mislaid. Mr Pot not only never repaid me the money but never conveyed nor offered to convey to me an interest in said journal. This and the fact that I afterwards learned that the said journal was not a profitable investment constituted the false pretences to which I referred in the article alluded to in this interrogatory.

To the 5th interrogatory [State what you know of the charge of forgery imputed to Edgar A. Poe in an article alluded to in last interrogatory] he saith: The charge of forgery referred to was made against Mr Poe by a merchant in Broad street, whose name I forget. Mr Poe stated to me that this gentleman was jealous of him and of his visits to Mrs Frances S. Osgood, the writer, the wife of S. S. Osgood, the artist; that this gentleman was desirous of having criminal connection with Mrs Osgood; and that, supposing he, Mr Poe, to be a favored rival, he had cautioned Mrs Osgood against receiving his, Poe's, visits, alleging to her that he, Poe, had been guilty of forgery upon his, Poe's, uncle. Mr Poe then said to me that his rival was a great rascal & with a profuse flood of tears asked my advice as to what course he should pursue. As the charge was a serious one, I advised that some friend of Mr Poe should wait upon the gentleman who had made the charges and request either a denial or a retraction. Mr Poe requested me to perform this office & I consented. I called on the gentleman, who would not on his own responsibility avow the truth of the charge nor would he retract, saying he was not sure whether he had heard it from a certain other person whom he named, or whether he himself had told it to that person. He declined holding any further conversation on the subject from the contempt which he held for Mr Poe, avowing at the same time, in answer to an inquiry from me, that his refusal arose from *no* want of respect for myself. On communicating these facts to Mr Poe, he asked my advice as to what course he should next pursue. I told him that he had his alternative, as long as his adversary would not retract, either to fight or bring suit. The latter he preferred; &, as he said he had no money to fee a lawyer, I induced a friend of mine to take charge of his suit without a fee to oblige me. Mr Poe afterwards informed me that he had received an unsatisfactory apology from his adversary. I am not certain whether he read me portions of this apology or stated to me its general nature, but the impression on my mind at the time was that the apology was by no means sufficient. I advised him to prosecute the matter until a retraction or an atonement could be obtained. This, so far as I know, was never obtained. I should mention also that I bore a note from Mr Poe to his adversary, which he refused to answer.

To the 6th [general] interrogatory [State any thing further within your knowledge pertinent to the matter in issue] he saith: He knows nothing further in the matter.

[signed] Thos Dunn English   [signed] J. B. H. Smith
                Acting Commissioner

Answers to Cross-Interrogatories

To the 1^t cross-interrogatory [What is your present business or profession, and in what have you been engaged for the last two years?] he saith: That of an author & editor, & I have been the same for the last two years with the exception of some eight or nine months or more, during which I held the office of weigher of the customs at New York.

To the 2^d cross-interrogatory [Do you know the defendants in this suit and how long have you known them?] he saith: I do. Mr Fuller I have known some time but not intimately; Mr. Clason less time & less intimately; cannot say now how long.

To the 3^d cross-interrogatory [Are you acquainted with, or were you, in and about the month of June last, in the habit of seeing or reading a paper published in the City of New York called "The Evening Mirror"? If yea, do you know who at that time was the editor, and who the proprietor of that paper, and if so state] he saith: I was in June last and am now. The editor and proprietor of the paper in June last was Mr Hiram Fuller, one of the defendants.

To the 4th cross-interrogatory [Did you see or read in the Evening Mirror, of the date of the 23^d day of June 1846, a card or article entitled "Mr English's Reply to Mr Poe," and signed "Thomas Dunn English"? If yea, are you the author and writer of that article?] he saith: I did see and read the article referred to in this interrogatory, and I am its author & writer.

To the 5th [cross-]interrogatory [Had you any and what agency in procuring the publication of that article in the Evening Mirror? To whom did you hand the manuscript, and what inducement or offer, if any, did you make for its publication?] he saith: I handed the article referred to, to Mr Fuller, the editor & proprietor of the Mirror, with a request that he would publish it. I made no inducement or offer for its publication beyond the fact that, as Mr. Poe had libelled me, I urged that the Mirror as a public newspaper should be open to my reply.

To the 6th cross-interrogatory [Supposing this suit to be an action for alleged libellous matter contained in that article, and that a recovery should be had against the defendants for such publication, are you in any manner obligated, or under promise to the defendants or either of them, to indemnify them from such recovery, or to share or pay the damages and costs? If so, state particularly] he saith: I am not.

To the 7th cross-interrogatory [Did Edgar A. Poe personally ever receive from your hands any money for which you now hold or in June last held acknowledgements? If so, state when and where, and produce such acknowledgements and set forth a copy of it] he saith: Not to Mr Poe personally but to Mr Bisco for Mr Poe I paid the sum of $30 under the circumstances stated in my answer to the 4th direct interrogatory. The acknowledgment for which sum I held in June last but have since mislaid.

To the 8th cross-interrogatory [Did not Mr John Bisco apply to you and receive the money alluded to when Mr Poe was not present, and what was the amount? And at the time you gave Mr Bisco such money, were you not indebted to Mr Poe for an article relating to American poetry published by you in a periodical called "The Aristidean"?] he saith: Mr John Bisco did apply to me, as stated in my answer to the 4th direct interrogatory, & received from me the sum of $30. I was not indebted to Mr Poe at the time for the article referred to, nor was I indebted to him at all.

To the 9th cross-interrogatory [Had you not, previous to Mr Bisco's calling on you, caused to be published in "The Aristidean" articles or an article or some portion thereof from Mr Poe's manuscript which had been written by him, and for which you had never paid him?] he saith: I did not. I never published any thing from the pen of Mr Poe for which I did not pay him promptly on the delivery to me of the manuscript, except an article on American Poetry, or a portion of an article on said subject, which was given to me by Mr Poe without solicitation in the presence of Mr Thomas H. Lane.

To the 10th cross-interrogatory [Have you ever and how often paid Mr Poe for literary articles to be published by you, or which you had published?] he saith: I have, but do not recollect how often.

[signed] Thos Dunn English   [signed] J. B. H. Smith
                                               Acting Commissioner

Examination taken, reduced to writing, and by the witness subscribed and sworn to this eleventh day of February 1847, before
                                               [signed] J. B. H. Smith
                                               Acting Commissioner

I, J. B. H. Smith, Commissioner, acting by virtue of the annexed commission, do further certify that I notified & requested J. Ross Browne, one of the Commissioners mentioned in annexed commission, to attend the taking of the deposition of Thomas Dunn English, but he said he could not attend the same on account of his official duties as a Clerk in the Treasury Department of the W. T.; and further, that John L. Graham, the other Commissioner named in said commission, was not notified to attend because he could not be found.

Feb. 11, 1847.   [signed] J. B. H. Smith
                                               Acting Commissioner

I also certify that the erasure in the answer to the 8th cross-interrogatory was made in the presence of the witness and before this deposition was signed.
                                               [signed] J. B. H. Smith
                                               Act. Comm.

---

77. 17 February 1847: Hiram Fuller Announces He Stands Trial Today

[English's deposition enabled the court to hold the trial for libel. On the day of that trial, Fuller made one brief and amused comment in the Evening Mirror. He failed to mention that his chief witness, Thomas Dunn English, had gone to Washington, D.C., to escape involvement in the proceedings and would not be present in court.]

We are undergoing the luxury to-day of a trial for libel on *Edgar A Poe*, contained in a card of Thomas Dunn English. E. L. Fancher, persecuting [*sic*] attorney. Particulars to-morrow.

---

78. *17 February 1847: Verdict in the Case of Edgar A. Poe vs. Hiram Fuller and Augustus W. Clason, Jr.*

[*The trial was held on February 17 before Samuel Jones, Chief Justice of New York Superior Court, some seven months after Poe first filed his Declaration of Grievances against Fuller and Clason. There is no verbatim transcript of the proceedings in the New York Hall of Records, for it was only during the second decade of the twentieth century that New York court rules required in the case of civil suits a verbatim transcript prepared by a court reporter. If a reporter had been present at this trial, his duty was prescribed by statute. Upon order of the attorneys engaged in the trial, he was to prepare a transcript at their cost. If ordered, this verbatim transcript would be retained by the attorneys as their own property, and only a narrative condensation of the verbatim record, such as is reprinted below, would be filed in the Hall of Records.*

Fuller kept a transcript of the trial, according to his statements in the Evening Mirror *(Documents 82, "Law and Libel," and 88), as Poe's attorney may have, but he refused to make it public on the grounds that "it involves a good deal of delicate matter, and introduces the names of several literary ladies." Actually, the name of only one lady appears in the record, that of Mrs. Osgood, and her name was genteelly passed over in court (Document 81).*

For more information than appears in the summary reprinted below, we have to turn to collateral accounts. From them we learn that Poe's attorney called Edward J. Thomas to clear Poe of the charge of forgery and two men to act as character witnesses, Mordecai Manuel Noah and Freeman Hunt. Thomas was a well-to-do merchant conducting business in Broad Street. Major Noah was a politician and journalist; according to Duyckinck, "there was no man better known in his day in New York." (When he ran for sheriff of New York City, he was taunted for his religion. "Pity," his opponent said, "that Christians are hereafter to be hung by a Jew." "Pretty Christians," retorted the Major, "to require hanging at all.") Hunt was best known for originating and editing the first magazine in America concerned exclusively with commerce, Hunt's Merchants' Magazine.

Thomas admitted under questioning that Poe frequently got drunk, but testified that the charge of forgery was baseless. Noah's and Hunt's testimony was that they never "heard anything" against Poe "except that he is occasionally addicted to intoxication." Hunt probably did not regard this statement as damaging, for his obituary in the New York Times of 4 March 1858 states that "he had an unfortunate foible for drink." To establish Clason's guilt, Poe's attorney took the stand to testify that Clason was Fuller's partner in the Mirror enterprise, a proceeding whose legality Fuller subsequently challenged in his paper.

Clason conducted the defense on his own behalf and Fuller's, supplanting William H. Paine, the original lawyer in the case. He introduced English's deposition, though it conceded, contrary to English's original charge in Document 13, that English did not "hold Mr. Poe's acknowledgement for a sum of money" which Poe had allegedly obtained from him "under false pretenses," and that, in fact, Poe had never written him such an acknowledgment. English's deposition also made it clear that he had not paid to have his so-called Card printed in the Mirror; his article, therefore, was not considered an advertisement by the court and blame redounded to the defendants for giving it circulation. Clason moved for a dismissal of himself as a defendant in the suit on the grounds that he was not a co-owner of the Mirror, but his motion was denied in the light of Fancher's testimony. Clason then moved for a verdict of acquittal, which was also denied. Whether Clason called Colonel William Lummis (Mrs. Ellet's brother) and O. W. Sturtevant(?), an unidentified person who remains a mystery, cannot be determined, though no doubt they were intended as character witnesses against Poe.

Clason summed up the case for the defense, arguing that he was not a partner in the Mirror firm and that Poe was not entitled to favorable consideration by the jury on account of his disreputable character. What Fancher said to the jury is not known, but no doubt he refuted Clason's arguments and reviewed the evidence which showed that Poe had not committed forgery; that he had not taken money from English under false pretenses; that, except for a weakness for intoxicants, he was of good character and reputation; and that the defendants were guilty of circulating libels against Poe that did him severe injury.

*Chief Justice Jones then instructed the jury to decide whether En-
glish's charges were libelous and, if so, whether there was "mitigation in
relation to them as to the character of Mr. P(oe)." Given the evidence,
the jury had no recourse but to return a verdict of guilty against the defendants, and Poe was awarded $225.06 in damages, the six cents being
the token that the defendants had to bear court costs, adjudged to be
$101.42. The award of $225.06 was considerably less, of course, than the
$5,000 Poe had sued for, but it was equivalent to awards wrested by
James Fenimore Cooper in the libel suits he brought against the American press from 1837 to 1845.*

*The news that his name had been cleared in court must have been
anticlimactic for Poe at this time. His wife Virginia had died less than
three weeks earlier. Broken in health and spirit, he was not present at
court when the verdict was read.]*

Afterwards, that is to say another day, and at the place last above
mentioned, to wit, on the seventeenth day of February, one thousand
eight hundred and forty-seven, before the Hon. Samuel Jones, Chief Justice of the said Superior Court of the City of New York, according to the
form of the statute in such case made and provided, come as well the
above-named plaintiff as the above-named defendants, by their respective attorneys above mentioned; and the jurors of the jury summoned to
try the said issue, being called, also come, who to speak the truth of the
matters aforesaid, being chosen, tried and sworn, say upon their oath
that the said defendants are guilty of the premises above laid to their
charge, in manner and form as the said plaintiff hath above complained
against them; and they assess the damages of the said plaintiff by reason
of the premises, over and above his costs and charges by him about his
suit in this behalf expended, to two hundred and twenty-five dollars, and
for those costs and charges to six cents.

Therefore it is considered that the said plaintiff do recover against
the said defendants, his said damages, costs, and charges, by the jurors
aforesaid in form aforesaid assessed, and also the sum of one hundred
and one dollars and forty-two cents, for his said costs and charges by the
said court nowhere adjudged of increase to the said plaintiff, and with
his assent; which said damages, costs, and charges in the whole amount
to three hundred and twenty-six dollars and forty-eight cents.

And the said defendants in mercy, &c

Judgment signed this twenty-second day of February, one thousand eight hundred and forty-seven.

[signed] J. Oakley [court clerk]

---

79. 17 February 1847: "Rough Minutes" of the Trial

[*The "Rough Minutes" of the trial, though brief, supply information found in no other record—the names of the jurymen, the persons called as witnesses, and the order of the proceedings.*

Though the roles played at the trial by Edward J. Thomas, M. M. Noah, and Freeman Hunt have been explained (headnote to Document 78), there is no information that explains the identities and testimony of James L. Smith, E. R. Webb, and Officer Galligher, though no doubt they were called to the witness stand. The same is true for O. W. Sturtevant(?) and William Lummis, except that we know Lummis was Mrs. Ellet's brother who frightened Poe into declaring himself temporarily insane to avoid a duel (see headnote to Document 89).

Since I could not obtain a photostatic copy of these "Rough Minutes" from the Office of the New York County Clerk, I have had to reply upon a handwritten copy of the original record that was generously sent me by William Henry Gravely, Jr., the biographer of Thomas Dunn English, who was the first to discover the "Minutes" in the Hall of Records.]

[*Rough Minutes*, Dec. 1846, to Dec. 1847—Superior Court]
Wednesday Morning Febry 17, 1847
The Court met pursuant to adjournment

Present

His Honor
The Ch. Justice

The Court is opened

Edgar A. Poe		E. L. Fancher
vs		Atty for Ptff
Hiram Fuller &		
Augustus Clason Jr[.]		Trial
Mr Fancher opens the case		Wm H. Paine
		Atty for Defts

Evdce for Ptff	Jurors &c &c	

Edwin Miles	Thos. Shannon
A. Arnold	S. Munn
John C. Hashagan	Wm Quackinbush
M. H. Duckworth	Wm B. Marsh
Chester Jennings	Richd McKim
Moses Gregory	M. M. Hendricks

Jas. L. Smith
Evening Mirror 23 June 1846
Weekly Mirror 27   ”   ”
E. R. Webb
Libel read
Edward J. Thomas
Letter from Thomas
  to Ptff
M. M. Noah
Freeman Hunt
  —Ptff rests—
E. L. Fancher
  Ptff. again rests

Officer Sworn

   "Galligher"

Mr. Clason opens the Defence
Evidce for Defts—

Depn of Thos. D. English
  Wm Lummis
  O. W. Sturtevant [?]

Mr. Clason moves for the Dis-
charge of Def[endan]t Clason & for
a verdict of acquit[t]al.
Jury who retire ————
  Defts rest
Mr Clason sums up for the de-
f[endan]ts
Mr Fancher   ”   ”   ”   ” Ptff
The Court charges the
Mo. denied ————————

The Jury return into Court, and say that they find a verdict for the Ptff for $225—Damages and six cents costs[.]
(Judg[men]t final thereon)

Paid

**80. *18 February 1847: The Trial as Reported in the New York* Sun,
Morning Express, *and* Daily Tribune**

[*A nameless reporter, who sometimes called himself "Yorick," made a
living by syndicating his reports of New York court cases to any news-*

paper that wished his services. House style aside, the reports in the three newspapers specified above are identical, except that the Morning Express *printed, "The Jury returned a verdict for Plaintiff of $2,25," an error that it corrected the next day as follows: "*THE MIRROR LIBEL SUIT.—*The verdict obtained by Mr. Poe in his Libel Suit against the Evening Mirror was '$225 and 6 cents cost,' instead of '$2,25' (as misprinted yesterday)."*

The Evening Mirror *also subscribed to "Yorick's" services, but in this instance Hiram Fuller adapted his report to his own purposes (Document 82, "The Court Journal").*

For reasons of decorum, the names of Mrs. Frances Osgood and Edward J. Thomas were deleted from the report.]

SUPERIOR COURT.—Before Chief Justice Jones.—*Edgar A. Poe,* vs. *Hiram Fuller and A. W. Clason, Jr.*—Mr. P. is known as an eminent writer and contributor to magazines, &c. Messrs. F. & C. are proprietors of the Evening Mirror. Mr. P. in an article published in Godey's Lady's Book, on literary men, made some mention of Mr. Thomas Dunn English, which caused that gentleman to publish, over his own name, one or two severe articles against Mr. Poe in the Evening Mirror. The sentences on which the suit for libel are [*sic*] founded are as follows:

"I hold Mr. Poe's acknowledgement for a sum of money which he obtained of me under false pretences."

"I know Mr. Poe by a succession of his acts, one of which is rather costly. I hold Mr. P.'s acknowledgement," &c. (As above.) "Another act of his gives me some knowledge of him. A merchant of this City [Edward J. Thomas] had accused him of committing forgery, and he consulted me on the mode of punishing his accuser, and as he was afraid to challenge him to the field, or chastise him personally, I suggested a legal prosecution as his sole remedy, and at his request I obtained a counsel who was willing, as a compliment to me, to conduct his suit without the customary retaining fee. But though so eager at first to commence proceedings, he dropped the matter altogether when the time came for him to act, thus virtually admitting the truth of the charge."

Proof was taken as to the proprietorship of the paper, &c. Mr. Clason, who defended the case, moved that a verdict for defendant [should not] be taken as related to himself, as it had not been shown that he was a proprietor. This was objected to by Mr. Fancher, counsel for plaintiff, who testified that Mr. Clason told him that he (Mr. Clason) in fact owned the establishment, and that Mr. Fuller was but a nominal proprietor. The motion was denied. For defence a justification was put in, also that the character of Mr. Poe was such as not to entitle him to the favorable consideration of a Jury.

The deposition of Mr. English, taken at Washington, was read. He states that Mr. Poe solicited of him the loan of $30 to get the Broadway Journal in his own hands, and promising to get Mr. E. a share of the profits; that Mr. E. lent him the money, taking his note, but Mr. P. never afterward offered to transfer an interest in the Journal, and deponent understood that the paper had not yielded any profits. As to the idea of forgery, Mr. P. had told him that a merchant of this City had designs upon a lady of their mutual acquaintance [Mrs. Frances Osgood], whom he supposed Mr. Poe to have great influence with, &c. and the said merchant in order to get the lady against Mr. Poe had told her he was a forger. Mr. English, in that deposition, also stated "the general character of said Poe is that of a notorious liar, a common drunkard, and of one utterly lost to all the obligations of honor."

Mr. T. the merchant named, testified to having met with the party at the New-York House, where he put up—he was called upon by Mr. Poe in relation to what was said about forgery—witness immediately sought out the person who told him; that person denied that he had ever made any such charge about Mr. Poe, and I supposed, said the witness, that I had misunderstood him. I wrote a letter to Mr. Poe, informing him of the denial and retraction. This witness, also Judge Noah, and Mr. Freeman Hunt, testified as to the character of Mr. Poe.—Never heard anything against him except that he is occasionally addicted to intoxication.

The respective counsel summed up the case. Mr. Fancher, on behalf of Mr. P. stated that Mr. P. has recently buried his wife, and his own health was such as to prevent him being present.

The Court charged the question of the Jury to be whether the publications were true or not, or if there is mitigation in relation to them as to the character of Mr. P.

The Jury returned a verdict for plaintiff of $225.—For plaintiff, Mr. E. L. Fancher; for defendants, Mr. Clason in person.

AFTER THE LAWSUIT

81. 15 March 1847: Letter to Mrs. Frances Sargent Osgood
Edward J. Thomas

[*Thomas had spread the rumor that Poe had committed forgery, a rumor that English rashly included in his "Reply to Mr. Poe" (Document 13). The reason Thomas slandered Poe is that he had designs upon the flirtatious Mrs. Osgood and thought he could damage Poe in her eyes, a man he regarded as a rival for her affection. Thomas was subpoenaed as a witness for the plaintiff to clear Poe of the charge, which he did. Having already incriminated himself, he was not disposed to incriminate himself still further, and obviously proved an unsatisfactory witness under cross-examination.*

The interesting point of his letter is the information that Mrs. Osgood's name was left unmentioned for the sake of delicacy when English's deposition was read to the jury. Contrary to Thomas's statement in this letter, Poe did not lose "his home." Though his rent was sometimes in arrears, he passed his remaining years there with Maria Clemm. "Sam" is Mrs. Osgood's husband, a portrait painter, who seemed to be down on his luck at this time. The "children" are Ellen and May, Mrs. Osgood's two daughters.

This letter is in the Boston Public Library.]

New York March 15/47.

I do not know as my kind friend will receive a line from one of her first & best well wishers with the slightest regard as he has so long delayed to discharge what to him is not only a duty but a pleasure. Be that as it may I know that I have thought of you daily and this I cannot help— for by some way or the other I never find myself giving up a few moments to reflection but in runs Mrs. Osgood—occupies the chief place— says a great many kind things—scolds now and then in jest and then departs until the next evening when again comes the same little witch. Well I like it for if I cannot see her I can think of her.

But I am getting along too fast—I meant to scold for your last little hasty note—it was a vex to get such a letter from such a friend. I forgive however as usual.

I am anxious to know how you are doing in Phil[a] and how you like the quiet of the City. I fancy you have been there about long enough to want a change and that change our good City of York. This is the City for people of fancy and I know you fancy it say what you may and the result will be you will settle here as much as any where else.

You know the result of Poe's suit vs Fuller. It went as I thought it would for I always believed the article a libel in reality. I had strong apprehension that your name would come out under English's affadavit in a way I would not like for I believed Poe had told him things (when they were friends) that English would sweare to; but they left the names blank in reading his testimony so that a "Mrs ———" and "a merchant in Broad St" were all the Jury knew, except on the latter point which I made clear by swearing on the stand that I was "the merchant in Broad St." I got fifty cents as a witness for which sum I swore that Poe frequently "got drunk" and that was all I could afford to sweare to for fifty cents.

Poor Poe—he has lost his wife—his home—may the folly of the past make him contrite for the future—may he live to be what he can be if he has but the will. He is now alone & his good or his evil will not so much afflict others. I have nothing in particular to tell you. I was very sorry to be so poor when Sam was here for I declare from my heart that I refused with the greatest reluctance & partly because I fear when I say I cannot[,] parties think otherwise. It is not so however for those whose business I have to do urge me for every $10 note that I can advance them —particularly in the winter. I am glad he obtained at the quarter I mentioned—it is all well there—if he had not—I would have raised it somehow for I had determined he should not go back without it.

Give him my best regards and say to him that I hope he is full of health and full of work—employment—encouragement or whatsoever other word is proper to apply to an artiste.

Let me hear from you soon and in my next I will promise to give you more about our friends. I want to "know what you are about and what you mean to do".

Love to the children and believe me as I am ever your friend

E. J. T.

82. *18 February 1847: Three Articles on Poe in the* Evening Mirror: *"The Court Journal," "Law and Libel," and "The Secret Out"*
Hiram Fuller

[*The evening following the day of the trial, Fuller published three articles which corroborate or add to our knowledge of the case and, in addition, reflect Fuller's reaction to the man who had bested him in court. The four major points that Fuller makes are that Poe's attorney had offered to settle the case out of court; that Fancher had taken the stand as a witness against the defense to establish Clason's financial culpability; that Poe had been offered free use of the* Evening Mirror's *columns to reply to English; and that the statutes hold a publisher guilty for "printing and publishing only," that is, lending his journal to the circulation of libel.*

"The Court Journal" article also appeared in the Weekly Mirror *on February 27.*]

THE COURT JOURNAL.—Chief Justice Jones was yesterday aroused from his slumbers in the Superior Court, at the particular request of Mr. Edgar A. Poe, who, after contributing for many years to the magazines and reviews, wished to add his mite to the records of a court. The gratification of this wish is a privilege which is readily granted in this litigation-loving community, and Mr. Poe could not of course be denied the pleasure which the lawyers and judges are ever anxious to extend to others, or be made an exception to the general rule.

The ladies are always causing mischief, as everybody knows. They will not permit a man to rest in peace, but delight in tormenting him. Our readers therefore will not be astonished to learn that Mr. Poe's complaints had their origin in Godey's *Lady's* Book, in which Mr. Poe published sundry un-literary articles on literary men, including in the latter category Mr. Thomas Dunn English. Although the sketch of Mr. E. was a mere scratch, still the latter, being quite as sharp a marksman with the quill as the former, determined to give a shot for a shot, and selected as his revolver the Evening Mirror. Mr. Poe's attack was a mere snapping of a percussion cap, compared to Mr. English's fusee, and as he found the pen fight an unequal one, he resorted to a libel suit, which, as we said in the commencement, opened the ocular demonstrations of our very worthy friend, the Chief Justice.

Mr. English, in his reply in the Mirror, published under *his own signature,* accused Mr. Poe of acts not very creditable to his character, but the sentences in which the libel was sought to be founded were as follows:

"I hold Mr. Poe's acknowledgement for a sum of money which he obtained of me under false pretences."

"I know Mr. Poe by a succession of his acts, one of which is rather costly. I hold Mr. P.'s acknowledgement," &c. (as above). "Another act of his gives me some knowledge of him. A merchant of this city had accused him of committing forgery, and he consulted me on the mode of punishing his accuser, and as he was afraid to challenge him to the field, or chastise him personally, I suggested a legal prosecution as his sole remedy, and at his request I obtained a counsel who was willing, as a compliment to me, to conduct his suit without the customary retaining fee. But though so eager at first to commence proceedings, he dropped the matter altogether when the time came for him to act, thus virtually admitting the truth of the charge."

The first step Mr. Fancher took was to prove the proprietorship of the paper. Failing to show by other witnesses that any other person than Mr. Fuller was the owner, the *Counsel for the plaintiff volunteered to take the stand, and testify to some private conversation with Mr. Clason, the counsel for the defence.* Mr. Fancher should have usurped the place of the jury, and decided the case forthwith. Mr. Clason then opened the defence by reading the deposition of Mr. English, to confirm all his charges, and winding up by the grand peroration: 'The general character of said Poe is that of a notorious liar, a common drunkard, and of one utterly lost to all the obligations of honor.'

Judge Noah and Mr. Freeman Hunt also testified that Mr. Poe was addicted to intoxication, and notwithstanding this, the jury returned a verdict for *the plaintiff of two hundred and twenty five dollars, and costs!*

Mr. Fancher had previously offered to settle the suit by the payment of $100—thus proving that even he, with his own testimony, was by no means confident of the justice of his cause.

We were always of the opinion that no man of character and reputation gained one jot of respectability by a libel suit, for if he cannot by his own efforts rise above the imputation, the verdict of a jury can never buy him the good will of the people. We have a higher opinion of the praise or censure of the public than to look upon it in the same light with a house and lot in New York at this season of the year, 'For Sale or to Let.' Reputation may be more easily made than bought, for we are unwilling to believe that he who has the greatest wealth is therefore entitled to the greater esteem.

In the case before us the attack was commenced by Mr. Poe, and the Mirror was in no wise a party to it, except by the *mere publication of a card* which every gentleman has a right to ask. We are well aware that the books are full of verdicts for 'printing and publishing only,' but two wrongs never made a right. By the same rule it might be shown that Mr. Colt, who manufactures pistols, is guilty of every death caused by the use of his fire-arms. If Tom Nooks has a good gun, which Bills [*sic*] Snooks hires and then shoots a man, what jury would say that Tom is guilty of the act?

LAW AND LIBEL.—It is customary with editors when they have been mulcted for any considerable amount in a case of libel, to come out in a bitter tirade against judge, jury and law, and to propose an immediate reform of the statute under which they have been tried and victimized. We do not intend to indulge in any such strictures, notwithstanding the remarkable verdict rendered against us yesterday in the Supreme Court, for allowing one literary individual to reply to another through our columns, in the shape of a 'Card to the Public.' The facts in the case are well known to our readers, and also the parties, who by resorting to low personal abuse of each other, have lost more in character than they have gained either in money or fame. We regret that we consented to the publication of the 'Card' containing the libel; but it was brought to us, *printed in a morning paper* [the New York *Morning Telegraph*], and we were assured that it was to be published in every newspaper in the city on the day that it appeared in the Mirror, and that every word it contained was true. An appeal was made to us on the score of *justice*; a gross attack had been made upon the literary reputation of a man who depended on his pen for bread, and it was but fair that a strong reply should be made. We did not suppose that a libel suit would be resorted to, in defence, by one who, with the exception, perhaps, of [James Gordon] Bennett [of the *New York Herald*], has probably written and published more libellous articles than any other man in the whole country. This is the first instance in our recollection of an action brought against an editor for publishing 'a card.' The principal is always the individual who stands or falls, suffers or is acquitted upon the truth of the charges set forth in the publication. However, we do not complain, though in justice to ourselves we must state that we offered the plaintiff the free use of our columns to vindicate himself from the charges contained in the 'card,' an offer which he at the time accepted, but was probably advised differently by counsel, who hoped to find something worth picking from this 'bone of contention.' Those editors who have allowed the said plaintiff to vilify us in their columns, will please consider that we have sued *them* for libel, and recovered the sum of $225 and 6 cents costs. One word more, and we dismiss the subject for to-day.

The action we have alluded to was brought against another gentleman conjointly with ourselves [Augustus Clason, Jr.], whose only connection with this paper consisted in a bill of sale taken by him of Morris & Willis, as security for money loaned. The Mirror, since the dissolution of partnership in 1845, has had but *one* editor and *one* proprietor, whose name duly appears as such on every copy of the paper issued [H. Fuller]. No other person has any control over its columns or affairs.

The testimony given on the trial has been written out by our reporter, and we may hereafter conclude to publish it entire. In the meantime we shall beware of contending with lawyers, who, when the testimony of their witnesses falls short, do not hesitate to go upon the stand and swear to the *private conversation of their opposing counsel* [Augustus Clason, Jr.].

THE SECRET OUT.—We have often been at loss to account for the bitter and persevering attacks of the *True Sun* on the editor of the Tribune. We find the following explanation in one of Mr. Greeley's articles of this morning:

> When we were called upon to indorse a note for them to help them start their paper, we did it cheerfully, though its payment by the makers depended on the extremely dubious success of their enterprise, asking only that the Whig party and policy should receive fair and candid treatment through their columns, and this we were promised. Instead of it, our party and ourselves have been misrepresented and vilified in that piratical concern for years past with an assiduity and recklessness of malignity entirely without precedent. We have been stung by many vipers in the course of our brief experience, but

rarely by any so persistently and with such palpable baseness of purpose as in this case.

This is the gratitude of the world. Do a man a favor and he will *pay you for it in some left handed way if he can.* We gave a certain *Poe-t* $15 a week for three months, at a time when we neither needed his services nor could afford to pay for them, and have during the present winter contributed our mite to relieve his distresses, who in return gives us a viper's gratitude. Mr. Greeley is not alone in his "experiences."

---

83. *19 February 1847:* "*Genius and the Law of Libel*"
Horace Greeley

[*Having read Hiram Fuller's comments on the trial in the* Evening Mirror, *as well as his expression of sympathy for "the editor of the Tribune" in "The Secret Out" (preceding document), Greeley himself discussed Poe's libel case in the* Daily Tribune, *obviously siding with the "helpless publisher." He commended Poe for having refrained from shooting English (a means of retaliation less common in the East than in the South and West) or from horsewhipping him (as William Cullen Bryant had horsewhipped William Leete Stone of the New York* Commercial Advertiser, *or as Augustus Clason had cowhided James Gordon Bennett of the* New York Herald *in similar instances, or as Greeley himself was to be caned in 1855 by the Honorable Albert Rust, a political foe). But for Poe to have sued Fuller for publishing English's article, not English for writing it, seemed, in Greeley's judgment, "mistaken and silly."*

Greeley also found fault with Poe for not having availed himself of "the columns of the Mirror," which "were impartially tendered him for a rejoinder. . . ." (Poe in his reply—Document 86—asserted that the invitation was hedged "with a proviso that I should forego a suit and omit this passage and that passage, to suit the purposes of Mr Fuller.") Greeley, no doubt, was remembering his own experiences with James Fenimore Cooper a few years back. Having lost one libel suit brought against him by the novelist, and facing the prospect of losing another one to him, Greeley pleaded with Cooper: "Why not settle this difference at the point of the pen? We hereby tender you a column of The Tribune for ten days, promising to publish verbatim *whatever you may write and put your name to—and to publish it in both our daily and weekly papers. . . . We will further agree not to write over two columns in reply to the whole"* (Tribune, *31 December 1842*). *Cooper, of course, had refused Greeley's invitation, as Poe had refused Fuller's, which seemed unreasonable to Greeley.*

The editor of the Tribune *also felt that a verdict of $25 "would have been a liberal estimate of damages," not $225.06, sufficient indication of Greeley's view of the harm done Poe's reputation. His remark about Poe's failure to fulfill his "pecuniary engagements" refers to the fact that Poe had borrowed $50 from Greeley to help him buy the* Broadway Journal, *a debt he had not repaid. What we learn here, among other things, is that Clason was Fuller's brother-in-law.*

For more information about the Greeley-Poe relationship, see head-note to Document 64.]

GENIUS AND THE LAW OF LIBEL.—Mr. Edgar A. Poe, well known as a Poet, having of course more wit than wisdom, and we think making no pretensions to exemplary faultlessness in morals, still less to the scrupulous fulfillment of his pecuniary engagements, wrote for Godey's Lady's Book a series of Literary Portraits of New-York notables, both of the major and minor order.—They were plain, sincere, free, off-hand criticisms —seldom flattering, sometimes savagely otherwise. Of this latter class was an account of Mr. Thomas Dunn English, which seemed to us impelled by personal spite. To this birching Mr. English very naturally replied, charging Mr. Poe with gross pecuniary delinquency and personal dishonesty, and the *Evening Mirror* was so good-natured as to give him a hearing. Mr. English is a disbeliever in Capital Punishment, but you would hardly have suspected the fact from the tenor of this retort acidulous upon Poe. Mr. P. therefore threw away the goose-quill, (though the columns of the Mirror were impartially tendered him for a rejoinder,) and most commendably refrained from catching up instead the horse-whip or the pistol; but he did something equally mistaken and silly, if not equally wicked, in suing—not his self-roused castigator, but the harmless publisher, for a libel! The case came to trial on Wednesday, and the Jury condemned the Mirror to pay Mr. P. $225 damages and six cents costs.— This was all wrong; $25 would have been a liberal estimate of damages, all things considered, including the severe provocation; and this should have been rendered, not against the Mirror, but against English, if, upon a fair comparison of the two articles, it appeared that Mr. P. had got more than he gave. Mr. Fuller of the Mirror talks very philosophically of the matter, and seems only anxious for the preservation of his Editorial laurels.—In reference to the joinder of his brother-in-law in the action as a co-proprietor of the Mirror, he says:

"The action we have alluded to was brought against another gentleman, conjointly with ourselves, whose only connection with this paper consisted in a bill of sale taken by him of Morris & Willis, as security for money loaned. The Mirror, since the dissolution of partnership in 1845, has had but *one* editor and *one* proprietor, whose name daily appears as such on every copy of the paper issued. No other person has any control over its columns or affairs."

---

84. *19 February 1847: "What Has Become of the Funds?"* Hiram Fuller

[*Having made his contribution to the Poe fund, however involuntarily, and taking Poe at his word—in his open letter to Nathaniel P. Willis (Document 70)—that he needed no charity, Fuller in evident pique published the following paragraph, which also appeared in the* Weekly Mirror *on February 27.*

The answer to Fuller's question is that Poe, for all the newspaper clamor about the Poes' poverty and sickness, received, so far as is known, a total of $60.]

WHAT HAS BECOME OF THE FUNDS?—We know of three several persons —an old lady, a Christian minister, and a benevolent editor, who have during the past winter been about soliciting money for the support of poor *Poe*. In a recent communication to *N. P. Willis, Poe* declares that he has *never been in want of pecuniary assistance*, and in case he had, he knew of a hundred persons to whom he could apply with confidence for aid. We again ask, with some emphasis, what has become of the funds?

---

85. *19 February 1847: "Mr. Edgar A. Poe"*
John S. Du Solle

[*Du Solle, whom Louis Godey had paid ten dollars to print Poe's "Reply to Mr. English and Others" (Document 24) in his* Spirit of the Times, *now commented briefly on Poe's libel suit in his paper.*

For earlier statements by Du Solle, see Documents 17 and 71.]

MR. EDGAR A. POE has just recovered in New York $225 and costs in an action for libel against the proprietors of the Evening Mirror, for publishing an article written by T. Dunn English, reflecting severely on the character of Mr. Poe. We regret to see Mr. Poe bring libel suits against authors, for with all his consummate ability he is not himself apt to speak mincingly of other writers. "Bear and forbear" is a very good motto.

---

86. *21 February 1847: Letter to Horace Greeley*
Edgar A. Poe

[*Poe was offended by Greeley's "Genius and the Law of Libel" (Document 83) because of the further damage it did his reputation (the* Tribune *had a circulation of about 11,000 copies at this time), for he desperately needed to regain entrée into the journals if he was to earn a livelihood. He had no option, however, but to appeal to Greeley's sense of "truth and love of justice." He claimed that, barring one sentence, he had not engaged in personalities in writing his sketch of English (Document 11), an obvious distortion of the truth, and pointed out truthfully that English, overreacting, had libeled him on two counts. Poe did not explain, though Greeley had raised the question, why he had sued Fuller and Clason rather than English, or why he had not sued all three.*

Greeley did not print Poe's letter nor feel the need to rectify the impression he had created. He simply ignored the matter entirely.

For more information on the Greeley-Poe relationship, see the headnote to Document 64. This letter appears in Ostrom, II, 344–5.]

New-York: Feb. 21—47.

My Dear Mr Greeley,

Enclosed is an editorial article which I cut from "The Tribune" of the 19th ult. When I first saw it I did not know you were in Washington and yet I said to myself—"this misrepresentation is *not* the work of Horace Greeley".

The facts of my case are these:—In "Godey's Magazine" I wrote a *literary criticism* having reference to T. D. English. The only thing in it which resembled a "personality," was contained in these words—"I have no acquaintance, personally, with Mr English"—meaning, of course, as every body understood, that I wished to decline his acquaintance for the future. This, English retaliates by asserting under his own name, in the Mirror, that he *holds my acknowledgment for a sum of money obtained under false pretences,* and by creating the impression on the public mind that I have been *guilty of forgery.* These charges (being false and, if false, easily shown to be so) could have been ventured upon by English only in the hope that on account of my illness and expected death, it would be impossible for me to reply to them at all. Their baseness is thus trebly aggravated by their cowardice. I sue; to redeem my character from these foul accusations. Of the obtaining money under false pretences from E. not a shadow of proof is shown:—the "acknowledgment" is *not forthcoming.* The "forgery," by reference to the very man who originated the charge, is shown to be *totally, radically baseless.* The jury returned a verdict in my favor—and the paragraphs enclosed are the comments of *the "Tribune"*!

You are a man, Mr Greeley—an honest and a generous man—or I should not venture to tell you so, and to your face; and *as* a man you must imagine what I feel at finding those paragraphs to my discredit going the rounds of the country, *as the opinions of Horace Greeley.* Every body supposes that *you* have said these things. The weight of your character—the general sense of your truth and love of justice—cause those few sentences (which in almost any other paper in America I would treat with contempt) to do me a vital injury—to wound and oppress me beyond measure. I therefore ask you to do me what justice you can find it in your heart to do under the circumstances.

In the printed matter I have underscored two passages. As regards the first:—it alone would have sufficed to assure me that *you* did not write the article. I owe you money—I have been ill, unfortunate, no doubt weak, and as yet unable to refund the money—but on this ground *you*, Mr Greeley, could *never* have accused me of being habitually "unscrupulous in the fulfillment of my pecuniary engagements." The charge is *horribly false*—I have a hundred times left myself destitute of bread for myself and family that I might discharge debts which the very writer of this infamous accusation (Fuller) would have left undischarged to the day of his death.

The 2ᵈ passage underscored embodies a falsehood—and *therefore you* did not write it. I did *not* "throw away the quill". I arose from a sick-bed (although scarcely able to stand or see) and wrote a reply which was published in the Phil. "Sp. of the Times", and a copy of which reply I enclose you. The "columns of the Mirror" were tendered to me—with a proviso that I should forego a suit and omit this passage and that passage, to suit the purposes of Mr Fuller.

I have now placed the matter before you—I should not hope or ask for justice from any other man (except perhaps one) in America—but from you I demand and expect it. You will see, at once, that so gross a wrong, done in your name, dishonors yourself and me. If you do differ then, as I know you do, from these editorial opinions supposed to be yours—I beg of you to do by me as you would have me do by you in a similar case—disavow them.

With high respect Yours
Edgar A. Poe

---

87. *23 February 1847: Two Squibs on Poe in the* Evening Mirror
Hiram Fuller

[*The two items below require no explanation, though Poe, the object of the attacks, is unnamed.*]

LIBEL SUITS.—A more aggravated case of libel, we understand, came off at Troy last week than we suffered under here, but in which, however, our neighbors of the Express had better luck than we had, thus showing that the New York jury set a higher estimate on such cases than a jury in the interior.

The Freeholder, (Anti-Rent paper) in Albany, sued the editor of the

Express for libelling his editor, who was indeed pretty roughly handled, after provoking such handling, however. Counsel were employed and the case was argued at length last week, the plaintiff in person and another gentleman of the Bar *vs* Mr Brooks in person. The result was 6¼ cents damages and 6¼ cents cost, the jury being out about ten minutes. The jury properly thought, that it was one of those ridiculous libel suits with which a Court ought never to be troubled.

We believe in the case that the counsel for the plaintiff did not turn *witness* to help out his case.

The *Sunday Dispatch* in alluding to libel suits very justly remarks:—

Sound reputations as rarely go to the Courts, as healthy constitutions go to the doctors. It is your weak, sickly man that swallows the apothecaries' stuff; it is your rickety, rotten reputation that asks the contemptible prop of a verdict to sustain it.

---

88. 27 February 1847: "To Correspondents"
Hiram Fuller

[*The item below is of interest for its reiteration of the statement made in "Law and Libel" (Document 82) that Fuller had a transcript of the trial, a document that has not yet come to light.*

Two distortions occur in this brief item, which appeared in the Evening Mirror. One is that the "names of several literary ladies" were mentioned at the trial. The available information shows that the name of only one literary lady was mentioned, that of Mrs. Frances Osgood, for her name appears in English's deposition. However, as Thomas tells us (Document 81), the court left her name, as well as his, "blank in reading English's testimony so that a 'Mrs————' and a 'merchant in Broad St' were all the Jury knew. . . ." The other distortion is the suggestion that Poe was planning to bring another suit "involving some of the same parties. . . ." There is nothing in the record that bears this out, though the rumor spread (see Document 91).]

To Correspondents.—"B." wishes to know why we do not publish the whole of the testimony in *Poe's libel suit*. We answer, because it involves a good deal of delicate matter, and introduces the names of several literary ladies, for whom we have too much respect to publish their names in the connection in which they unfortunately appear. We understand that another suit is about to be brought on the tapis involving some of the same parties, and if "B." feels particularly curious on the subject, we advise him to be present on the trial.

---

89. *27 February 1847: A Passage from* The Trippings of Tom Pepper: or, The Results of Romancing
Harry Franco (Charles F. Briggs)

[*During the course of the serialization of an innocuous picaresque novel in the* Weekly Mirror, *a satirical passage on Poe was introduced on 27 February 1847, ten days after the verdict was rendered in the libel suit. The same passage also appeared on 4 and 5 March 1847 in the* Evening Mirror, *which was also running the serial.*

"Ferocious" was probably intended to be Cornelius Mathews, "Myrtle Pipps" William Gilmore Simms, and "Tibbings" Evert A. Duyckinck, though only suggestive identifications are made. Nowhere in the surviving correspondence of these men is there any reference to The Trippings, *which there probably would be if any of them felt they had been caricatured in it. In the passage from the novel reprinted below, the author claims to treat only one real person, though in his preface and final chapter, not reprinted here, he disowns having caricatured anyone. However, the* Literary World *on 31 July 1847 stated: "we could not help, despite the disclaimer of all personalities in his preface, questioning . . . whether, in fact, his book was not a gallery of portraits of well-known living people. . . . If this be really so, the author must settle it with his own conscience and the parties whom he has libelled. . . ." Likewise, in his "Editor's Table" in the* Knickerbocker (February 1847), *Lewis Gaylord Clark, whose favorite target of late was Cornelius Mathews, wrote: "these 'Trippings' are from the pen of an exceedingly clever writer, who copies character with the faithfulness of a daguerreotype. We wonder who is* 'MR. FEROCIOUS,'" *he added, and proceeded to identify him as Mathews in all but name. And* Yankee Doodle, *edited by the Duyckinck circle, wrote under the heading "A Hopeless Case" (2 January 1847): "We under-*

stand that the proprietors of the Evening Mirror *intend dipping the remaining chapters of 'The Trippings of Tom Pepper' in nitric acid, hoping that they may make them go off."*

Whether Mathews, Simms, and Duyckinck were caricatured in the novel, the unarguable fact is that Poe, under the sobriquet of Austin Wicks, and Elizabeth Frieze Ellet, who appears as Annie Elizabeth Gilson, were ridiculed.

The author of the serial, which appeared anonymously on the front pages of both Mirrors, *became known when the first volume of his book appeared in June 1847 in the Mirror Library. It was Briggs, better known as Harry Franco, who was then assisting Hiram Fuller in producing the* Mirror. *(Following the libel suit, Fuller began to carry the following notice in large bold type in the* Mirror: *H. Fuller, Proprietor and Editor, Assisted by Charles F. Briggs. . . .")*

Briggs, the original editor of the Broadway Journal, *had invited Poe to serve as his co-editor on that magazine. Poe, accepting the offer, soon dislodged Briggs to become the sole editor and, eventually, the sole owner of the* Broadway Journal. *To compound the injury he had done Briggs, Poe attacked him in the first installment of "The Literati." In his sketch he remarked that Briggs's novels were obvious imitations of Smollett's, that he "never composed in his life three consecutive sentences of grammatical English," and that he was "grossly uneducated" (this of the man to whom James Russell Lowell had dedicated his* Fable for Critics*).*

As for Mrs. Ellet, her connection with Poe is rather complex (for what is known of the story, see Moss, Poe's Literary Battles, *pages 207–21). Jealous of Poe and Mrs. Osgood's flirtation, she proceeded to slander them both. In addition, she prompted Margaret Fuller and Anne C. Lynch (both of whom appeared in "The Literati") to retrieve from Poe the letters Mrs. Osgood had sent him, ostensibly because they were compromising and Poe untrustworthy, though her motive was only to embarrass them. Incensed at the affront, Poe told the ladies that Mrs. Ellet had better look after her own compromising letters to him. Later, feeling he had betrayed Mrs. Ellet's confidence and had proved her point that he was untrustworthy, he in his own words "made a package of her letters . . . . and with my own hands left them at the door" (Ostrom, II, 407–8). Mrs. Ellet, exposed as a meddling hypocrite, and a jealous one at that, urged her brother, Colonel William Lummis, to make Poe prove his charge that he possessed compromising letters from her or else declare himself a slanderer. Caught in this desperate situation, Poe adopted an extreme "solution": He claimed he made his remark about Mrs. Ellet's letters in a fit of insanity, and had this explanation conveyed to the lady by Dr. John W. Francis (whom Poe had praised in the first installment of "The Literati"). If he had not been insane when he exposed Mrs. Ellet, he had by this time been driven to, if not over the edge of, insanity by her implacable persecution of him. As he wrote in the letter cited, "Is it any wonder that I was driven mad by the intolerable sense of wrong?" His self-confessed madness was, of course, exploited by his enemies, as is evident in the passages on Hammerhead in English's 1844, in Lewis Clark's comments in the* Knickerbocker *(Document 1), in the* Gazette *and* Times's *observations (Document 2), and in Fuller's editorial in the* Mirror *(Document 8).*

The passage that appears below is identical in all three versions of The Trippings. *It forms a part of Volume 1, Book 1, Chapter XVI, pages 156–64, in the Mirror Library version that appeared in June 1847. Volume 2 of the novel was published belatedly in April 1850.]*

. . . Nothing is more painful to my feelings than to know that I have inflicted pain upon others, and I have always looked upon those authors who write histories of their own contemporaries from mercenary motives, with abhorrence. Such a person I became acquainted with while residing in the family of old Gil, whose character shall form the only episode in my autobiography, and the reader may skip it or not, without danger of being greatly a loser in either case. . . .

One of old Gil's daughters, Lizzy, had a passion for literature, and, greatly to the grief of her parents, she would associate with literary people, and send her compositions to the magazines signed with her full name, Annie Elizabeth Gilson. This gave old Gil a good deal of uneasiness, for he classed the literati with dancing-masters, players and artists, for all of whom he entertained unmeasured contempt. He thought that the pen could be put to no higher or better use, than making entries in a ledger, unless, indeed, it were in writing sermons, and an author and a beggar being synonymous terms, he naturally looked upon his daughter Lizzy as a lost sheep, when he discovered the direction of her ambition. He could tolerate music because it formed a part of the church service, and a music-master was endurable, because he could be made serviceable to the cause of religion, but as for "a parcel of poets, and such kind of blackguards," he used to say "they ought all to be sent to Sing Sing, where they could learn to earn an honest living."

Poor Lizzy took all the scoldings of her parents as good naturedly as she could, and instead of trying to argue them out of their prejudices, which she knew would be a hopeless task, she used to utter her complaints to the Muse, and vent her griefs mysteriously in a magazine. She had addressed lines to every member of the family, and had even done me a similar favor, in Mr. Post's Magazine, in a sonnet, To "——," which I have unfortunately forgotten, and cannot, therefore, furnish the reader with a copy, but I remember that it was highly complimentary to my truthfulness, and that I was compared to a rose with drab-colored petals. It was the height of Lizzy's ambition to give a conversazione, and invite all the literati and famous artists about town, and taking advantage of a revival of religion in the church of which her father was an elder, gave out that she would be at home on a certain evening, when she knew he would be engaged at a prayer meeting. Pauline [Lizzy's sister] had entrusted me with the secret, and requested me to remain at home, promising me delightful fun with her sister's visiters, for she had hardly a better opinion of the literati than her father. Old Gil and his wife went off to the prayer meeting, taking their children with them. . . .

The family library of old Gil consisted chiefly of Bibles, with one or two Concordances, the works of Charlotte Elizabeth, the Presbyterian Confession of Faith, Doddridge's "Rise and Progress," the writings of Hannah More, and the complete works of Mrs. Sherwood, besides a collection of little books, with such titles as "Charles Davis, or the Power of Grace," "Matilda Brown, or the Sinner Saved by Charles Burdett," etc., etc. These books were carefully arranged in a small book-case in the back parlor, but the moment that old Gil left the house, Lizzy had them all removed, excepting only the complete works of Mrs. Sherwood, and their places supplied with "Moore's Byron," "Griswold's Poets," and some bound volumes of the "Lady's Book." The candelabras in the parlor were lighted up, a decanter of wine borrowed from her married sister, for old Gil would allow no fermented liquor in his house of any kind, some other refreshments were procured, and Lizzy stood in the middle of the room to receive her guests. Pauline and I seated ourselves as much out of the way as possible, that we might enjoy each other's conversation without being overheard, as well as watch the literati without mixing among them, and soon after they began to arrive. They were so unlike the usual visiters at old Gil's, that they probably appeared to us more *outre* than they would have done elsewhere. Pauline was delighted with the opportunity of sitting by me and showing her wit by making remarks upon the company as they entered the room. The first who entered was an artist, whose name I have forgotten; they called him the American Sir Martin Archer Shee, because he had written verses and painted portraits. He was a little man, with high-heeled boots, which pitched him forward as he walked; he was tightly strapped and buttoned, and he wore his lank black hair very long, and his mustache in imitation of Reubens. The American Shee talked but little, and so lisped his words that we could not make out what he said. A pensive lady, in a black silk dress, with very long curls, came next, accompanied by a learned Pole, who could speak all languages but English. The greeting between Lizzy and this lady was very cordial, she was the celebrated Miss Arabella Andrews, the American L. E. L., and the "Sappho" of the magazines. Then followed a Unitarian clergyman, and a German professor; another authoress, in spectacles, who was called the American Joanna Bailie, but there was nothing notable about her, except that she was dreadfully ugly, and wore a pink gauze cap, with a large bunch of yellow roses. A very pompous gentleman was next introduced as Mr. Myrtle Pipps. Lizzy said she was happy to have the honor of seeing the American George Paul Rainsford James in her father's house. Mr. Pipps bowed very low, rested his right hand inside of his outrageously fine vest, and elevating his head a little, remarked that there was no hospitality at the North, and that the only true article was to be found in the Palmetto State, where the domestic institutions encouraged the growth of a chivalric public sentiment. Two or three gentlemen of the press came next, whose names I suppress, and then Mr. Fitch Greenwood and his lady, the joint authors of a translation from the Swedish. Mr. Fitch Greenwood wore spectacles, and he looked through them as though it cost him an effort and didn't think much of anything that he saw through them. He spoke to nobody, but he looked at everything. Mrs. Fitz [*sic*] Greenwood was a slender little body, with red eyes; she talked to everybody, and looked at nothing. I was startled to see Mr. Ferocious and his friend Tibbings enter next, followed by a gentleman who was announced as the celebrated critic, Austin Wicks, author of the "Castle of Duntriewell," a metaphysical romance, and a pscychological [*sic*] essay on the sensations of shadows. Mr. Wicks entered the room like an automaton just set a going; he was a small man, with a very pale, small face, which terminated at a narrow point in the place of a chin; the shape of the lower part of his face gave to his head the appearance of a balloon, and as he had but little hair, his forehead had an intellectual appearance, but in that part of it which phrenologists appropriate for the home of the moral sentiments, it was quite flat; Pauline said, if he had any moral sentiments, they must be somewhere else, for it was very evident that there was no room for them there. He was small in person, his eyes were heavy and watery, his hands small and wiry, and his motions were like those of an automaton. He was dressed primly, and seemed to be conscious of having on a clean shirt, as though it were a novelty to him. Pauline was excessively amused at the monstrously absurd air of superiority with which this little creature carried himself, and was vexed with her sister Lizzy for receiving him with such marked respect. But the truth was, he had praised some of Lizzy's verses, and had talked to her about spondees and dactyls until she thought him a miracle of learning. He was shallow enough on almost all subjects which tend to make a man respectable in the world, but he had committed to memory a few pedantic terms, and contrived to pass himself off among literary ladies, like Lizzy, for a profound critic. Mr. Ferocious, and his follower, Mr. Tibbings, listened with open-mouthed admiration to Wicks, and declared he was the most profound critic of the age. There were many more notable people dropped in during the evening, among them a native tragedian, with a round and inexpressive countenance, a stoop in his shoulders, and a halt in his gait; he was called, I think, the American Kemble, for it was a peculiarity of those originals to call themselves after some English prototype. Mr. Wicks was the American Jeffrey, a singularly unfortunate name to apply to the poor creature, as he had neither the learning, the wit, the respectability, the honesty, the independence, nor a tithe part of the talents of the great Scotch critic. But Mr. Wick[s] called Jeffrey a humbug, and sneered at the pretensions of everybody who attempted criticism, although his highest efforts in literature had been contributions to a lady's magazine. The literati conducted themselves with great propriety during the evening, doing nothing worse than saying the most ill-natured things they could utter about all their acquaintances who were not present, and complimenting each other in the most fulsome and laughable manner, until the refreshments were introduced, when Mr. Wicks, having drank a glass full of wine, the little spirit that it contained flew into his weak head, and he began to abuse all present in such profane and scurrilous terms, that all the ladies went into hysterics, and poor Lizzy was in great tribulation, for fear that her father should return before he could be got out of the house. Mr. Ferocious and Tibbings were lamenting in dismal tones that a man of such splendid abilities should have such an unfortunate propensity. "However," said Mr. Ferocious, "I like it. It shows the inner life of the individual being!"

"I endorse the remark of Ferocious," said Tibbings; "it is one of the infirmities of genius; Savage used to drink, and Byron was fond of gin. I think that an American author should be allowed quite as much liberty as an English one, for you know, Ferocious, this is a free country."

"Tibbings," said the American Jeffrey, staggering towards that slender gentleman, "you are a fool."

"Don't notice him," said Mr. Ferocious; "keep cool, quiet, sedate. It's only a phase of his genius. I like it. It's original, peculiar, American. He will bring up something fine, directly, out of the depths of his inner existence."

"Ferocious!" said Mr. Wicks.

"Listen, ladies," said Mr. Ferocious, winking at the ladies, who were standing aloof in terror.

"Ferocious," said Mr. Wicks, again, "do you know what I think of you?"

"In vino veritas. What is it?" said Mr. Ferocious, smiling complacently towards the ladies.

"Ferocious you are an ass!" hiccupped Mr. Wicks, "a dunce; you can't write English; I praised you once, but I am sorry for it; I said that you were one of our greatest poets, but I now say you are one of our greatest asses."

The revulsion of feeling with Mr. Ferocious and Tibbings was so sudden, and their admiration of the critic so completely changed to raging scorn, contempt and hatred, that the natural language of their passions, instead of clothing itself in words, found a more forcible expression in actions, and utterly regardless of the presence of the ladies, they fell upon the helpless critic, and would probably have done him a serious injury if the tragedian and I had not jumped to his rescue and saved him from the terrible revenge of the enraged author and his friend. The poor wretch being entirely unconscious of his danger, immediately began at me and the player, bestowing upon us a string of scurrilous epithets, which must have been quite familiar to him when he was sober, or he could not have used them so freely. The company now broke up in great disorder, and we took the drunken critic home to his boarding-house, and delivered him into the hands of his wife, who thanked us meekly for the care we had taken of her poor husband. This incident was rather fortunate for Lizzy, as she got rid of her guests in time to put the house in order before the return of her parents. Her admiration for Mr. Wicks was not in the least diminished by this scandalous occurrence; she regarded it as an eccentricity of genius, and wrote a sonnet about it, which she published in a weekly paper. Mr. Wicks sent her a letter, lamenting his destiny, praising her poetical abilities, and asking for the loan of five dollars. The kind-hearted Lizzy was so shocked at the idea of so great a genius being in want of so trifling a sum, that she made a collection among her friends, for a man of genius in distress, and sent him fifty dollars, accompanied by a note so full of tender compassion, for his misfortune, and respect for his genius, that any man possessed of the common feelings of humanity must have valued it more than the money. But Mr. Wicks had no such feelings, and with a baseness that only those can believe possible who have known him, he exhibited Lizzy's note to some of her acquaintances, as an evidence that she had made improper advances to him. The scandal had been very widely circulated, before some candid friend brought it to Lizzy, who, on hearing it, was thrown into an agony of grief and shame, which nearly deprived her of reason. She could not call upon her father to avenge the wrong that had been done her, but one of her married sisters having heard of it, told it to her husband, who sought for the cowardly slanderer, with the intention of chastising him for his villa[i]ny. But he had become alarmed for the consequences of his slanders, and had persuaded a good natured physician to give him a certificate to the effect that he was of unsound mind, and not responsible for his actions. Having showed this to Lizzy's brother-in-law, and signed another paper acknowledging that he had slandered her and was sorry for it, he was allowed to escape without a personal chastisement. But shortly after, being empolyed to write for a fashionable magazine, he took an occasion, in a series of pretended biographical sketches of literary men and women who had been so unfortunate as to become known to him, to hold poor Lizzy up to ridicule, by imputing to her actions of which she was never guilty, and by misquoting from her verses. Lizzy had the good sense to laugh at such imbecile spite, and when the poor wretch had brought himself and his family into a starving condition by his irregularities, she had the goodness to contribute her quarterly allowance of pocket-money to the gatherings of some benevolent ladies who had exerted themselves in his behalf.

The conduct of Wicks had a very wholesome effect on Lizzy. It opened her eyes to the meretricious and worthless character of a mere literateur, and cured her forever from hankering after the transitory fame of a magazine contributor. She had seen her verses in print, and had been traduced and criticised by a mercenary writer, and was ever after content to remain unknown except to those whom she loved. Her first and last literary *soiree* had afforded her a source of unfailing merriment, whenever it was mentioned, and she describes with great gusto the tragical encounter between Wicks, Tibbings and Ferocious, for the amusement of her intimate friends. The poor creature, Wicks, having tried a great variety of literary employments, and growing too dishonest for anything respectable, at last fell into the congenial occupation of writing authentic accounts of marvellous cures for quack physicians, and having had the imprudence to swallow some of the medicine whose virtues he had been extolling, fell a victim to his own arts, and was buried at the expense of the public.

---

90. *11 March 1847: Letter to George W. Eveleth*
    Edgar A. Poe

[*On 19 January 1847 Eveleth had informed Poe that he had been accused by the Philadelphia* Saturday Evening Post *of plagiarizing his* Conchologist's First Book *(Philadelphia, 1839) from* The Conchologist's Text Book *(Glasgow, 1833). There was some basis for the charge, as Arthur Hobson Quinn points out in* Edgar Allan Poe, *pages 275–6. In a letter dated 16 February 1847, Poe asked Eveleth for particulars and asserted that the "charge is infamous and I shall prosecute for it, as soon as I settle my accounts with the 'Mirror.'" Poe, however, neither sued the Post nor made it retract its charge.*

In answering Eveleth's queries, Poe avers in the letter printed below that he suffered no actual damage from the lawsuit or the notoriety attending it, a mistaken assessment of the situation, as Poe well knew, but

*he was attempting as usual to put on a good face for his young admirer.
This also accounts for his exaggerating the damage done to Fuller and
Clason, whose actual assessment (unless Poe was including their legal
fees) was $326.48–$225.06 in damages and $101.42 in court costs. Poe
does not mention his own legal fees. The "acknowledgment" Poe speaks
of refers to English's allegation: "I hold Mr. Poe's acknowledgement for a
sum of money which he obtained from me under false pretences." If Poe
had brought a criminal suit against English, as he alleges he might have,
he would not have received damages in a sum of money; and English, if
he had been found guilty, would have been punished by fine or imprison-
ment or both (see headnote to Document 37 for a discussion of the legal
situation). The Mirror, contrary to Poe's statement, did have a witness to
testify against Poe, if we ignore Lummis and Sturtevant (?), whose roles at
the trial cannot be determined. It was English who by means of his deposition declared that the "general character of . . . Poe is that of a notorious
liar, a common drunkard, and of one utterly lost to all the obligations of
honor."*

The full version of this letter appears in Ostrom, II, 348–9.]

New-York March 11. 47.

My Dear Sir,

I am still quite sick and overwhelmed with business—but I snatch a
few moments to reply to yours of the 21rst ult. . . .

I fear that according to the law technicalities there is nothing "actionable" in the Post's paragraphs—but I shall make them retract by *some*
means.

My suit against "The Mirror" has terminated, by a verdict of $225, in
my favor. The costs and all will make them a bill of $492. Pretty well—
considering that there was *no* actual "damage" done to me.

I enclose you my reply to English—which will enable you to comprehend his accusations. The vagabond, at the period of the suit's coming on,
ran off to Washington for fear of being criminally prosecuted. The "acknowledgment" referred to was not forthcoming, and "the Mirror" could
not get *a single witness* to testify *one word* against my character. . . .

Most truly your friend

Edgar A Poe

91. *21 March 1847: "More Libel Suits"*
   New York Dispatch

[*The first person to suggest in print that Poe was about to bring "another suit . . . involving some of the same parties" was Hiram Fuller, a suggestion he made on 27 February 1847 (Document 88). Now the* New York Dispatch *in its Sunday edition repeated the rumor, not citing the* Evening Mirror *but the Philadelphia* Galaxy *as its source; and Fuller in his turn quoted the* Dispatch *to the same effect (next document).*

This matter raises some questions which I am not able to answer with conviction but which suggest a "plant." Why should the rumor have apparently arisen in Philadelphia and not in New York where Poe's affairs were better known? More to the point, was there a Philadelphia Galaxy *at all? Neither the* Union List of Serials *nor the* Union List of Newspapers *indicates that the* Galaxy *ever existed, nor has the National Union Catalog any record that it existed. One can understand why the* Atlanta Enterprise *might not have survived General Sherman's burning of the city (one would like to see a file of that paper since Chivers told Poe that he had republished "the Home-Journal Article" in it, probably Duyckinck's "An Author in Europe and America"), but one has difficulty in understanding why a Philadelphia journal of the nineteenth century should totally disappear as if it had never existed. To add to my suspicion, the* New York Dispatch, *according to the* Evening Mirror *of 1 May 1846, was "to be issued from the Mirror Building. . . ."*]

MORE LIBEL SUITS.—The Philadelphia *Galaxy* promises another action growing out of Mr. Poe's suit against the *Mirror*, in which several literary ladies will figure. We hope not. We trust that we love the ladies, and honor and cherish them, all that sort of thing—but according to our experience and observation in all cases, where literature is not used to second benevolence, a literary lady is a *blue bore*. We write *bas bleu*—bah! blue!

Literature as a *means*, is all very well—but literature as an end, is a shocking perversion of the female intellect. Just in proportion as a woman is a good writer, she is a bad woman—not a bad character—but as a *woman*, bad. The proverb—'When the devil wishes to ruin a woman he puts a pen in her hand,' is so true, that when you see a woman, taking up a pen as an avocation, you may consider her done for, as far as a woman's proper object is concerned.

A literary woman never ought to marry—her husband is sure to be ill treated, and her children neglected. The most melancholy, miserable looking men we ever saw were the unfortunate husbands of 'literary ladies.'

---

92. 24 March 1847: "More Libel Suits"
Hiram Fuller

[*Quoting from the Sunday edition of the* New York Dispatch *(preceding document), Fuller in the* Evening Mirror *reported the rumor that Poe and his attorney were planning a lawsuit against "several literary ladies. . . ." The announcement in the* Dispatch *should not have surprised Fuller, for he had anticipated the rumor on 27 February 1847 (Document 88).*

Given the conventions of the time, even contemplating legal action against ladies was considered outrageous.]

MORE LIBEL SUITS.—The Philadelphia *Galaxy* promises another action growing out of Mr. Poe's suit against the *Mirror*, in which several literary ladies will figure.—*Sunday Dispatch.*

We shouldn't wonder. Mr. Poe and his lawyer having made so good a speculation by their infamous prosecution of the Mirror, will very naturally be tempted to try their hand upon some other victim. The counsellor and client were worthy of each other.

---

93. 28 March 1847: Letter to Enoch L. Fancher
Edgar A. Poe

[*Maria Clemm was still living with Poe in Fordham, though Virginia had died some two months earlier, on January 30. Still reluctant to appear in the city, Poe sent her to Fancher to pick up the award money from his libel suit.*

How much Fancher charged for his services to Poe is unknown. Hiram Fuller asserted, with more spite than knowledge, that "the greater por-

tion" of the award money "went into the pocket of the poet's sympathetic attorney" (Document 94).

The year-date of the letter below is wrong; it should be 1847. A Freudian would have a ready explanation for the slip: Poe was at once wishing himself back to 1846 when he was at the peak of his fame and wishing away the events of 1847 that had reduced him to ruin.

This letter appears in Ostrom, II, 716.]

E. L. FANCHER ESQ^{re}

Dr Sir,

Mrs Maria Clemm is hereby authorized to receive the amount of damages lately awarded in my suit, conducted by yourself, against the proprietors of the New-York Evening Mirror, and to give a receipt for the same.

Resp^y Yours
Edgar A Poe

Fordham, N.Y.
March 28th 1846.

---

94. 7 June 1847: "Prenez Garde, Chrony"
Hiram Fuller

[Fuller permitted some two months to elapse before referring again to the libel suit in which he had been a defendant. He swore he would never again "confide to the smooth words and fair promises of irresponsible literary humbugs," an allusion to English who had promised to make his charges good by the most ample and satisfactory evidence if Poe resorted to a legal prosecution, yet who not only deserted Fuller but failed to provide any testimony in his deposition to support his charges. English, discredited in New York, decided when he left Washington, D.C., in March 1847, to settle in Philadelphia, his old stamping ground, where he remained until 1852. Fuller, no doubt, had some bitter things to say about English in private, and English, vexed with Fuller, proceeded to satirize him oftener than he did Poe in the John-Donkey, a weekly he and George G. Foster edited from 1 January to 21 October 1848, when the seven libel

suits filed against the magazine forced the publisher to discontinue the journal.

Fuller in his Evening Mirror article reprinted below is correct in saying that English's "Card" was first published in a morning newspaper, for the Morning Telegraph did carry English's article; but there is no evidence that the "Card" was "also published in one or two of the weekly papers." What is patently untrue is that English's article appeared in "his advertising columns." The first, third, and fourth pages of the four-page Evening Mirror were almost wholly given over to advertisements; the second, though containing two or three columns of advertising, also carried four or five columns of news and gossip. English's "Card" appeared on the second page and was definitely not among the advertisements. The page of the Weekly Mirror containing the "Card" carried no advertisements at all.

The Home Journal's proposal for founding what Fuller here calls "an Asylum for used-up authors" appears as Document 61. The actual assessment of damages and court costs was $326.48, not $353, as Fuller asserts, and only $225.06 of this amount went to Poe and his attorney.

This and Document 34 are the only ones that specify the occasions when Poe broke his seclusion at Fordham to appear in person in the literary district of the city, though he may have been in attendance at court during the Preliminary Hearing (Document 43). No doubt his walk on Nassau Street was an ordeal for him, for on that street were located the editorial offices of the Mirror, the Knickerbocker, and the Tribune, among others, and he was more than likely to meet a number of enemies. No doubt too, as Fuller seems pleased to report, he had braced himself for that ordeal by drinking too much. And doubtless too the imp of the perverse, which Poe knew so well, impelled him to do the very thing he felt he ought not to do—namely, visit the publishing office of the Mirror where Fuller had his editorial quarters. Apparently Poe did not stop to see Duyckinck, for Duyckinck remarked on 24 June 1847 in his unpublished diary, "With Mathews, visited Poe at Fordham. . . ."]

Prenez Garde, Chrony.—We regret to learn that the bold, clever, and rather reckless editor of the Boston Chronotype has been sued for a libel. He had better apologize and compromise at once. We speak from experience—having now before our eyes a document (which we intend to frame and hang up in our sanctum as a perpetual caution) showing the utter folly of trusting for justice to the law, and at the same time teaching us never again to confide to the smooth words and fair promises of irresponsible literary humbugs. The interesting document we allude to certifies that we have paid *Edgar A. Poe* and his attorney, *E. L. Fancher,* the sum of *three hundred and fifty-three dollars* to satisfy the offended majesty of the law, which we unwittingly violated by allowing *Thomas Dunn English* to insert "*A Card*" which he brought to us in the columns of a morning paper, and which was also published in one or two of the weekly papers. The verdict of the jury was $225 and costs, being the exact amount of damage which twelve "good men and true" conscientiously believed the character of the poet had suffered by the publication of the said English's "Card"; and the greater portion of the balance, of course, went into the pocket of the poet's sympathetic attorney.

We notice that Judge Wilde, of Massachusetts, a most excellent and learned Judge, has recently decided a similar case in favor of the *publisher,* who should *not* be held responsible for what appears in his *advertising* columns. But notwithstanding this decision, we advise our contemporaries never to resort to the law for protection or defence in cases of libel. Litigation is always vexatious, and the result of a trial by jury is always uncertain, especially when desperate lawyers—to eke out a poor cause, leave the bar for the witness stand, and instead of pleading, *swear* a case through, per force. We regret to add that all the pecuniary losses and troubles that we have ever experienced have been occasioned by unfortunate connections with men who take pride in the name of Poet, and whose themes *on paper* have always been Honor, Love, and Religion. We can count on our fingers no less than four of these "ornaments of literature," who have cost us in the aggregate a pretty big figure,—and the worst of all is the loss of faith in the integrity of human nature, which the rascality of a few individuals may forever inflict upon one's social philosophy and affections. . . . So we will reiterate our advice to the Press generally, and to our little "*Chrony*" particularly, to eschew libels and *live* poets; the former will get you into difficulty, the latter into debt. . . .

Since writing the above we have had a striking demonstration of the truth of our remarks: the poor wretch who succeeded by aid of the law and a sharp attorney in filching our money, staggered into our publishing office this morning, clad in a decent suit of black, which had doubtless been purchased by the money so infamously obtained, and behaved himself in so indecent a manner that we were compelled to send for a posse of the police to take him away.

The last thing that we heard him say, as they took him up Nassau street, was something about *home*, and we suppose that he wanted to go to his friend of the *Home Journal*, who a short time since proposed founding an Asylum for used-up authors. Poor wretch! We looked upon him with sincere pity, and forgave him all the wrong he had done us, only reserving our wrath for the instruments which give such people power to inflict injury upon innocent victims.

---

95. *10 June 1847: "An Attorney in Search of Practice"*
Hiram Fuller

[*Responding to the libelous comments made about him by Fuller on June 7 (Document 94), Enoch L. Fancher, Poe's attorney, evidently served a bill of complaint upon Fuller preparatory to filing it at court. Fuller decided to make the matter public in the* Evening Mirror.]

AN ATTORNEY IN SEARCH OF PRACTICE.—The legal gentlemen [*sic*] of whom we spoke the other day as having assisted Mr. Poe to ease us of nearly four hundred dollars, thinks his character damaged by having the truth told of him, to the extent of 5,000 dollars, and has very quietly commenced a suit against us for that amount. For our own part, we think from a short acquaintance with this gentleman that he quite over estimates the value of his character, in supposing it possible that it could be so extensively damaged; and so, we think a jury will decide. But truly, we live in a pretty time when, if one man assists another to obtain the contents of your purse by employing the little crooks and cranks of the law, you are debarred from the privilege of announcing that fact to your friends. If telling the simple truth of an attorney will give him any right to ask the public authorites [*sic*] to assist him in obtaining 5,000 dollars, on the score of damage done to his character, what a character the attorney must have that would be seriously injured! and what magnificent damages might not some of the rogues of the Court of Sessions obtain from the press for assaults upon their characters. Jack Williams, who attempted to break jail the other day, should immediately commence suits against every paper in the city for publishing the truth about him. If it is an offence to tell the truth of an attorney, we do not see upon what principle it should be less an offence to tell the truth of a pick-pocket, particularly when the attorney has been instrumental in doing, you a serious injury. We have looked carefully over our remarks and have not been able to discover anything libellous in them, they contain not a syllable of untruth; but a legal friend has suggested, that calling an attorney "sharp" is an offence in the eye of the law. If so, we think the law very sharp-sighted, (we hope there is nothing libellous in that) for the term is a very general one, and we thought, that, applied to an attorney, it was highly complimentary; but we are perfectly willing to make the amende honorable and eat our words, if it will save us from the horrors of a suit at law. If the gentleman will be satisfied by a recantation, we will admit that he is not a sharp attorney but quite the reverse, viz: a very dull one. But perhaps that would be libellous. We have one very great comfort in our affliction, we shall have the privilege of being tried before an upright and intelligent Bench; men who came out of the law and have never had to appeal to a jury to ascertain the precise legal value of their characters.

---

96. *12 June 1847: "From the* Express"
Hiram Fuller

[*Finding an item in the New York* Express *bearing on his article, "An Attorney in Search of Practice" (preceding document), Fuller quoted it and again discussed Fancher's threatened libel suit against him.*

This article also appeared in the Weekly Mirror *on June 19.*]

From the Express.—The MIRROR tells us under the head of "AN ATTORNEY IN SEARCH OF PRACTICE," of some "sharp," practice upon that paper in the way of another libel suit. Some gentleman of the Bar, it seems, alledges [*sic*] himself damaged, $5000 worth. It is quite time that so respectable a profession as that of the Law sets its face against this sort of practice, and abandon it all to "Quirk, Gammon and Snap." Sueing [*sic*] Editors for alledged libels has become in this State, under the monstrous decisions of the late Supreme Court, a trade, a traffic, a regular pursuit. It is nearly overdone, however, just now, or left in very small hands. If the Mirror fights its case well before a Jury, the legal gentleman will be left to pay his own costs.

As we have been repeatedly asked the *name* of the "legal gentleman," alluded to in the above paragraph [New York *Express*], we will guardedly publish it for the admiration of the press and the public. ENOCH L. FANCHER, formerly a methodist minister, the friend and attorney of *Edgar A. Poe*, is the aggrieved and damaged party. His late success in prosecuting us for a libel on Mr. Poe, has probably inspired him with new ardor in his profession, while our recent advice to our contemporaries to settle libel suits without resorting to trial by jury may have led him to believe that he had only to issue another *capias* to obtain $5000. But we rather think he will find himself mistaken. There is a law that protects men from malicious prosecution—and there is such a thing as public opinion, an influence which we had much rather trust to than the law. But in the present case we are disposed to follow the advice of the Express, a good authority in these matters, and fight our adversary before a jury to his heart's content. We shall learn in what the liberty of the press consists, and whether truth and justice form any protection before the legal tribunals of the State. Our friends of the Express have had no less than *sixty* libel suits commenced against them, and in no case, we believe, has a jury rendered a verdict against them of more than *six cents*. Mr. Brooks has generally appeared in person in his own defence, proving the untruthfulness of the legal maxim that a man who pleads his own cause has a fool for a client. Probably Mr. Fancher thinks that he can put us to some expense by his ridiculous suit, even though he should not recover anything himself; but to show the kind of estimation in which such conduct as his, is held by the honorable members of his profession, many of whom we are happy to number among our most intimate friends, we would inform him for his consolation that several gentlemen of great legal ability have volunteered to defend us agains[t] this second attempt to harrass [*sic*] us and obtain our money. We cannot say with any degree of sincerity that we wish he may get it, for nothing would give us greater annoyance than to know that the quondam Methodist parson was clothing and feeding himself at our expense. It is greatly to be lamented that he had not experienced a little religion while he was engaged in the unprofitable business of preaching the gospel, for there is little hope of a man learning to be a christian at the bar who failed while in the pulpit.

---

97. *14 June 1847:* **The** Evening Mirror *Quotes the* **Express**

[*The editor of the New York* Express, *responding to Fuller's remarks (preceding document), explained that the* "Mirror *misunderstands us as having some sixty libel suits commenced against us," and offered advice on handling such lawsuits. Fuller published the item without comment, trusting, very likely, that subscribers to the* Mirror *would read it in connection with his earlier remarks on Enoch Fancher.*]

The *Mirror* misunderstands us as having some sixty libel suits commenced against us, although it is a fact that since the rumor of a verdict obtained against us in Rochester, the legal gentlemen who mistake the Bar for the Road, have been in hot pursuit of paragraphs, out of which they thought they could make money, or extort fees to settle. A class of lawyers has arisen in this State since the monstrous decisions of the Courts, who are trying to live on the Press. The true rule is, to fight them and compel them to starve. When an Editor has been mistaken, or is innocently guilty of a libel, he himself owes to the party injured every honorable reparation,—but he is under no obligations to pay lawyers *black mail*. The Juries will take care of us, against these prosecutors, if cases are attended to with earnestness and determination.—*Express*.

---

98. *8 July 1847:* "*Attorney and Client*"
Hiram Fuller

[*E. L. Fancher either settled with Fuller out of court or, as seems more likely, accepted the apology he published in the* Evening Mirror *(reprinted below). In any event, he dropped his suit against Fuller, for my search in the New York Hall of Records shows that Fancher did not file his bill of complaint against him.*

Fuller here corroborates the charges Poe made in his letter of 18 Oc-

tober 1847 (see headnote to Document 70) when he writes: "There have been actors behind the scenes in all this business. . . ." Unlike Poe, however, he does not name them.

This apology was also published in the Weekly Mirror of July 10.]

ATTORNEY AND CLIENT.—In our remarks on the libel suit of Edgar A. Poe, brought by Mr. Fancher against us—we did not mean to dispute the right of counsel to bring a suit on the complaint of a client, but we thought then, and think now, that when men of questionable character and intemperate habits desire to have a libel suit brought against an editor of a paper for a libel, which he did not himself write, a discretion should be used on the part of counsel, because an absence of that discretion would seriously affect the liberty of the press. In conducting that case, we imputed to Mr. Fancher the betrayal of a confidential communication—we are now assured by a disinterested friend, that his information was not obtained in any confidential way, and therefore our information was incorrect. In conducting Poe's suit, we did not intend charging Mr. Fancher with any dishonorable confederacy in extorting money from us. There have been actors *behind the scenes* in all this business, whom we may yet have to call before the footlights. When a man has robbed you he will kill you also if he can, for the reason that "dead men tell no tales."

---

99. 27 July 1847: Letter to Poe
George W. Eveleth

[*Poe had sent a clipping of his "Reply to Mr. English and Others" (Document 24) to Eveleth, upon which his admirer made some candid comments. ". . . There are some things in it which I had rather not seen," he wrote, and added: "In some instances you have come down too nearly on a level with English himself. This, as the editor of the paper"—Hiram Fuller—"says . . . is in bad taste." Eveleth nevertheless excused his "especial favorite" on the grounds that his illness must have made him "a little peevish. . . ."*

The "book" Eveleth mentions is Literary America, *which Poe was probably working on spasmodically (see headnote to Document 58).*

[213]

This letter, only a portion of which is given below, appears in Mab-bott, 182–4.]

Phillips, Me. Tuesday evening, 27

Friend Poe.

I received yours of March 11, inclosing the reply to Dunn English, in due season. . . .

I am impatient to hear from you. I *haven't* heard a word since your last letter, neither of good nor of bad—and I have watched pretty snugly the papers that have come to our office, in the hope of coming across your name. I would almost rather have seen it, written with a slanderer's pen, as I have seen it before, than not at all. How is it that you contrive to keep so still?—it must be contrary to your disposition to do so—it is contrary to the order of the Mind that gifted you so bountifully with the active principle, *mind*—it is not in accordance with the idea in your letter to Willis—"The truth is, I have a great deal to do; and I have made up my mind not to die till it is done." It may be though, that you are very busy with your "book," so that you haven't time to make a noise—pretty likely *it* will make a noise when it appears—when is it to appear?—or it may be that illness keeps you still. I should indeed be afflicted to know that this is the case. Are you better than when you last wrote? Your reply to English is severe, and should be so—but there are some things in it which I had rather not seen. In some instances you have *come down* too nearly on a level with English himself. This, as the editor of the paper (what paper is it?) says on the other side, is in bad taste—You laid yourself liable to be laughed at by answering in such a spirit, more than you would have done if you had kept calm—I imagine that your illness made you a little peevish. . . .

Your faithfully.
Geo. W. Eveleth.

---

100. *4 January 1848: Letter to George W. Eveleth*
Edgar A. Poe

[Poe was months late in answering Eveleth's letter (preceding document) and was at once self-justifying and self-congratulatory about his libel suit when he did. Poe may have liked his "Reply to Mr. English and

Others" (Document 24), but it would be hard to find anyone then or now who shares his taste. The peevishness and indignation which at times mark his "Reply," Poe insists, were "put on." One cannot help wondering how much he was putting Eveleth on in this letter, since he liked to play at being Dupin who was nothing if not rational and in that sense superior to circumstance.

The "magazine campaign" which Poe mentions in the opening portion of the letter printed below refers to his efforts "to establish a journal in which," as he said, "the men of genius may fight their battles; upon some terms of equality, with these dunces the men of talent." This, to quote Poe again, had become the "one great purpose of my literary life." If he succeeded, he said, he would within two years put himself "in possession of a fortune and infinitely more," the "infinitely more" being perhaps the power to redress the grievances done him.

The full letter appears in Ostrom, II, 354-7.]

New-York—Jan. 4, 1848.

My Dear Sir—

. . . I have been "so still" on account of preparation for the magazine campaign—also have been working at my book—nevertheless I have written some trifles not yet published—some which have been. . . . My health is better—best. I have never been so well. . . . I do not well see how I could have otherwise replied to English. You must know him, (English) before you can well estimate my reply. He is so thorough a "blatherskite" that [to] have replied to him with *dignity* would have been the extreme of the ludicrous. The only true plan—not to have replied to him at all—was precluded on account of the nature of some of his accusations —forgery for instance. To such charges, even from the Auto[crat] of all the Asses—a man is *compelled* to answer. There he had me. Answer him I must[.] But how? Believe me there exists no such dilemma as that in which a gentleman [is] placed when he is forced to reply to a blackguard. If he have any genius then is the time for its display. I confess to you that I rather *like* that reply of mine in a literary sense—and so do a great many of my friends. It fully answered its purpose beyond a doubt— would to Heaven every work of art did as much! You err in supposing me to have been "peevish" when I wrote the reply:—the peevishness was all "put on" as a part of my argument—of my plan:—so was the "indignation" with which I wound up. *How* could I be either [peev]ish or indignant about a matter so well adapted to further my purposes? Were I able

[215]

to afford so expensive a luxury as personal and especially as *refutable* abuse, I would [w]illingly pay any man $2000 per annum, to hammer away at me all the year round. I suppose you know that I sued the Mirror & got a verdict. English eloped. . . .

Truly Yours—

E A Poe.

---

101. *8 September 1847: "Important Legal Ruling"*
Hiram Fuller

[*Despite his apology to Enoch L. Fancher (Document 98), Fuller continued to make an issue of the fact that he had taken the stand to testify that Clason, his brother-in-law, was a partner in the* Mirror *firm. This time his target of attack was Justice Samuel Jones, the judge in the case, who had allowed Poe's attorney to act as a witness.*]

IMPORTANT LEGAL RULING.—In the course of a trial yesterday in the Court of Common Pleas, Judge Daly, presiding, R. N. Morrison, Esq., of counsel for the plaintiff, offered to take the stand as witness for his client. Blunt, counsel for the defendant, objected on the ground of incompetency. In support of the objection, the learned counsel introduced and read two decisions lately made by the Queens Bench of England. After able argument on both sides of the question, Judge Daly ruled the evidence offered as inadmissible, thus sustaining the decisions of the English bench.

This is a most important and most just decision. In a recent libel suit in which we were defendants, the principal witness was the plaintiff's counsel, and it was on his testimony solely that an innocent party [Augustus W. Clason, Jr.] was mulcted in heavy damages. Judge Jones admitted this kind of testimony, which Judge Daly rules out. And this is Law. Opposite ends of the City Hall are governed by opposite principles. What is admissible in the Supreme Court is inadmissible in an inferior one. In this case the inferior Court has the superior Judge. Such mockery of Justice, with the recollection of a heavy verdict, makes one's gorge rise.

---

102. 16 November 1847: An Untitled Article in the Evening Mirror
   Hiram Fuller

[*This documentary began with Lewis Clark's attack on Poe, an attack that was vigorously joined by Hiram Fuller, and it seems only fitting to end the account with Fuller's protestations that he had had "no quarrels with . . . cotemporaries that have occasioned any unpleasant feelings on either side," as well as with his expression of gratitude for the "words of 'brotherly love'" that came from the "lips and pen" of Clark.*

The record presented here shows how Poe as a person was reduced to ruin by the New York literati and their sponsors, who used the occasion while he was defenseless to work out old grudges or new ones. What the record fails to show clearly enough is that Poe, up to the time he had written "The Literati" sketches, had achieved an unparalleled national reputation as a critic, whatever notoriety he earned in gaining that reputation; that, on the strength of "The Raven," he became famous as a poet, however parodied and mocked "The Raven" was; and that his narratives, widely if not invariably accepted as brilliant at home, were beginning to be acclaimed in England and France.

His encounters with English, Fuller, and company, however, brought his career to a grinding halt, for his personal reputation, smeared beyond recovery by his enemies, soured his literary reputation, so that his manuscripts often went begging for publication or he was forced, "anxious," as he says, "to get out of . . . pecuniary difficulties," to publish in a journal such as the Boston Flag of Our Union. *His bibliography shows that from June 1846 to the time of his death he chiefly wrote poetry, probably because, being least likely to offend, it was most likely to be published. The few critical articles he wrote were with three exceptions all innocuous and inoffensive. The bibliography also shows that Poe, who had a record of being published in more than fifty magazines, annuals, and daily papers, now had access to only four New York journals—the* American Whig Review, *the* Columbian Magazine, *the* Democratic Review, *and the* Home Journal—*and that these magazines accepted only one contribution of his which was remotely critical. That contribution was "The Literati of New York—S. Anna Lewis," which was published in the* Democratic Review, *very likely with Duyckinck's help. (Duyckinck's connection with the* Democratic Review *was so well known that Lowell in his* Fable for Critics *could portray him as urging a critic to review a book, saying: "And*

I think I can promise your thoughts, if you do, / A place in the next Democratic Review.") Impoverished and desperate, Poe had edited and applauded Mrs. Lewis's poems "for a consideration," because, as he "fiercely" told Mary Gove who rebuked him for this "unpardonable sin," "Would you blame a man for not allowing his sick wife to starve?" (Mary Gove Nichols, "Reminiscences of Edgar Allan Poe.") The title of this essay led English in his John-Donkey *to hail "Poe's New Dunciad," if only to disturb the New York literati again. "We hear it stated in certain quarters," he wrote, "that Mr. POE is about to resume his sketches of character, commenced in the Lady's Book something more than a year ago. . . . Mr. POE . . . is a perfect windfall of a critic. He is a ripe scholar, too; dead ripe; rather too ripe; perhaps gone to seed."*

The three reviews Poe wrote that were not innocuous he had to publish in magazines outside New York. These were his critiques of Hawthorne's Mosses from an Old Manse, *which he published in Philadelphia in* Godey's Lady's Book, Lowell's Fable for Critics, *and* Joel T. Headley's The Sacred Mountains, *both of which he published in Richmond, in the* Southern Literary Messenger. *Yet even this statement glosses the situation. For in the summer of 1849 Poe was complaining to Annie Richmond that the New York magazines to which he had access had either failed (the* Columbian Magazine*) or were "forced to stop paying for contributions" (the* American Whig Review *and the* Democratic Review*), and that other magazines outside New York (the* Southern Literary Messenger *in Richmond,* Graham's Magazine *and* Sartain's Union Magazine *in Philadelphia) were "very precarious." The only book he published during the period was* Eureka (1848), *which, of course, was noncritical and anomalous in every sense. For that work he received from George P. Putnam, a former partner in the firm of Wiley and Putnam which had published his* Tales *and* Raven *volume, only fourteen dollars, and that amount only as a loan to be repaid "in case the sales of said work do not cover the expenses." Furthermore, despite the fact that under his guidance the* Southern Literary Messenger, *against fantastic odds, had come to rival the* Knickerbocker *in popularity and that he had made* Graham's Magazine *the leading literary journal in the country, no one, as Duyckinck pointed out (Document 68), offered him a berth on a magazine, let alone an editorship. In short, though totally committed to literature, Poe was almost literally starved out of the profession. The poverty and persecution he suffered, which exhausted his energies and drained his self-esteem*

—a self-esteem he vainly tried to recoup by efforts to establish his own magazine—led to his being found semiconscious on a street in Baltimore and to his death on 7 October 1849 at Washington College Hospital, having gone through a "state," to quote Arthur Hobson Quinn, "of utter despair and self-reproach" that "passed into a violent delirium."

We may leave the final word on this score to Duyckinck who, as a pivotal figure of the period, was an authority on the matter. In his unpublished diary Duyckinck wrote on 1 November 1875:

. . . Poe came into the world, for America a little too soon, at a period when there was the least possible encouragement for a man of genius; when the public was indifferent and in an inverse way of mending the matter the writers themselves were often absurdly antagonistic to each other. . . .

Poe, cool and fastidious, aristocratic in his taste in literature, should have been nurtured in a proud academic society. . . . As it was, he was compelled to splash among the minnows, entangling himself in the weeds and mud. Two things demoralized the man, his faulty temperament . . . and his daily necessities. . . . If he was insincere at times, it was because he was indifferent. The stake was too trifling for him to preserve the honour of the game. . . .

What if he had lived a little longer to enjoy the European fame which his works were on the eve of receiving when he died? A few months longer and "Fame that the clear spirit doth raise" might have proved the beacon and incentive to a better and higher life.

One curious incident is worth recording before we turn to the article below. The Weekly Mirror *on 22 May 1847 changed its name to the* American Literary Gazette and New York Weekly Mirror. *In anticipation of the "new" literary journal, the* Weekly Mirror *of May 8 announced that Jedidiah B. Auld, Duyckinck's friend who had written for* Yankee Doodle, *would be the new editor and that he would be assisted by Duyckinck himself, not to mention Charles F. Briggs and H. C. Watson, the music and art critic, who were already on the* Mirror *staff. Despite continuing announcements that Auld and Duyckinck would be added to the staff, there was never any official notice that they helped to conduct the magazine. In fact, the last announcement to mention Auld and Duyckinck appeared on 19 June 1847, after which Fuller dropped their names, though he continued to announce the new journal. On July 24, to* dispel any misunderstanding that may have developed, Fuller announced that he was the sole editor and proprietor of the American Literary Gazette and New York Weekly Mirror.

Auld's position in all this is made clear by a letter he wrote to George Duyckinck, Evert's young brother, who was traveling in Europe. The letter is dated September 1847 and is in the Duyckinck Manuscript Collection in the New York Public Library. Auld said that he would like to publish George's letters about his travels abroad in "my little Mirror but alas I abdicated three months ago the sceptre. With me it was but a reign of one hundred days. . . ." The reasons he gave for having accepted the editorship were that Cornelius Mathews, who was then editing Yankee Doodle, "was very anxious . . . that I should EDITORSHIP" and that he himself was willing to "go into the scribbling to get paid." The reasons he gave for relinquishing the editorship were that he "saw no [monetary] compensation was likely to be gained" and that he felt "sensibly the disgrace of a failure [in his management of the journal] which I believed inevitable from the first."

Evert Duyckinck's role in this affair, while more intriguing, is less clear. He had edited the newly founded Literary World from 6 February to 24 April 1847, after which time he abruptly "retired" from the editorship in favor of Charles Fenno Hoffman, only to become connected with the magazine again on 7 October 1848 when he and his brother bought the journal and jointly edited it. Duyckinck retired as editor of the Literary World on account of a dispute with the publishers. He had allegedly broken an unwritten agreement with them that Cornelius Mathews, his best friend, would have nothing to do with the magazine. (The angry exchange of correspondence between Duyckinck and his publishers is in the Duyckinck Manuscript Collection.) It seems likely that, following his retirement from the Literary World, Fuller offered him the editorship of the American Literary Gazette, a position he declined in favor of Auld, though probably agreeing upon Fuller's urging to assist Auld if the need arose. What services, if any, he actually rendered is not clear from Auld's letter. All that Auld says on this score is that "Evert received the offer of the affair and his name was connected with the Mirror more than I desired, since it seemed in some measure like a display of feeling against the [Literary] World."

Among other errors that Perry Miller (The Raven and the Whale, pages 206, 209) made in discussing this situation—for instance, that Fuller

sold the Weekly Mirror *to the Duyckinck group and then bought it back
—is that the "first volume" of the* Trippings of Tom Pepper *(Document
89) carried on "its cover the statement that it was edited by Auld and
Duyckinck." There is no indication on the title page, any preliminary
pages, or outside cover of either one of the two volumes that Auld and
Duyckinck "edited" the novel.*

In the article below, Fuller's quotation from the Knickerbocker *of
November 1847 is accurate. The* Gazette and Times, *probably the first
journal to deride Poe's "Literati" and the author himself (Document 2),
was obviously congenial to Fuller.* Yankee Doodle, *whose expiration on
the eve of its third volume (2 October 1847) surprised its own staff (it had
announced the contents of the next number, which never appeared), did
not, of course, send Fuller its love. Instead, in its final number,* Yankee
Doodle *observed: "The* Gazette and Times, *having been incorporated
with the* (Evening) Mirror, *has ceased to exist—that is, it has resolved
itself into nothing—alias, the* Mirror."]

The 'New York Evening Mirror' daily journal has received into
itself the 'Daily Gazette and Times,' and is now among the liveliest,
best conducted and widest circulated of our daily sheets. Mr. FULLER
is indefatigable in his efforts, and his capable assistants second well
his exertions. A second series of 'Tom Pepper' is commenced as a
feuilleton, which is continued in the 'Weekly Mirror,' now a very
handsomely printed sheet, in the folio form.

We copy the above from the *Knickerbocker* of November, not for the
purpose of promulgating our own praise, but as an excuse for publicly
thanking *Mr. Clark* for the many words of fraternal kindness, or, to use
a good old scriptural expression, words of "brotherly love" that we have
received both from his lips and pen. We do not feel over-burthened with
indebtedness to our contemporaries, some of whom have carefully visited
upon us as it were "the sins of the fathers;" and it is pleasant occasionally
to let out some expressions of gratitude in return for kindness received.
We have had in our editorial career to contend with enemies that we
never made, and many adverse influences which were not easily overcome. We took the Mirror with forty mortal quarrels on its face; and,
like the sons of the old houses of Capulet and Montague, inherited feuds
which we could not feel. There was a *Courier* quarrel—a *Commercial*
quarrel—a *Herald* quarrel—an *Express* quarrel, an *Onderdonk* quarrel,

with other minor quarrels scattered about the country too numerous to mention.—Our first effort was to bury the editorial hatchet, rub out old scores and begin anew. And we are happy to state that, with many of the old enemies of this paper, we have long since smoked the pipe of peace. But some of them, to use a more expressive than elegant word, are still *grouty* and will remain so, for aught we know or care, till doomsday. Such occasionally do us the honor to steal, from our columns, and when compelled to notice us it is only as an "evening paper." But it is something to boast of, that independent and plain spoken as the Mirror has always been, we have thus far had no libel suit to answer on our own account, and no quarrels with our cotemporaries that have occasioned any unpleasant feelings on either side. *Yankee Doodle* on his death bed sent us his love, and begged forgiveness for the poor jokes he had attempted at our expense. We ejaculated in return the common prayer for all departed *sinners—requiescat in pace.* But we are straying from our purpose, which was to thank our friend Clark for his ever welcome Monthly with its words of cheer. It is enough to reconcile one to many severities and asperities to find here and there a generous specimen of humanity. It enables us to appreciate the remark of Coleridge, who declared that he was preserved from misanthropy by the thought that Wordsworth lived.

In contrast with the treatment of the Knickerbocker, we may be allowed to mention that the editor of one of the oldest and wealthiest newspaper establishments in this city was requested by a person belonging to this office to notice editorially the fact that the *Evening Gazette* had been united to the Mirror. The request was compiled with, *and a bill sent in for about two dollars.*

WORKS PERTINENT TO POE'S LIBEL SUIT

Dedmond, Francis B. "Poe's Libel Suit Against T. D. English." *Boston Public Library Quarterly,* V (Jan. 1953), 31–7.
[*Despite the misleading title, for Poe did not bring a suit against English but against Hiram Fuller and Augustus Clason, this article accurately sketches the outlines of Poe's lawsuit.*]

———. "The War of the Literati: Documents of the Legal Phase." *Notes and Queries,* CXCVIII (July 1953), 303–8.
[*This article presents Poe's Declaration of Grievances and English's Deposition.*]

Gravely, William Henry, Jr. "The Early Political and Literary Career of Thomas Dunn English." Unpublished Ph.D. dissertation. University of Virginia, 1953.
[*This is the fullest and most thorough biography of Thomas Dunn English available, though it concludes with English's leaving Philadelphia for Virginia in 1852 and though, given the obscurity of the man, some of the information is necessarily fragmentary and conjectural. The most pertinent chapters are 6, 8, and 9.*]

Harrison, James A., ed. *The Literati* (Vol. 15) and *Letters of Edgar Allan Poe* (Vol. 17) in *The Complete Works of Edgar Allan Poe,* 17 vols. New York: AMS Press, 1965.
[*Reprinted from the original 1902 Virginia edition, these two volumes in this still standard, though incomplete, edition are quite pertinent to Poe's lawsuit. Volume 17, in addition to containing "Mr. English's Reply to Mr. Poe," "Mr. Poe's Reply to Mr. English and Others," English's "In Reply to Mr. Poe's Rejoinder," also contains letters from certain crucial correspondents to Poe, which I have drawn upon in this study. Harrison makes some mistakes in discussing the lawsuit, the most glaring of which is that "English brought criminal charges of obtaining money under false pretences and of forgery against Poe" (XVII, 233). It was Poe who brought charges, not against English but against Fuller and Clason, and the lawsuit was not a criminal prosecution but a civil one.*]

Hurley, Leonard B. "A New Note in the War of the Literati." *American Literature,* VII (Jan. 1936), 376–94.

[*Hurley presents his discovery of the Poe-Hammerhead satires in English's novel, 1844; or, The Power of the "S.F."*]

Mabbott, Thomas Ollive, ed. "The Letters from George W. Eveleth to Edgar Allan Poe." *Bulletin of the New York Public Library,* XXVI (March 1922), 171–95.

[*A valuable collection of letters from a young medical student in Maine whose favorite author was Poe. His inquiries induced Poe to comment often on the lawsuit as well as on other relevant matters, such as the authorship of "An Author in Europe and America." This work is especially helpful when read in conjunction with Poe's own letters to Eveleth.*]

Moriarty, Jos. F. *A Literary Tomahawking: The Libel Action of Edgar Allan Poe vs. Thomas Dunn English—A Complete Report of the Documents of the Case and Materials about Poe Published for the First Time.* Privately printed, 1963.

[*This narrative of Poe's lawsuit contains some of the better known documents such as Poe's articles on Thomas Dunn English, English's replies to Poe's articles, many of the trial documents, and a few of Hiram Fuller's statements on the libel action. Despite its subtitle, this study is an incomplete report of the case and much of the material in it had prior publication. Inasmuch as this work has eluded Poe bibliographers, and myself too until my own manuscript was in press, a word about it seems in order. It consists of eleven pages of typewritten front matter, eleven unpaginated illustrations, and 149 typewritten pages of text, all reproduced by planograph. According to the Union Card Catalog, three libraries have copies of this work, the Library of Congress, New York Public Library, and the California State Library at Sacramento.*]

Moss, Sidney P. "Poe, Hiram Fuller and the Duyckinck Circle." *American Book Collector,* XVIII (Oct. 1967), 8–18.

[*This article traces Fuller's persecution of Poe and how the Duyckinck circle, especially Simms, Duyckinck, Mathews, and Poe, sought to offset the effects.*]

———. *Poe's Literary Battles: The Critic in the Context of His Literary Milieu.* Durham, N.C.: Duke University Press, 1963.

[*A work that puts Poe's critical documents in their contemporary con-*

text, it provides a thoroughgoing account of Poe's major quarrels with the Boston and New York coteries, and traces, along with other events, the Longfellow war, the Boston Lyceum "hoax," and the episode involving Frances Osgood and Elizabeth Ellet—essential background for understanding the libel suit.]

Nichols, Mary Gove. "Reminiscences of Edgar Allan Poe." New York: The Union Square Book Shop, 1931.
[These reminiscences by a friend of Poe and one of the literati (reprinted from an article that first appeared in the Six Penny Magazine of February 1863) help us to see Poe in his Fordham retreat.]

Oliphant, Mary C. Simms, Alfred Taylor Odell, and T. C. Duncan Eaves, eds. The Letters of William Gilmore Simms, 5 vols. Columbia: University of South Carolina Press, 1952–1956.
[Volume 2, which contains Simms's letters written from 1845–1849, is especially pertinent to the lawsuit. I have drawn upon this volume for the one Simms letter reproduced in this study.]

Ostrom, John Ward, ed. The Letters of Edgar Allan Poe, 2 vols. New York: Gordian Press, 1966.
[Reprinted from the Harvard University Press publication with a Supplement that brings the work up to date, volume 2 is especially valuable for Poe letters pertaining to the libel suit. I have not hesitated to draw upon this work for transcriptions of Poe letters, because I have found only one transcriptual error in it in all the years I have used it.]

Reece, James B. "Poe and the New York Literati: A Study of the 'Literati' Sketches and of Poe's Relations with the New York Writers." Unpublished Ph.D. dissertation. Duke University, 1954.
[This work contains detailed biographical sketches of the thirty-eight writers whom Poe touched upon in "The Literati" series and traces Poe's relations to them.]

Schreiber, Carl. "A Close-Up of Poe." Saturday Review of Literature, III (9 Oct. 1926), 165–7.
[This article deserves mention only because it was the first to print a fragment of the court record, namely, portions of English's Deposition.]

INDEX

Aldrich, James, Poe accuses of plagiarism, 46, 47

Allen, Hervey, 31

American Literary Gazette and New York Weekly Mirror, 219–21. *See also Weekly Mirror*

American Review: A Whig Journal (New York): Poe contributes to, 217; stops paying contributors, 218; mentioned, 17

Anthon, Charles, in "Literati," 18

Appleton and Company publish Halleck, 93

Aristidean, The (New York): as Poe's ally, 26–7; Poe's relations with, 27; reviews Hirst, 27, 44; reviews Longfellow, 27; Poe on, 29, 32; Poe publishes in, 164, 165, 169; mentioned, 33. *See also* English, Thomas Dunn

Arthur, Timothy Shay, 7. *See also Arthur's Ladies' Magazine*

Arthur's Ladies' Magazine (Philadelphia) merges with *Godey's*, 7, 8, 12–3, 15

Athenæum, The (London): Poe cites on *Tales and Poems*, 23; Clark quotes on Poe, 111, 113

Atlanta Enterprise, Chivers reprints Duyckinck's defense of Poe in, 204

Auld, Jedidiah B.: edits *Yankee Doodle*, 219, and *American Literary Gazette*, 219–20; writes to George Duyckinck, 220; did not edit *Trippings of Tom Pepper*, 221

Barnum, P. T., 51, 62

Barrett, Miss Elizabeth Barrett: Poe quotes letter of, 21, 23–4; Poe dedicates *Raven* volume to, 25; letter of to Poe, 25–6; on English reception of "The Raven" and "Valdemar Case," 26; Poe reviews, 118; English alleges Poe asked for favorable notice, 121; Poe sends letter of to Duyckinck, 141; Duyckinck quotes from letter of to Poe, 143; mentioned, 140

Baudelaire, Charles, Forgues helps bring Poe to attention of, 144

Bayless, Joy, quotes Griswold on Mrs. Ellet, 156

Behrin, Nathan, viii

Benjamin, Park, denies starting rumor that Poe engaged in forgery, 58

Bennett, James Gordon: Fuller threatens with libel suit, 87; Fuller compares Poe to, 185; Clason cowhides, 187

Bisco, John: English pays to help Poe buy *Broadway Journal*, 34, 49, 164, 167, 169; Poe's letter to, 68–9. *See also Broadway Journal*

Boston *Chronotype*: sued for libel, 207; Fuller advises to eschew libels, 208

Boston Flag of Our Union, Poe reduced to publishing in, 217

Boston Lyceum: Poe's performance at, xv, 35, 36, 89; Poe's appearance at announced by Morris, 41; Poe ignores English's charges on his performance at, 49; reactions to Poe's performance at, 127

Boston *Transcript. See* Walter, Cornelia Wells

Bostonian, The: announces distress of the Poes, 127; Miss Walter cites, 136

Botta, Mrs. Anne C. L. *See* Lynch, Anne Charlotte

Briggs, Charles Frederick ("Harry Franco"): Fuller on, 18, 49; Poe on, 46, 50, 51; said to squib Poe in *Mirror*, 48; connection of with *Mirror*, 49, 195, 219; "quotes" Horne on Poe, 118; lures Poe away from *Mirror*, 128; editor of *Broadway Journal*, 195; *Fable for Critics* dedicated to, 195; mentioned, 9

—*Trippings of Tom Pepper, The*: Knickerbocker, *Literary World*, and *Yankee Doodle* on, 194–5; serialized in *Mirror*, 194, 195, 196; satirizes Duyckinck, Mrs. Ellet, Mathews, Simms, and Poe, 194–202 *passim*; book version of misreported as edited by Auld and Duyckinck, 221

British Critic, The (London), Poe cites on *Tales and Poems*, 23

Chief Justice Jones presides over, 171, 173, 176; transcripts of, 171, 186, 193–4; witnesses called in, 171–2, 174, 175; Fancher turns witness in, 172, 183, 184, 193, 208, 216; verdict in, 173, 175, 194, 207; "Rough Minutes" of, 174–5; jurymen in, 175; English's deposition read in, 175, 181; "Yorick" reports, 175–7; Fancher offers to settle out of court, 183, 184; Greeley on, 188–9; alleged that Poe will bring another against several ladies, 193–4, 204, 205; Poe on, 203, 214, 216; Mrs. Clemm collects "award money" from, 206; mentioned, vii, xv, 123, 132, 139, 155, 195, 202
—Poe's Declaration of Grievances: text of, 79–85; filed, 86; somewhat exaggerated, 88; mentioned, 171
—Preliminary Hearing: text of, 95–8; mentioned, 207
—Case of Poe *vs.* Fuller and Clason Postponed, 105
—Creation of a Commission To Obtain English's Deposition, 161–2, 165
—Direct and Cross-Interrogatories To Be Put to English, 162–5
—English's Deposition, 166–70
—Verdict of the Trial, 171–4. *See also* English, Thomas Dunn, Fancher, Enoch L., and Fuller, Hiram
Library of American Books: Duyckinck edits, and Mrs. Kirkland and Simms in, 42, and Poe, 138; *North American Review* on, 142; Headley in, 142
Literary America. See Poe, Edgar A.
Literary Gazette (London), Poe cites on *Tales and Poems,* 23
Literary World (New York): on *1844,* 100; Melville reviews for, 161; on *Trippings of Tom Pepper,* 194; Duyckinck edits, and Hoffman, 220. *See also* Duyckinck, Evert Augustus
"Literati of New York City, The." *See* Poe, Edgar A.
Literati, The. See Griswold, Rufus Wilmot
Locke, Mrs. Jane, Poe writes to, 156
Locke, Richard Adams: in "Literati," 30, 113, 124; in *Literary America,* 30, 124; alluded to as author of "Moon Hoax," 114
London *Athenæum. See Athenæum, The*
London *Literary Gazette,* Poe cites on *Tales and Poems,* 23

Longfellow, Henry Wadsworth: Poe's "war" on, xv, 26, 126–7, 128, 135; *Aristidean* on, 27; Miss Fuller on, 85; Fuller charges Poe made "lying insinuations" about, 85, 86; in *1844,* 107–9 *passim,* 121; Clark "quotes" Poe on, 113; Poe reviews *Waif* edited by, 128; *Yankee Doodle* on, 159; mentioned, 19, 93, 117
Lowell, James Russell: on *Yankee Doodle,* 160; dedicates *Fable for Critics* to Briggs, 195; on Duyckinck's connection with *Democratic Review,* 217–8; Poe reviews, 218
Lummis, Col. William: threatens Poe, 28, 37, 174, 195–6; at libel trial, 172 174, 203; alluded to in *Trippings of Tom Pepper,* 201. *See also* Ellet, Mrs. Elizabeth Frieze Lummis
Lynch, Miss Anne Charlotte, prompted by Mrs. Ellet to retrieve Mrs. Osgood's letters from Poe, 195

Mabbott, Thomas Ollive, edits *Raven* volume, 161, and Eveleth's letters to Poe, 224
Mathews, Cornelius: Duyckinck's closest friend, 45, 159; Poe reverses critical judgment on, 118; satirized in *1844,* 121; *North American Review* on, 142, 159; edits *Yankee Doodle,* 159; satirized in *Trippings of Tom Pepper,* 194–202 *passim;* Clark on, 194; visits Poe, 207; urges Auld to edit *American Literary Gazette,* 220
Melville, Herman: writes for *Yankee Doodle,* 159, and *Literary World,* 161; mentioned, 144
Mercury (New York) reports murder of Mary Rogers, 152
Mexican War: beginning of, 60; General Taylor in, 61; called "heathenish," 127
Miller, Perry, 220–1
Mirror. See Evening Mirror and *Weekly Mirror*
Mirror Library publishes *1844,* 100, and *Trippings of Tom Pepper,* 195, 196
Moore, Thomas, Fuller cites to burlesque Poe, 106
Moriarty, Jos. F., on libel suit, 224
Morning Express (New York): on illness of the Poes, 126, 128, 130; Greeley quotes on Poe, 134, 135; on libel trial, 175–7; mentioned, 133
Morning News (New York): on English's

"Reply to Mr. Poe," 39; on Poe's "Reply to Mr. English and Others," 59–60, 63; announces Poe will prosecute *Mirror*, 60, 63; reprints article from *Public Ledger* on Poe's proposed libel suit, 64; on Fuller's vituperation of Poe, 71; on Poe's "brain fever," 92; mentioned, 40

Morning Post (London) reprints "Valdemar Case," 140, 141

Morning Telegraph (New York): first to print English's "Reply to Mr. Poe," 34, 48, 77, 87, 137, 185, 207; why Poe may not have sued, 77

Morris, George Pope: as editor, 15, 21, 127–8, 137, 138; Poe on, 22; on Poe, 41; on English's "Reply to Mr. Poe," 42; *Home Journal* of open to Duyckinck, 141; at Mrs. Poe's funeral, 165; sells *Mirror* to Fuller, 186, 189. *See also Home Journal*

Moss, Sidney P., provides background on Poe's career, 224–5

"Mustard Mace" on Poe, 13

National Press: A Journal for Home. See Home Journal

Neal, Joseph C.: publishes "Mustard Mace" on Poe, 13; reprints and comments on Poe's "Reply to Mr. English and Others," 60–1

New Orleans *Daily Picayune. See Picayune, Daily*

New York City, literary capital of America, 134

New York City Hall: New York's literary world clustered around, xvii, 68, 134; preliminary hearing in Poe's libel suit held in, 78, 95; mentioned, 105

New York *Commercial Advertiser*, 187

New York *Daily Tribune. See Tribune, Daily*

New York Dispatch spreads rumor Poe plans libel suit against several ladies, 204, 205

New York *Evening Post*, Simms mentions, 93

New York *Express*, Fuller quotes on libel suits, 210–1, 212

New York Hall of Records, documents in Poe's libel suit stored in, 78, 171, 174, 212. *See also Libel Suit*

New York Herald. See Bennett, James Gordon

New York Mercury reports murder of Mary Rogers, 152

New York Mirror. See Evening Mirror and Weekly Mirror

New York *Morning Express. See Morning Express*

New York *Sun* reports Poe's libel trial, 175–7

New York Superior Court, Poe's libel suit tried in, viii, 77, 98, 160–3 *passim*, 166, 171, 173, 174, 176. *See also* Libel Suit

New York Supreme Court. *See* New York Superior Court

New York Times, obituary of Hunt in, 172

New York *Tribune. See Tribune, Daily.*

New York University, Poe fails to make scheduled appearance at, 35, 36, 49

Nichols, Mrs. Mary Gove. *See* Gove, Mrs. Mary

Noah, Maj. Mordecai Manuel, at libel trial, 171–7 *passim*, 184

North American Review (Boston): Poe feuds with coterie of, xv; on Duyckinck's Library of American Books, 142, 159; reported calling Poe's *Tales* "trash," 143; *Yankee Doodle* on, 159; on Poe, Simms, and Mathews, 159

Odell, Alfred Taylor, co-editor of Simms's letters, 225

Oliphant, Mary C. Simms, co-editor of Simms's letters, 225

Osgood, Mrs. Frances Sargent: Poe involved with, xv, 89, 91; Poe alludes to as "common friend," 57, 58; Fuller on, 98; satirized as Mrs. Flighty in *1844*, 99, 103; Mrs. Hewitt writes to on distress of the Poes, 125–6, 138: English mentions in deposition, 167, 193; not mentioned in court, 171, 177, or in report of libel trial, 176, 182; family of, 181

Osgood, Samuel Stillman: husband of Mrs. Osgood, 167; asks Thomas for financial help, 182

Ostrom, John Ward: on Mrs. Ellet, 156; editor of Poe's letters, 225

Paine, William H.: Fuller's and Clason's attorney in libel suit, 95, 96–7, 105, 106, 162, 174; Clason supplants at libel trial, 172

Pascal, Blaise, 144, 147

satirized in *Trippings of Tom Pepper*, 194, 195, 198; mentioned, 140

Smith, J. B. L., court appoints to take English's testimony, 161, 163, 165, 168, 170

Smith, James L., at libel trial, 175

Southern Literary Messenger (Richmond), Poe's work for, 218

Southern Patriot (Charleston): Simms defends Poe in, 41, 89; Simms on "Literati" in, 92

Spectator, The (London), Poe cites on *Tales and Poems*, 23

Spirit of the Times (Philadelphia): on English's "Reply to Mr. Poe," 40–1; prints "Mr. Poe's Reply to Mr. English and Others," 49, 60, 61, 62, 67, 87, 190; Fuller alludes to as "Philadelphia paper," 138; on Poe's open letter to Willis, 158; mentioned, 44, 53, 192. *See also* Du Solle, John Stephenson

Stephens, Mrs. Ann Sophia, Poe mentions, 52

Stone, William Leete, horsewhipped by Bryant, 187

Sturtevant (?), O. W., at Poe's libel trial, 172, 174, 175

Sun (New York) reports Poe's libel trial, 175–7

Superior Court. *See* New York Superior Court

Taylor, Gen. Zachary, 39, 61

Telegraph. See Morning Telegraph

Ten Nights in a Bar-Room (Arthur) outsold by *Uncle Tom's Cabin*, 7

Thackeray, William Makepeace: "Snobs of England" by, 5; mentioned, 144

Thomas, Edward J.: alluded to as "merchant," 36, 81, 96, 167, 176, 177, 182; spreads libel on Poe, 57; Poe's letter to, 57–8; letter of to Poe, 58; at libel trial, 171, 172, 175; letter of to Mrs. Osgood, 181–2; mentioned, 174

Thorp, Willard, on "Walter Woolfe," 101

Times. See Spirit of the Times

Times, The (London), reprints "Valdemar Case," 23

Transcript, Daily Evening. See Walter, Miss Cornelia Wells

Tribune, Daily (New York): on "Literati," 11; Graham's ad in, 12; on Poe's libel suit, 34, 175–7, 187–9; Miss Fuller reviews for, 85, 134; called "Sly

Coon" in *1844*, 99; prints Griswold's "Ludwig," obituary of Poe, 134; Greeley's notice of Poe in, 134–5, and Miss Walter's quotation from, 136; Fuller alludes to as "New York paper," 137; Foster on staff of, 159; open to Cooper for reply to Greeley, 187–8; circulation of, 190; Poe sends clipping from to Greeley, 191; address of, 207; mentioned, 186. *See also* Greeley, Horace

Trippings of Tom Pepper, The. See Briggs, Charles Frederick

True Sun (New York) on Greeley, 186

Tupper, Martin Farquhar, Poe cites on *Tales*, 23

Uncle Tom's Cabin (Stowe), 7, 114

Union Magazine. See Sartain's Union Magazine of Literature and Art

United States Magazine and Democratic Review. See Democratic Review

Valentine, John, at Mrs. Poe's funeral, 165

Vanderpoel, Justice Aaron H.: role of in libel suit, 160–1; *Mirror* on, 161; creates commission to obtain English's testimony, 162, 163; mentioned, 18

Verplanck, Gulian C., in "Literati," 18

Voltaire: Poe indebted to, 147n; Forgues mentions, 154

Walter, Miss Cornelia Wells: Poe quarrels with, xv; on Poe, 5–7, 135, 136; mentioned, 8, 9, 15

"Walter Woolfe." *See* English, Thomas Dunn

"War of the Literati, The," 50, 64. *See also* English, Thomas Dunn, Fuller, Hiram, and Poe, Edgar A.

Waters, John. *See* Cary, Henry

Watson, H. C., on *Mirror* staff, 219

Webb, E. H., at libel trial, 174, 175

Weekly Mirror (New York): prints extra copies for "exchange," 20; Poe's alleged reasons for Willis and Morris abandoning, 22; Poe cites disapproval of himself by, 24; Clason and Fuller as co-owners of, 42, 68, 77, 128, 172, 184, 186, 189, 216, 220; frequently notices "Literati," 48; publishes English's Cards, 50, 60, 61, 137, 169, 208; Poe estimates circulation of, 51; Poe suggests criminal prosecution of, 57; Poe refers to as "filthy sheet,"

59, 87; *Morning News* announces Poe will prosecute, 60; Philadelphia correspondent of on Poe, 66–7; Briggs's connection with, 118; under Willis and Morris, 128, 137; Poe on staff of, 128, 137; chief target of *Yankee Doodle*, 159; serializes *1844*, 159, 194, 195; open to Poe for rejoinder to English, 187, 192; serializes *Trippings of Tom Pepper*, 194, 196; address of, 207; changes name, 219; Duyckinck's and Auld's association with, 219–21. *See also* Fuller, Hiram

Welby, Mrs. Amelia B., Poe mentions, 52

Western Clearings (Mrs. Kirkland), 7

Wetmore, Gen. Prosper M., in "Literati," 85, 86

Whitman, Mrs. Sarah Helen, on Poe, 4

Wiley and Putnam: publish Poe, 25, 126, 218; Duyckinck edits for, 42; publish Miss Fuller, 93; Simms mentions, 94; publish Hawthorne, 95; *North American Review* mentions, 142

Willis, Nathaniel Parker: in "Literati," 8, 17; Fuller resents, 15; as writer and editor, 21, 22, 93, 127–8, 132; departs for Europe, 41; letter of to Poe, 128; on Poe, 129, 130–2; Fuller answers editorial on Poe by, 132–3; seeks to collect money for Poe, 134, 135; on *Mirror* staff, 137, 138; writes obituary of Poe, 138; reports French libel suit involving Poe, 139–40; publishes Poe's letter, 141, 156–7, 189, 214, and Duyckinck's defense of Poe, 141; invites Poe to reply to his editorial, 155; announces Mrs. Poe's death, 165. *See also Evening Mirror, Home Journal,* and *Weekly Mirror*

Winwar, Frances, 31

Wise, Henry A., English on, 40, 44, 54, 56

Yankee Doodle (New York): Simms announces founding of, 95; on *1844*, 99; on Willis's defense of Poe, 132, 160; editors, contributors, and targets of, 159–60, 219, 220; rebukes press for persecuting Poe, 160; on *Trippings of Tom Pepper*, 194–5; expiration of, 221; Fuller on, 222

"Yorick" reports Poe's libel trial, 175–7

Zadig (Voltaire), Poe indebted to, 147